NINE LIVES OF A FREE SPIRIT

NINE LIVES OF A FREE SPIRIT

An Autobiography by

EUNICE BLACK

Matador
9 De Montfort Mews
Leicester LE1 7FW, UK
Tel: (+44) 116 255 9311 / 9312
Email: books@troubador.co.uk
Web: www.troubador.co.uk/matador

ISBN 978 1906221 553

A Cataloguing-in-Publication (CIP) catalogue record for this book
is available from the British Library.

Cover photograph: as Lady Bracknell in The Importance of being Earnest

Typeset in 12pt Stempel Garamond by Troubador Publishing Ltd, Leicester, UK

Matador is an imprint of Troubador Publishing Ltd

This book, my life story, is dedicated to my mother Florence
and to my brother George.
Both, to whom I owe so much.

CONTENTS

INTRODUCTION

"Whether I shall turn out to be the hero of my own life, or whether that station will be held by anybody else, these pages must show…"

from *The personal history and experience of David Copperfield the younger* by Charles Dickens.

On a recent hospital visit, the doctor asked me: "Mrs. Black, are you allergic to anything?"

"Only bores and boredom" I said.

"Life is an adventure, live it."

Here is my story.

Any life is a river. We start with spring – our birth, we change to a small stream – our childhood, to a flowing river – our adulthood, then swirl, wide, through a great city – our maturity, and so, into the ocean – our death and eternity.

In the spring of 1992 I was told I would never be able to read again in the conventional manner and would be registered blind. I was seen by Doctor Hector Chawla, the eye specialist at Edinburgh's Alexandra Hospital. He said: "Today, Mrs. Black I must operate on the retina. Sadly, the damage I shall attempt to repair with a very fine laser is located near the optic nerve and is the area that controls the ability to focus on words and figures. You will never read again. I will save the nerve and peripheral vision if possible."

He then asked me to sign the consent form.

"What if I refuse" I asked.

"You will be blind within three months in any case."

I had little choice. I agreed and thereafter entered a closed world.

No driving my MGB GT, no theatres, films, television; no viewing paintings, no seeing faces of loved ones, no reading, no studying, no acting.

But there were consolations. The great kindness of friends and neighbours, car drivers and complete strangers offering to help me cross busy streets. Talking books and talking newspapers, both spoken by wonderful voluntary actors and local people. They saved my life. Special performances of plays, operas and museum visits for the deaf and blind. The Kensington home care shopping and housework service has been invaluable.

I soon discovered that one made mistakes. I cried "Hello" to a friend across the road and thought... she's put on weight! When I got there I realised I had been addressing a red letter box... Mr. Falvey, my builder at the time, entered my kitchen just as I knocked over a full teapot, two glasses and crockery onto the floor. I could not read the labels on tins. I wept with frustration.

"Sit down" he said.

"Here's a cup of tea."

"Now Mrs. Black, think ears, forget eyes. Buy audios set to different stations, a CD player, a small TV, arrange regular positions for all utensils, carry a stick as an extra hand, carry a cordless telephone."

Invaluable advice on my first day of blindness.

* * *

In August 1995 I had a knee replacement and in July 1997 a terrible fall. My kind American friend Doctor Robert Vitale, Professor of Modern Languages invited me to convalesce in his delightful house in the Coconut Grove area of Miami surrounded by waving palms and tropical flowers. I was in heaven. One day he gave me a microphone, dozens of blank cassettes and ordered me to talk of my life story. It was very quiet during week-days whilst my friends were working, silence the perfect opportunity to begin chatting. It required an enormous amount of concentration to think back, names, people, places of such a long time ago. I have lived virtually throughout the 20th Century, living so many different types of life. From the age of 22, apart from my married years, I have lived alone. I have worked for 55 years, worked very hard, have been so lucky to work at teaching, lecturing, directing and acting. My great loves, the arts and the theatre. I missed the company of a close family, my mother, father, grand-parents, cousins and children all taken early or non-existent. So friends, have been my special family.

Here is the transcribed result of several months' dictation, comfortable on a chaise longue under the palm trees; and a further year's work in London. It would have been impossible without the support, expertise and encouragement of my very dear friend Mr. Leonard Amborski. His kindness and patience and translating of the edited tapes have been indispensable. Without his help there would be no book.

So, here is a twentieth century life story of an East End Cockney

Londoner. A life of constant switchback, like the tributaries of a river, a life of many and varied activities, mainly academic and artistic – theatre and television. I have lived intensively through these two mediums during a century of great invention and many changes. I was born into the Edwardian era which very quickly gave way to the frenetic twenties and thirties. The war then followed and that changed our perspective completely, the rest of the 40's and the 50's were an austere recovery from the privations of war time. The "swinging 60's" were a renaissance when the new generation of young people wanted changes to society. Homosexuality was legalised and women's lib. became an everyday expression. Women had more freedom to choose between a career or domesticity, resulting in, alas, the decline of religious belief and family values. What was high moral standard in the first part of the century virtually no longer existed in the second half, a great sadness in my view. The children of modern day Britain are deprived of moral education. Not a question of attending church every Sunday but the building of a solid base on which to guide one's life. It would be a good thing if religious education began from the age of five. This teaches the young to understand civilized manners, about being kind and loving to others. The inner-cities are plagued with serious problems regarding youth in the 90's, crime and violence and drug addiction now degrade youth. It is difficult to be a teenager. I have taught thousands in my classes over the years; the transition of puberty now made all the more difficult by sexual pressures, social demands, career difficulties and choices. Many do not have caring parents and there are more and more single parent families, many mothers under the age of 18. I firmly believe that it is wrong and selfish for girls to have a baby so young. Children should be able to benefit from having two parents to care for them. Children should be cherished and loved.

When young, I lived on quotations which guided my ideas on love and marriage. For instance: "Englishmen never make love by day, but at night they are all right." Anonymous.

Or "Marriage is the exchange of the hurly-burly of the chaise longue for the deep, deep peace of the double bed." Dorothy Parker.

Or "Love is for men a thing apart, 'tis woman's whole existence." Byron

I wish to disagree with all three, although these opinions are very witty and funny.

Our generation in the early part of this century were brought up, in the working class, to be very proper. It was considered a great disgrace if a girl became pregnant before marriage. The working class were far more well behaved, sexually, than the upper classes, who could no doubt manage their affairs more discretely. But working class people were very proper, their daughter had to have a proper husband and the children must be legitimate. The cockneys had an expression for a girl who had become pregnant before marriage: "She has fallen."

Her parents would say: "Who is the father?"

They would see his parents and tell them that their son has put their daughter in the family way – marriage as soon as possible. These unions were called shot-gun marriages. They were successful quite often. Both pairs of parents, combined forces to make the girl respectable. It was much better than the present laxity of responsibility, the lack of family commitment, jeopardizing the welfare of the child.

The working class up-bringing of days gone by were far more respectful of religion and propriety. You imagined, or at least I did, that when adult, you met one man in your lifetime who loved you and whom you loved; he would propose marriage having secured your father's permission and satisfying the question of suitability to him. After marriage you would become a mother eventually and live with and be faithful to your husband until death. This type of life and commitment was what most girls aspired to when I was young. This correct, Christian up-bringing was accepted as a secure family tradition. Girls (in particular) grew up slowly. Their monthly period, at the age of 12 or 13 was often a mystery to them. My mother told me: "You will have that now until middle-age."

She never explained, it was taboo. At the bottom of the bookcase, I found "Married Love" by Marie Stopes (famous in her time for explaining sexual mystery and the provenance of babies). I sat and read it and didn't understand a word. Later I wondered if my brother George had not left this book in plain sight especially for me to read and learn for myself. I suppose my experience was probably the same as a great many teenagers, chatting and laughing with our girl friends and not bothering with boys at all. If we had been in a mixed school, we would have had a completely different outlook. I think now, girls and boys should be educated separately between the ages of 12 and 16. I have taught so many children and think they are happier when in separate schools. There are too many distractions during puberty. The changes of body, sexual diversions, boys' beards, girls' breasts; voice, height, extra weight, awareness of good looks (or lack of beauty).

Alas, women today, do not wish so eagerly for a domestic life especially if they have received a better education. However many still do opt for the housewife choice. It is a personal matter that should not be judged by the feminists who consider it degrading to the woman. Naturally there are always two arguments for the same cause. If you received further education and found that you had talent and had trained and passed exams and had been to University perhaps, you might feel that being a wife and mother only, was boring, restrictive and unfulfilling…

I was quite naïve as a young teenager I suppose, not aware of the ways of the world until the age of 15 or 16 when I found that I liked being escorted home from school play rehearsals by a young man with whom I was friendly. His name was Ron Duboc, my first boyfriend. He would hold my hand, I thought that was marvellous. Later at 17 or 18 he saw me home and gave me a peck on the cheek and that was heaven. Sex never occurred to us. We grew up slowly. I would hop on a bus each morning in order to catch sight of him on his way to his school. That made my day...I had seen Ronald on his way to school!...it must sound terribly feeble to modern young ladies who grow up so quickly, the pressure to have a boyfriend and experience sexual life is so great. One feels abnormal if one is innocent.

Sexual promiscuity has become decadent since the 60's. The Mary Quant revolution with throw-away dresses and very short mini-skirts started a debacle in the fashion world. Correct dress became old hat. Long hair hanging right down to the waist and over the face. All inhibitions were gone, abortion became legal and the pill was invented making sex free and easy. I found this so-called freedom rather sad, because it cheapened sexual pleasure. Sex is beautiful when you are in love with someone and old enough to love with tenderness and passion. "Bonking", the new expression for free sex better describes the sexual habits of rabbits, not humans. I am very happy to have been brought up as I was, to be initiated slowly into the joys of growing up and discovering sex.

It was quite late before I had my first sexual experience. It was with a man who proposed marriage to me offering love, children and a lifetime of happiness until death. Just like I had imagined...

I

AN APPRECIATION OF OTHERS
(on stage and before the camera)

Whilst at Walthamstow High School I would often go on outings to the Old Vic Theatre and I saw actors early on in their careers who became legends in their own lifetime. Olivier, Redgrave, Edith Evans and others. I would go as often as possible, take two shillings from my brother George and get the tram across London. One would queue for balcony seats hoping to get in the front row. I remember an amusing incident which occurred on one occasion when I was waiting in the queue in the normal manner. A drunken man wandered up and down begging for money with his cap. He said that he would not perform that day if we did not give him some money. Most people ignored him. But to my utter amazement I later recognized him on stage, and, playing a drunk. Which was the act? This was Wilfred Lawson, a very famous and talented actor with a weakness for the bottle. The Old Vic has marvellous accoustics. We nearly lost it recently when it was put up for sale by Ed Mirvish, the Canadian businessman who had bought and restored it in the early 80's. But he was now getting quite old, had enough and was retiring. The building came very close to falling into the hands of unscrupulous property developers who's ideas were far more commercial. At the last moment a consortium of theatre people led by Sally Greene (she had ensured the continued success of the Richmond and Criterion theatres) acquired the Old Vic and it was saved. I do not understand why the Government does not step in to save these historic buildings for posterity.

'There are no small parts, only small actors." Laurence Olivier

A truly great performance which I was privileged to see was Ralph Richardson in Peer Gynt, a three hour play with Olivier playing a tiny role as the onion peeler. Sybil Thorndike played the mother. In my youth Olivier himself was the greatest star of the classic theatre. I saw his Richard III at the first night and on that occasion, a stroke of luck, I sat in the stalls. I spent all my money on theatre tickets. That particular night, the theatre was crowded with famous people and the Press. John Mills was in the audience and legend has it that he received a message, Sir Laurence wanted him backstage. Olivier had stage fright and could not remember the first line of the play. John Mills comforted him and told him to repeat the first line. Olivier went on stage to give the most brilliant performance of this part ever seen. He entered up-stage centre, limped down stage, glared at the audience and rasped:

"Now is the winter of our discontent, made glorious summer...."

We sat hypnotised. One of the most memorable evenings of my life. Having been in terror before going on stage, he gave a performance that made your hair stand up on your neck; he had magnetism and electricity that filled the theatre. He was able to make himself so evil and yet charming, you believed that having murdered her husband he could then enchant Anne into marrying him. I can see him on the throne, sitting, when he became King. One of the courtiers came to beg favours.

He snarled at him: "I am not in a giving mood."

My blood ran cold. Later I saw Olivier as Othello. He had agreed to give a special performance for actors. I couldn't believe that I was watching Olivier, he was a noble black soldier in voice, colour and personality.

Lilian Bayliss had enticed him from the West End where he was an admired matinee idol to come and act in the classics, south of the river at the Old Vic Theatre, for very little money. As a young student I had seen his full-length Hamlet and was mesmerized by this dynamic young actor. There is no comparison between the live theatre and film. But thankfully Olivier made a few early films and Hamlet and Henry V are recorded forever. I feel very privileged to have lived during his lifetime and seen these unique classical performances. Each century produces perhaps only one actor of this creative ability. Today, star performers are discouraged. Ensemble work with no "stars" is preferred. I disagree and believe these colossal plays need stars at their centre. It is depressing to underplay any such work. The audience should feel up-lifted, emotionally moved, even to tears, after experiencing a thrilling perform-ance of a great play.

The last time I saw Olivier was as Lear. He was quite an old man by then. His performance was realistic and very moving, especially when he dies and Cordelia, his favourite daughter is held in his arms. I was crying. Another Lear of note was Sir Donald Wolfitt which was performed just after the war at the Camden Theatre in Camden Town (an area of working class markets made famous by Dickens who had lived there at the age of eight working in a blacking factory before he became a successful novelist). Wolfitt led his own company. He toured Shakespeare throughout England. He was a great man. Paul Schofield played Lear at the Aldwych Theatre for the RSC as an irascible old bastard. In the first act, so stupid to ignore the love of his youngest daughter and give his land away to the other two waspish daughters. This interpretation was stunning and original. I had seen a much earlier Lear from Charles Laughton who played him as a very old man indeed, which was wrong because the character needs to progress into old age and senility, there was no decline into tragedy which is essential if to be believed.

I paid 6p for a wooden seat in the balcony at the Old Vic. Les Enfants du Paradis! I saw Edith Evans as Rosalind in "As you Like it"; not a conventionally beautiful woman but she conveyed youth and beauty with the most amazing voice and diction. I saw the newcomer Michael Redgrave who had come down from Cambridge playing Chekhov. He was tall and handsome and later played a variety of classical character parts. So enthralling for a young girl to experience at first hand great acting in plays she was studying. How lucky to live in London.

Lilian Bayliss had made theatre accessible to the poor of London. She offered them cultural experiences as an alternative to merrily drinking gin night after night sitting in the pub. Ordinary people could come, watch and listen to excellence. She would sit in the wings during performances of The Marriage of Figaro or The Magic Flute (she had occasional Opera evenings as well) and pluck her little banjo. She would fry onions on a small stove in the wings for her supper. A remarkable lady, if maybe a little eccentric. She was without doubt one of the great theatrical personalities of the 20th Century.

I went to Stratford-upon-Avon to see Olivier as Coriolanus. He looked much younger and slim. He loved good costumes and make-up. During the death scene at the end, he ran to the top of a twelve foot rostrum pursued by his enemies. When stabbed he did not fall to the floor but fell backwards from the rostrum to the main stage. The whole audience gasped in horror at this extraordinary death. The young actors who had killed him held him by the ankles. There he died hanging upside down...rather like the death of Mussolini.

In living memory the most outstanding production of Romeo and Juliet remains that of Olivier and Gielgud as young men alternating the roles of Romeo and Mercutio at the New Theatre with Peggy Ashcroft as Juliet, she was young and beautiful, a talent without boundaries; the brilliant heroine and Olivier the young passionate teenage Italian, madly in love with her. Their scenes together were breathtakingly emotional. In comparison Gielgud spoke beautifully but lacked Olivier's passion. It was fascinating to see two contrasting performances.

After Olivier founded The National Theatre, originally at the Old Vic and now on the South Bank, one knew where to go for constant excellence. I saw Harold Pinter's "No Man's Land" with Ralph Richardson and John Gielgud at a pro's matinée. Brilliant comedy performances much appreciated by an audience containing many actors. It was a master class in comedy acting. Richardson played a drunken Hampstead type, a retired colonel and Gielgud the woolly-headed poet. Richardson oblivious, soaked in whisky attempted to lift a decanter and pour the contents into a glass without spilling any, which he did, to great applause. He called his man-servant to assist him to bed. Drunk, he walked two slow very deliberate steps towards the door then suddenly fell forward horizontally. It was absolutely hilarious. The man-servant then lifted him up and carried him off stage. These performances should have been recorded for posterity, a sublime duet by brilliant actors.

I saw Richardson as Bottom in "Midsummer Night's Dream," a surprising comic turn, very funny, a cheeky cockney pumped up with conceit, a know-all completely dominating his fellow workmen.

A few modern productions of Shakespeare have sometimes been quite ludicrous. In 1992, Titania was shown sleeping on a rusty old bed in a swamp. Shakespeare said that the setting should be beautiful and classic, with wild flowers... "There sleeps Titania. . . with dances of delight."

How can a modern director decide that on old bed in a swamp is what Shakespeare intended.

In a production of Hamlet the Queen sat on the floor with a bottle of

gin. Peter Brook experimented with this most famous scene in her
bedroom when she is confronted by her son Hamlet in sorrow. He was
most original. His all male "As you like it" was most imaginative, fascinating and well spoken. His Dream was brightly lighted throughout the
night, was poetical with the fairies swinging on trapezes. It was a
masque, quite magical, which of course this play should be.

Long live Shakespeare for the younger generations. Please may schools
not bury Shakespeare under examination schedules. Let teenagers see
live performances.

Dame Peggy Ashcroft who very sadly died a few years ago, finally won
international recognition late in her career when she was awarded an
Oscar for her performance in "A Passage to India"; and also as "Barbie"
in the highly acclaimed television production of "The Jewel in the
Crown." But her greatest acting was no doubt achieved as the Queen in
Shakespeare's "Histories" at Stratford-upon-Avon. She was extraordinary in her ability to grow from youth to old age in such convincing a
manner during the course of one day. How she managed to act those
three plays in one day was unforgettable. She had a beautiful voice and
great intelligence. A truly great Dame who devoted her long career to
the classics.

Another recollection is of Alec Clunes and the Arts Theatre in great
Newport Street, near Leicester Square. He was the Director and leading
actor. "The Recruiting Officer" and plays by George Bernard Shaw and
many Restoration Comedies were performed during his time there. He
was a brilliant actor, very tall and handsome. His son Martin has now
become famous in his own right winning awards for comedy on television. He is uncannily like his father in voice, style, face and impeccable
diction and sense of humour.

I went to one of the very first performances at The Arts Theatre of

"Waiting for Godot" by Sam Beckett. Alec Clunes had the courage to produce it and to choose a young unknown Director whose first professional job it was, Peter Hall... Beckett, an Irishman living in Paris is considered a great original of recent English theatre, because he dared to be so completely different from the orthodox three act plays. To be recognised as an original is an accomplishment in any field. This was 1946, my future husband and I went to the Arts Theatre to see a "comic play.".. "Waiting for Godot.".. we sat amazed during the first act. Nothing was happening, two old men sitting beneath a tree saying nothing at all. We decided to stay for the second act and became gripped by it. Later, during what should have been a romantic supper, we argued about the play. The chief argument being that the two men were in fact two aspects of one person. His earthy side and his intellectual and spiritual side. All the critics said the play was a load of rubbish, all except the Sunday Times' Harold Hobson who said that this was the work of a genius.

* * *

John Osborne's "Look back in Anger" originally produced at the Royal Court Theatre in 1956 was the first of many gritty dramas known as "kitchen sink drama." This was the story of a young working-class student who went to University and was married to a middle-class girl played by Mary Ure whom he constantly criticized. The character of Jimmy Porter is legendary. Audiences stood to protest at his appalling rudeness...

"Don't talk to her like that..."

He was so uncomfortably real, people believed him, thus creating emotional reactions from the audience. It was extraordinary. An age of socialist realism had begun. A Taste Of Honey premiered shortly afterwards. The Royal Court Theatre was and still is avant-garde. They invited Sir Laurence Olivier, then Director of the National Theatre to star in Osborne's next work "The Entertainer." Olivier had taken on a challenge once before to leave his more established comforts. He accepted the role and it remains one with which he will always be associated. He played a third rate northern comedian. For an actor of his calibre to play such a lowly no talent performer was a tour de force. His jokes were terrible and he knew it and he despised himself for using the same awful material night after night to virtually empty houses. There was sadness and despair behind the eyes... He had been doing this for thirty years and this was his tawdry life. He toured the northern Music Halls repeating his bad performance enlivened by the occasional slow tap dance. It was a brilliant portrayal of a tragic character. It was there that he met and later married the young actress Joan Plowright with whom he had three children. Already a much respected stage actress, her career has diversified to playing character parts in Hollywood films since her husband's death.

These plays were creations of new young left-wingers who although not Communist wanted to change the world. The working classes should not be dominated by the middle and upper classes. University education became accessible to all who had sufficient intelligence, both men and women. Now students are complaining that they cannot afford to pay back non-interest loans. It is ridiculous.

* * *

Most comedians now hold a microphone, but your face should be clear of an instrument that separates you from the audience. Eye to eye contact is vital and don't mumble; a line missed is a dead joke. Of the new comedians I particularly like Harry Enfield. Of the more established, Rowan Atkinson and John Cleese are both superb originals with great intelligence. Their humour comes from the heart which makes them see the world slightly askew. A genuine accolade to a solo comedian is reserved for Stanley Baxter, a Scottish magician of such varied talents, he amazes us with his elegance as a dancer, his singing voice and his impersonations of famous people. The wicked twinkle in his eye expressed his wit and humanity – a genius.

Fawlty Towers is probably the only truly great television farce. The whole series is a classic. Apparently the Spanish do not approve because the English make fun of Manuel the Spanish waiter. But they have missed the point completely. We love Manuel dearly, he is not a caricature that we laugh at. The wife, Sybil, as played by Prunella Scales is a truly inspired creation, a south coast catering lady assuming a grand refined accent. Quite hilarious. The Hotel is always full of the typically English who play their parts for truth: the retired Colonel, two elderly ladies and the varied customers.

After the war had finished I was asked to work in comedy for television at the BBC often with many of the great names, many of whom had worked in Music Hall. When I was very young I was most fortunate to have been taken to see Max Miller. This cockney wide boy in loud suits who spoke directly to the audience was bawdy by innuendo. Now this type of comedy is old fashioned. Rory Bremner is one who talks about his life and own experiences direct to the audience. I don't think that kind of comedy will ever die away, not as long as we have people who have the courage to stand alone. Ken Dodd is the greatest exponent of the solo act.

One afternoon, several years ago, I was feeling rather lonely, depressed and miserable; my wrists were in bandages. I walked by the London Palladium where the matinée was about to begin. To my joyful surprise Jimmy Edwards was the star comedian. During his solo he played the trombone, talked to the audience and was a genial buffoon, a clown, he held the audience in a comic spell of love and laughter. God Bless our comedians who restore humanity and tolerance to our spirits, and sanity to the world. I am honoured to have worked with them.

Ray Cooney is a marvellous writing actor and director in the world of farce. He converted the Playhouse Theatre on the Embankment from a radio studio to a perfect house for farce, small and theatrical. He carried on the great tradition of British farce.

Tony Hancock was another original comedian. He had a mobile face. His character was the modern equivalent of Charlie Chaplin who in the twenties created the "little man" on film, always surviving wearing large big flat shoes, baggy trousers and a most respectable waistcoat. He carried a little walking stick which he twirled around as he walked along to show his exuberant spirit that would never be conquered by any disaster. Tony Hancock sat in a suburban house in Cheam in Surrey wearing a rather smart trilby hat and a respectable middle class suit and coat. He dreamed of being different, wealthier and better educated. He had a wonderfully expressive face which was ideal for television. His script writers invented the unforgettable character of a working man constantly aspiring to greatness, but never succeeding. In one show he sat and said: "Oh God it's Sunday, what can I do?" Yawn, yawn...

A boring morning with no escape from his limited situation. His face expressed it all.

Paul Schofield, essentially a classical actor gave a memorable perform-ance as the Inspector in "A Government Inspector" by Gogol. A young clerk on a visit to provincial Russia is mistaken for the Government Inspector. The locals ingratiate themselves with forced humility to please him and overwhelm him with hospitality. He is amazed; he is not the Inspector but accepts this praise and adoration. They endlessly give him vodka, he becomes more and more drunk. A brilliant satire of syco-phancy. To act progressively drunk during a play is difficult. Schofield was brilliant, he knew he could play comedy effectively. Later, wiping tears from my eyes, I said:

"That performance should be recorded for Drama School students, as a master class in comedy."

Of late he has been concentrating on reading for the talking books, playing many of the parts written by Charles Dickens.

In my very early youth I was taken to see George Robey who walked on stage as a clergyman with huge semi-circular black eye brows. The audience laughed and laughed. Max Wall was another grotesque comic. The theatre was filled with his admirers, including myself. He came on slowly on to a bare stage, did a deep growl and then slowly recited a third rate joke, then said: "Oh God, what a way to earn a living."

These people had the ability to hold you in their hand and make you feel that you were the only person they were addressing.

Female comedians have traditionally not performed in the theatre as regularly as men, especially the Victorian Music Hall Theatre; there they dressed up as men or were eccentric characters. My favourite comedienne was Beatrice Lillie. She worked in revue, now sadly a forgotten art form, and played numerous parts mostly as herself. She was tall and elegant and undemonstrative. She always looked as if she was wandering about the stage, singing and reciting, and improvising; which of course she was not. She had a beautiful speaking voice, had been trained as an Opera singer. Her mother was determined that she should become a great singer, but she always failed her auditions. At her wits end she went for an audition with André Charlot the great impre-sario of revue at the time. He told her to sing serious Opera. He was not impressed. Drawing on her inner comic spirit, as yet unexposed, and in desperation, she gave him an insight of her true talent and sang burlesque opera. Legend has it that Charlot jumped up in amazement and offered a role on the spot, effectively she became a comedienne by accident. She sang a sad song: "Wind round my heart," at which the audience roared with laughter. She had a great style of nonchalance, you interpreted what she meant. Noël Coward, the whole of London and New York fell in love with her.

Ruth Draper filled the stage with many different characters playing all the parts herself. No artist has performed like that other than Marcel Marceau the great mime.

Joyce Grenfell, like Bea Lillie was tall, beautifully dressed and very elegant. Her songs and monologues were based on keen observation and love of all mankind. A teacher in a nursery school installing discipline among the children was remarkable; or at a musical soirée, a middle-class or high brow party exchanging conversation with different guests; she was quite outstandingly funny.

Patricia Routledge at sixty has achieved fame on television, her own series has created the now much imitated "Hyacinth Bucket" pronounced "bouquet" and has brought her to the attention of a much larger audience than the theatre. She was trained as an Opera singer, went to Liverpool University. She is a very funny character actress with a great sense of nonsense and fun.

Julie Walters and Victoria Wood who work together, both have hilarious comic gifts. Alas, I have only ever seen them on television and there is always such laughter from the audience that I often miss the punch-lines.

Two great actresses in comedy were Athéne Seyler often seen in Restoration comedy. This requires great elegance of speech and timing. She wrote a book entitled "The craft of comedy" which consists of her letters to a young actor who wrote to her and asked how to play comedy. She replied and the collection of letters were later published. It is a rare book, a true classic of the art of acting. I have given away my own copy to my friend and fellow actor Philip Bowen. Margaret Rutherford was the other. Her talent was first appreciated by the late Hugh (Binkie) Beaumont. She had immaculate diction, had been a teacher of elocution when young. She started acting quite late. Noel Coward saw her and wrote the part of Madame Arcati, an eccentric medium, in "Blythe Spirit" especially for her. The play has become a classic as a comedy farce. I have played the part in the fashion of a dotty academic with monocle.

Patricia Hayes and Irene Handl were two actresses who specialised in cockney characters. Handl was of middle European and middle class extraction. I once saw her sitting at the side of a rehearsal room at a television studio with a tiny lap dog. She was writing. I went up to pat it on the head and it snapped at me viciously. I asked her if that was how she learned her lines. She replied: "No, no, no, I'm writing my first novel, THE SIOUX." Amazing!

She was cast by Jonathan Miller, may God forgive him, to play Lady Bracknell. She was very short and famous for playing cockney characters. It was a failure. When asked why she agreed to play the part, she said: "I don't know why. Mr. Miller cast me in this part...at one dress rehearsal, he suddenly told us to act our part in whatever accent we wished other than our own"

She only knew a German Jewish accent and played her like that, which he thought was very funny. She added: "But I was never happy in the part."

I will never understand why Jonathan Miller thought she could play Lady Bracknell. Pat Hayes always played cockney parts. She moved us enormously when she played a bag lady on television, a truly great actress in my view.

It is true that those who can play comedy can play tragedy, but rarely the reverse. Comedy is based on tragedy. If your trousers fall down by mistake or you slip on a banana skin! Farce is a disaster played at great speed, unexpected and exaggerated. Beryl Reid was a brilliant comedienne, who played a memorable tragic part in "The Killing of Sister George" as a long running serial star on radio who started to drink on too many occasions and finally was dismissed. The scene in which the television executive called to tell her the news was memorable. Her life was over, she attempted suicide. She played the part with great conviction, very tragic.

Dame Edith Evans, a classical actress, is considered the greatest ever to have played Lady Bracknell. Many were holding their breath when Dame Maggie Smith did it, but Dame Edith remains foremost in our minds. I suppose it's the "hand bag" line that became immortal. "The Importance of being Earnest" is the greatest comedy in the English Language. She had appearance, poise and great style of speech which is essential for the delivery of the lines; they are Mozartian in economy and elegance. John Gielgud played Worthing in a rather funereal manner. She was dominating, infuriatingly snobbish in the wonderful first act. It is important to point the lines making them appear natural at the same time. I have played the part four times. I would rush to the theatre each evening so happy to have the pleasure of acting this part in this great comedy.

Both the RSC and The National have had ensemble playing in the last 25 years and do not encourage the making of star names. The theatre needs great stars in great parts. They lift the spirit and the imagination in a way that can only happen with a live performance. Anthony Sher is a star of the theatre. Everybody rushes to his performances. He has the gift of lifting the play into a higher level of excitement, interest and emotion. Which is what the theatre is all about.

Penelope Keith is a great comedy actress, always the epitome of middle-class snobbishness and pettiness often offered roles in plays by Ayckbourn who has already written 37. I saw her in one of his plays set around a dinner party in a lower middle-class household where a guest is very fussy about the setting of the table. The humble hostess doesn't care as she is too harassed. The situation was so perfect the audience cried with laughter. It was played very seriously, was so real. In fact when leaving the theatre we heard such comments as: "She's just like my aunt...my mother...."

It was the finest comedy acting.

The pretentions and weaknesses of the lower aspiring middle class, well observed with great affection. We are lucky indeed to have had Ayckbourn, Pinter and Stoppard as theatre writers in the latter half of the 20th Century, providing immense social commentary on our ways of life at this time in history.

There exists snobbery among intellectuals if one acts in comedy rather that tragedy or serious drama. To play comedy and farce well, requires the greatest ability and skill. Comedy provides a sense of balance and humanity to the actors, the audiences and the world in general and should be admired and respected.

Stanley Unwin was an original eccentric. A former Post Office worker who whilst repairing the telephone lines would talk down them speaking his own nonsensical language off the top of his head, very Edward Lear and funny. It was suggested that he should appear on television. I worked with him in a comedy sketch in Children's Hour for the BBC. I portrayed an elegant middle-aged lady who wished her cat to win first prize in a competition. The cat in question was a fake tricked up to have a life of its own, a puppet if you like. I was asking Professor Unwin to provide me with directives for the perfect cat. He replied in his own inimitable style. This originality is so precious in our lives and comes unexpectedly from almost anywhere.

The University wits, Dudley Moore a brilliant Doctor of Music from Oxford re-invented Benjamin Britten in a parody at the piano. Peter Cook, a complete original who could improvise anything. Jonathan Miller looked like a camel and Alan Bennett who was a Professor of History at Oxford and a playwright. They excelled in the revue "Beyond the Fringe" featuring their own material which went to the Edinburgh Festival. A wonderful quartet. It was the beginnings of modern satire. Later came "Monty Python's Flying Circus" which was broadcast late at night by the BBC. John Cleese invented the Ministry of Funny Walks, a send-up of bureaucracy. They saw life afresh from a completely different aspect. This led to "Fawlty Towers."

There is nothing worse than a bad farce. I remember Spike Milligan in one called "Oblomov" in which he played the Russian character who never wanted to get out of bed, he was too lazy. It opened in the West End and was to close after one week. Spike decided to enjoy himself for the week by improvising ad-libs through the evening. The audience roared with laughter, the news spread, queues formed outside the theatre. The show was suddenly a hit and ran several months. I went to the theatre with a group of teenagers who had passed their A level examinations and their choice was to see Spike Milligan. Bill Owen also in the cast was told I was in the front row. Spike came out in front of the curtain, looked down and said: "Wonderful knees" and ad-libbed inspired lunacy.

He was a maniac in overdrive. I went back stage to congratulate Bill. I asked if I might pay my compliments to Spike. Bill said: "Oh no, he's so exhausted at the end of a performance, he shuts himself in his dressing room and doesn't go home for quite a long time while he recovers from that inspired two hour performance"

It is sad that Spike, such a wonderful person, is so hyper-sensitive that any bad news will cause him to retreat in misery to the world in general. A dear man. I understand that he came on one night in front of the main tabs, feeling sad and said to the audience, roaring with laughter: "Shall I go home?" They replied:

"Yes."

"Shall I pull the main curtains."

"Yes, Spike."

He then walked off the stage, out of the theatre and went home. The Theatre Manager offered a refund or see the understudy. Bill told me that on another evening the entire front stalls were filled with Japanese tourists who had heard that this was a funny play with a very funny man. A little further back were members of the Goons is a row including Michael Bentine. It was hilarious to watch, Spike ignoring the front twelve rows as they sat in complete incomprehension of his sense of humour. Roars of laughter rose from the rest of the audience.

LIFE ONE
AN APPRECIATION OF MYSELF
(on stage and before the camera)

In 1956 I asked Spotlight about interviews in repertory theatres outside London. Northampton was suggested and I was lucky enough to be accepted by Alex Reeve, artistic director of their Repertory Company as the actress playing the character parts. Northampton was a highly respected well established theatre avidly supported by the wealthy local community. Each production was designed taking great care and the art studio where the sets were made and painted each week was first class. Weekly rep. requires great discipline from all those involved in order to produce a first night every Monday. My first role was in a Lancastrian comedy. The first week I learned the lines in the evenings and rehearsed during the day. I was paid £12. per week. In my second role I was an elegant lady, on stage for two hours. One's mind is divided between two characters, one in rehearsal by day and the other on stage in the evening. I would return home to eat a late supper and learn the lines of another play. It was an extraordinary double life and I enjoyed every minute of this routine. I was amazed that I could learn so many words in such a short time. The memory is sharpened and I was relieved that I could memorise quickly having been terrified at the prospect of weekly repertory. So we rehearsed Acts 1 & 2 on Thursday, on Friday Act 3 and on Saturday a complete run through in the morning and a costume fitting later. Sunday we rested. Monday morning there was a full dress rehearsal and finally the first performance in the evening with the local press in attendance ready to formulate their critiques.

Whilst at Northampton an agent asked me to go to Colchester and play the lead in Rattigan's "Separate Tables." An offer I could not refuse. The repertory theatre is situated on the High Street and was a former Art Gallery which had been transformed into a small rather uncomfortable theatre by a local wealthy man who loved theatre. I played Mrs. Railton-Bell. I received a proposal of marriage there from a twice divorced middle-aged gentleman who had seen me in the play. He invited me out to lunch which supplied great amusement to my fellow actors and I was astonished that he sent a Rolls Royce with a chauffeur to my Hotel the next day. We went to the beautiful Victorian Hotel in the High Street and he ordered oysters for me! His lunch consisted of whisky. Another day we met for afternoon tea, he wanted me to meet his friends in the country. We were served an elegant tea but my gentleman friend preferred whisky. I concluded that he was an alcoholic. Shame, he was kind and thoughtful but not, alas, future husband material.

I was playing a comic policewoman in panto on Christmas Eve matinée when great blankets of fog came rolling in from the North Sea. We had Christmas Eve (evening) and Christmas day off but were scheduled to return for the 2pm matinée on Boxing Day. The actors rushed to London to be with their families. I offered to take three in my mini along with my dog Sally. As soon as we left Colchester, visibility was reduced by the terrible fog. I put my headlights down to see the catseyes in the road and slowly drove towards Chelmsford. It was a frightening drive, no streetlights out in the country. I lost my sense of space and distance as if driving through a cloud and accidentally drove into a farmyard. We eventually reached Chelmsford and later London.

As Mrs. Railton-Bell, I was seen by the author who offered me the part in a National Tour lasting many months. Rattigan personally supervised the casting for this long tour as the play was still running in the West End. It was most enjoyable travelling to a different town each week, often through the famous station at Crewe. On Sunday bedraggled actors waited disconsolately around for their infrequent connections. One could be travelling all day from Plymouth to Newcastle or Manchester. An actor must have good health, strength, determination and a passion for the live theatre. It is very hard demanding work, unglamorous, with little money, no fame, just a desire to act and follow no other profession.

One must find lodgings in each town. Equity is able to offer suggestions and on one occasion I selected a Mrs. Prime's house thinking it would be spotless, I mean with that name...pity I knew Latin...She was a slovenly woman, the place was dirty beyond belief. I loathed getting into bed at night in fear of bugs. The windows were grey, the kitchen sink greasy, the floor deep in rubbish. Ghastly.

The greatest Landlady of all was Mrs. Tibbs in Nottingham who offered full board rental at a reasonable rate and was a wonderful cook. She loved actors as they afforded her the company she missed after the death of her husband. I remember she gave me a birthday party. The entire cast came, late at night after our performance of the classic farce "See How They Run." Actors are always hungry and were delighted to accept. Her son was present with a new recording device. She put her best linen, cutlery and china on a huge table. I offered to pay her for the party, she refused saying she enjoyed our company so much. A treasure, dear Mrs. Tibbs.

Another famous theatrical landlady was Mrs. McKay in Manchester, a formidable lady. The first time I arrived cold and wet after a long rehearsal, she said: "You're late."

"I'm sorry." I said.

'The other actors arrived over an hour ago, you are too late for supper."

I asked for a glass of water. Before I was sent up to my bedroom I said I was late because I had been detained at rehearsals by the director. Twenty minutes later, having confirmed my story with the other actors I was told to come down and have some supper. A ferocious, Victorian Head Mistress was Mrs. McKay. Inevitably we became the best of friends. The next time I asked if I could stay she was delighted and said she would prepare my favourite dinner on my first evening. She liked someone who was direct and honest. She was very proud of her job as a landlady. She loved to show you the photographs of all the famous people who had stayed with her. She was a wonderful person, gave you very good food, the accommodation was spotless and comfortable and she too loved her actors. But I shall never forget that first encounter.

Performing in pantomime is great fun, especially when you are playing a very tall fairy wearing a tutu and carrying a wand as the Fairy Queen in Cinderella. The children looked up in amazement at this huge Fairy with the huge voice! I imagine that their mothers brought them up to think Fairies are small dainty creatures with little voices. I remember a little voice from the audience asking: "Mummy, is that a fairy?" which made me laugh. I played the part in Peckham to a noisy afternoon school party of tough not so little boys. They heckled everybody but remained quiet when I entered. It was a tough neighbourhood with tough children with difficult family circumstances. For actors who usually play straight parts, panto can be a great source of comic relief. We are entertainers and this is our work at Christmas time. Pantomime, although Italian in origin, is a great British tradition and three to four hundred productions are mounted every year both amateur and professional. These days it is often the first opportunity for children to see live theatre. May Panto continue to prise children from their computer games and television.

For a year, I played the Grand Duchess Anastasia in a production of

"The Student Prince." In the grand ballroom scene, after an initial dance by the chorus, my entrance was announced. I looked magnificent – an enormously wide crinoline covered with sparkling jewels, a tiara, a necklace of diamonds, a very tall glittering feather head-dress, earrings and bracelets and rings on my fingers (and bells on my toes if they had been available!). I swept downstage to begin my dialogue with the Prince. From the front row of the stalls, a man spoke to his wife: "She looks like a Christmas tree."

Surprisingly I managed not to corpse, I just waved my enormous ostrich feather fan at him – in agreement.

I was travelling with Doris Hare in a farce called "Saturday Night at the Crown," set in a North Country pub. Doris and I played two middle-aged ladies who met every Saturday night to drink. It was hilarious, very low brow but great fun to act. We did a short tour which ended at the Cambridge Arts Theatre in term time. Oh Lord I thought, academics will despise us. We will play to empty houses. Cambridge has produced many fine comedians through the Cambridge footlights revues. The BBC go there to look for new talent. One year I saw Bill Oddie there and telephoned James Gilbert, Director of Comedy, and told him of this new talent. He had heard about him and had already signed him up.

My fears were without foundation, we played to packed houses. Everyone came, the Dons, the Masters of Colleges. Comedy is baffling. I had a fox fur with a bushy tail which I used as a stage prop. I thought I might wear it around my neck one night with the tail sewn by a thin cotton to the body of the fox. The idea was that Doris would stroke the tail of the fox and say: "Lovely fur dear, where did you get it?" and continue to stroke until it fell away into two pieces. It might get a laugh. Might... It was a roaring success, Doris sat holding the tail in her hand until the laughter died down. Not knowing what to do with it she gave it to me. My character, "Eunice Sidébeuttom" with a deep ploonge-line, indeed a deep cleavage, thrust the tail down there to gales of laughter that seemed to last for ever. One never knows what works in the theatre. It can often depend on the audience at that particular performance. Our run in Cambridge was most enjoyable. Doris made a curtain speech after each show. She thanked the audience and said that she had a great fondness for Cambridge because her husband had been to "Keys" College. Given the nature of the play, the audience assumed that this was a joke and that she had learned to pronounce "Caius" in the correct way especially for the curtain speech. But no, her husband was a doctor and had truly been to Caius College Cambridge.

While there I suggested to the other actors that we must have a day's punt to Grantchester two miles away as the river meanders. Punting up-stream is not easy and I was the only one who knew what to do, so the whole cast, with me at the helm set out up the river. As we approached our destination the heavens opened and we were soaked. We crossed the fields to see the famous Church where: "The clock was standing at a quarter to three and is there honey still for tea."

We had a hot cup of tea before starting back by bus for the evening performance, I was to return alone with the punt. But they would not desert their Captain and we all returned together on the punt. On arrival, drenched to the skin we gave Doris some hot whisky and lemon to assure her presence on the stage that evening! I shall never forget going back to Cambridge later as a Lecturer, informing the students that I had played there once, not as Lady Macbeth or Cleopatra, but as a north country lady in a farce. That was amusing.

It is quite strange that people with comedy spirit have telepathy. A bubble inside the heart that you are born with. One likes to laugh at human foibles and most importantly at oneself. Looking back I can now see that I have been attracted to people, and they to me, who have an instinctive comedy spirit.

Comedy can be interesting when repeated every night. In "Rookery Nook" by Ben Travers I was playing Aunt Gertrude always getting a laugh on my entrance. One night, no laugh. You wonder what has happened. Could it be that another actor on stage had moved an eye brow or scratched his nose to distract? This can kill an entrance. If the timing was wrong, maybe I entered a second too early or too late. You must be exactly on time to ensure laughs. I was on a fifteen week tour with Leslie Crowther. During our dialogue he asked me to give a certain line a beat and that would give him a laugh. But it did not. I imagined that he knew what he was doing, but night after night it did not work. We decided that we would not pause but continue at speed. Result – a huge laugh, don't know why, perhaps it was because we were relaxed not trying so hard.

When playing comedy and farce for a lengthy run, audiences can be very different from one night to the next with the week-ends usually more lively, you can hear the buzz in the auditorium, it's terrific. Bad weather influences the audiences' reaction to wit and satire. A first laugh is always a triumph. If they love you and work with you, unconsciously you give a better performance. To act in a bad farce is a painful experience. You long for each evening to end but have to continue to act to the unfortunate audience. I played in such a farce on stage with the great Hermione Gingold, "Highly Confidential" at the Cambridge Theatre. I was the feed and had to stand perfectly still. I stood on the side of the stage and punctuated her often hilarious monologues with "Yes Madam" – "No Madam." To my horror I would get the laughs. I know my job, as the feed I must not get the laughs. It is a crucifixion for the star comedienne. The audience has paid for their seats. The silence from the stalls at non-funny lines and actions is deafening.

* * *

I acted with Benny Hill and his three supporting actors. Henry McGee, the handsome young man, Bob Todd the older man and Jack Wright a tiny man whom Benny would pat on the head. I said to him: "Bob you only have to open your mouth to get a roar of laughter, you are so funny, are they going to give you your own series?"

"No, Eunice, I don't want it. I like my job here with Benny, we are a wonderful team, the four of us. Benny knows it, we know it, we all work together...ten years already."

That's a combination comedy team, a quartet. But Benny, the man who wrote the whole show, was a brilliant technician. He always had a bevy of beautiful girls whom he chased or who chased him. He loved the girls and they loved him. The chase was innocent and unsuccessful. His music hall humour with sexual innuendo was quite innocent. We would meet at 7am and go by coach into the country where they rented a house for the day's shooting. When I asked Benny why he limited his appearances to four main shows a year, he said: "99% of my income goes to the taxman. I'd rather have free time to travel around Europe with a notebook ready to jot down any ideas as I observe the human race. Better four good first-class one hour shows, never appear too often."

Audiences can be ruthless about comedians, so quick to criticise them if the show is not as original or as funny as usual. He told the studio staff exactly what he wanted and always knew what that was. He was a kind and brilliant and I miss him very much. That was comedy tailor-made for television, which has to be timed to fit the appointed slot. During rehearsals the show is chronometered to the last second to make sure it fits the schedule.

I found this most unnerving when I first worked with Jimmy Edwards. The brilliant and very experienced James Gilbert was directing a new series to be called "Faces of Jim." I was fortunate to be in the first episode. Frank Muir and Dennis Norden were the writers, a fantastic team. They wrote for Jimmy and his big personality. June Whitfield, Ronnie Barker and myself read the script every Thursday morning.

The writers came to supervise the rehearsals. We had forty minutes worth and from that after the cuts would be left with a first class thirty minutes of sheer comedy. Brilliant. We had a great deal of fun during those Thursday morning readings which would be followed by the walking and the plotting. When we reached the dress run, the expert BBC technicians would arrive and shoot the final version laughing all the way.

The subject of that first episode was to be "Come Dancing"; a group of ex-army men and women who decided to go into an Army competition for formation dancing. A great idea for comedy. The coach on the way to the competition would break down in the middle of the country. We went to rehearse on location in Surrey. We had to wade through a stream, thus getting our pretty costumes muddy and wet, bravely determined to get to the dance. It was hilarious. I remember Jimmy sitting on the bank of the river, laughing because he was safe, clean and dry whilst the rest of us had mud up to our necks. Because I am so tall I was asked to go in and test the river bed in case of unexpected holes. I didn't care about getting wet and muddy I was enjoying myself. We practiced several times, finally going for a take. We hadn't noticed a heard of cows crossing the river near us casually lifting their tails doing their various business. It was hysterical, we fell back into the river in laughter. The take was brilliant. Jim was so kind, afterwards he took us to the nearby village pub where we could have a hot shower, change, have a hot drink and something to eat. It was a wonderful day out, great experiences and good humour.

After that I was asked by Muir and Norden if I was available to be in the rest of the series. Yes I was and very pleased. There was a brilliant send-up of "Pride and Prejudice" condensed into thirty minutes. Jim was the father and the dotty mother part had been cut. He had to find husbands for his dopey daughters who were all short. He married them all to the first passer by, clergyman, mailman whatever. He was then left with me, six feet tall! He'd say: "Oh, my God how do I get rid of this one?"

They were brilliant scripts and I was so sorry that Frank recently passed away. They were the happiest times of my television career. To work with a brilliant team and a first class script each week, en rapport, happy, is heaven.

I played "Big Gladys" in "On the Buses." I greatly enjoyed acting with Reg Varney and the team. He was the bus conductor and the stories were of his adventures around London and in his cockney home where Doris Hare was the presiding matriarch. Reg's character's relationship with the inspector at the depot (a brilliant creation with a Hitler moustache) provided the conflict necessary for any comic situation. My character was also frequently in conflict with the inspector. A typical scene would be that I was in the ladies lavatory at the depot, Reg placed some mistletoe over the door. As the pretty conductresses came out he kissed each one. The inspector lifted up his arm to remove the mistletoe. At that moment I came out, thinking he was holding it for me, I blushed and said: "I didn't know you cared!" and gave him a big kiss. The audience laughed so much, the Director stopped the show and we had to re-take. Surprise is one of the elements required for comedy; shock, the unexpected, the puncturing of pomposity.

My agent informed me that I had been offered a couple of days work at an independent studio in Merton, South London, working on what we thought was a second rate film. In fact it starred John le Mesurier and Spike Milligan, was called "INVASION QUARTET" and became a classic often shown in University towns to admiring under-graduates. It is set in Northern France in 1942. I was playing a French country woman carrying a basket with a goose, chickens and eggs. Spike Milligan and John le Mesurier were Commandos leading a secret invasion to blow up a German installation where the deadly gun known as the "Big Bertha" was located. They would ride under-cover in a bus with other peasants. I loved the goons on the radio in the 50's, so original and hilarious. No one had acted with those voices; Peter Sellers, Harry Secombe, Michael Bentine and Spike. I arrived at the studio at 7am and saw the bus ready for the shoot, one side removed for filming reasons with several extras dressed as French peasants inside. One man was sitting in a deck chair in rags his eyes shut, sleeping. I realised that it was my favourite Goon and said: "Good morning Mr. Milligan."

He opened one eye and said: "Call me Spike."

"Good morning Spike" I replied.

He got up and took me by the arm and said: "Follow me."

We sat in the bus, he grabbed one of the sandwiches and a mug of tea intended for the extras and began ad-libbing a humorous sketch using them as props. I joined in when it seemed appropriate and the others were laughing heartily. The Director came over: "Spike, we must put all that in the film."

Spike said: "Eunice, what have we been doing?"

I told him: "I have no idea."

Neither of us could remember what exactly we had been doing such was the spontaneity of the great and always original Spike Milligan. You should try and see "Invasion Quartet" when next on television or a cinema somewhere.

I had a small part in "A Taste of Honey" directed by Tony Richardson, a Cambridge graduate married to Vanessa Redgrave. He often preferred location filming to studios. He took the truly original play by Shelagh Delaney and made a film. A true story about life as she knew it around the Manchester ship canal. The film's stars are Dora Bryan as the mother and Rita Tushingham as the teenage daughter. I was cast as the school teacher at the beginning of the film. The Director had wanted to convey the contrast between English Literature and Art, and the real life of this slum area in which the film was set. The girls in the class were day dreaming and not paying attention whilst I recited "Ode to Autumn" by John Keats. I looked as dour as the scenery, wore old shabby tweeds, was middle-aged without make-up. Tony Richardson used an old derelict school in South London. The story is of a fourteen year old girl with a feckless mother with many boy friends always short of money often forced into midnight flights to avoid paying the rent, poor desperate people. The film is a classic of British Cinema. Poverty was at last not romantic but ugly and desolate. How ever brief, I believe my cameo appearance to be poignant. My voice at the time was perfect for the role.

* * *

I acted at the Brewhouse Theatre in Taunton, Somerset. I admired these local people because they built their own theatre without the help of grants from the Arts Council. They love the theatre but had to go to Plymouth or Exeter to see a first class play. Local people worked in the box office, the restaurant and sold programmes. Touring professional companies used the theatre but sometimes local amateurs staged productions. One year they did not want a traditional panto but elected for a farce, "See How They Run." The auditorium was small, sloping to the stage. I have played Miss Skillon four times. She is a tweedy middle-age lady in love with the local vicar. All the classic plays of the last two hundred years, the farces of Ben Travers and

Oscar Wilde's works should be performed in period costume. "See How They Run" is set in 1942 and Miss Skillon is sort of the female equivalent of Captain Mannering in Dad's Army, too old for active war duty, so she's the bossy organizer in the village. The scene opens in the vicarage drawing room, the door bell rings, the maid answers. Miss Skillon enters wearing a steel helmet and a cardboard gas mask around her body. That entrance is guaranteed a roar of laughter. My deep voice accentuated her dominating character. A first class farce is difficult to achieve and has strictly defined rules. The pace must increase, no repeat actions or dialogue, add to the plot and in the final act, bring in new characters who install further complications to the situation. End fast, resolve all loose ends in the last few pages and bring the curtain down on a big laugh. It is important for the audience to gaze upon the mess at the end of Act two. They do not want an interval, they want to return as soon as possible to see what happens next. I was at the Whitehall Theatre with Brian Rix and Terry Scott, masters of comedy and farce. I admired them during rehearsals in their duologues, they worked out comedy reactions and how to make the situation funnier. They played two men who were not called up for war service but whose wives were. They were having a good time fooling around while their wives were away winning the war. Their wives returned on leave earlier than expected and these two were caught misbehaving, the classic theme of farce. It was a joy to see the accuracy and pace of their work. When the audience are laughing they do not realise the time and the skill it has taken to construct this entertainment, to make it look so easy and spontaneous, that is their art.

I worked with The Crazy Gang on one occasion. They had been a hit for years at the Victoria Palace with their own brand of slapstick. Each one had a distinct personality but they always worked as a team. An attempt was made to make this team into television stars, but it failed miserably. I played a small part in one of the recordings. This was a medium they did not understand. They needed a live audience and its reaction. If the laughter continued, the team reacted to increase it. But in television everything is timed to the split second. I thought it sad that they had come to television too late. Other established TV comedians attempted to help them but their style was theatrical. They acted in the Victorian/Edwardian Music Hall tradition that was out of fashion. Television humour is fast and witty, modern audiences at home are more sophisticated and concentrated in their response.

*   *   *

One of the most memorable and exciting acting experiences of my life was joining the Unity Theatre in London's King's Cross. This was a theatre for the working class and the school of thought was left wing. I was introduced to this by my friend Hylda's sister Lotte and her husband who said that a group had bought an old Methodist Church and intended to convert it into a small theatre. Many working class volunteers participated in the conversion of this building into an ultra modern theatre. Effectively this was a close knit and fairly secretive Communist Society with Marxist beliefs. Many were ordinary Labour Party members. To wish to perform one did not have to be a trained actor from RADA. The first Director was Herbert Marshall who had worked for 10 years in Moscow and had married a Russian lady. He introduced us to the Russian method acting of Stanislavsky which involved a lengthy character study for each role. Much has been written on this method. "The Actor Prepares" is an actor's Bible. As his first work he chose a translation from the Russian, "The Aristocrats." His style of directing was so new and fascinating. Many people in the company did not use their real names because they worked in the Civil Service. They thought they would become subject to investigation by the Police. Many other people had joined, a mixture of all classes. I joined because the acting experience was exciting, professional and adult. I was sympathetically left wing and voted Labour but was certainly not a Communist, as I had an independent mind – would never accept political theory without discussion and argument.

A famous black American actor/singer joined the company, Paul Robeson. He performed in a play with Alfie Bass. It gave the company great impetus to have such a personality, a black man in their theatre. One must remember that at this time in London's history, there were few black people around. James Gibbs, later an outstanding and famous pianist who accompanied all the greatest singers, was a student at the Royal College of Music and was a member of the Theatre. We were lucky to have him accompany us. Our first musical show, was a satirical and political pantomime, "Babes in the Wood." I was cast as Robin Hood (to my great surprise) leader of the working men. I wore a green hat, short tunic and long red tights. I looked most handsome, tall and stunning. The stage manager used to say that men would faint at the sight of my lovely long red legs, which made me laugh. I sang and was the leader of the Revolutionaries in the Company. The rest of the show had great gags. The Royal Family, the Aristocracy, Hitler and Mussolini were sent-up quite alarmingly.

One of the performers, Veda Hope, who became famous later, would bring the house down with her comic, silly and fatuous Fairy Wishfullfilment, representing the Conservative Party. I shared a dressing table with her. It was great fun, the first ever politically satirical show in Britain. The show was a tremendous success and the news of it went around the world and particularly to America. Under-graduates from Oxford and Cambridge also loved it and would return many times. At Christmas, Veda and I were abducted by these young lads when we attempted to leave the stage door and were taken to their University parties. We loved their enthusiasm. We sang our songs and a good time was had by all.

Veda later went to work in a revue by Herbert Fargeon at the Little

Theatre in the Adelphi, the theatre where Joyce Grenfell made her debut. In 1938 some material was banned by the Censors, for example:

> "I may be last
> I may be loose
> I may be easy to seduce
> I may not be particular
> To keep the perpendicular
> But all my horizontal friends
> Are Princes, Peers or Reverends
> When Tom or Dick or Bertie call
> They leave me strictly vertical."

Fargeon posted this verse in the foyer of the theatre stating that it had been banned and invited the audience to enjoy it notwithstanding.

"Babes in the Woods" played to full houses for eight months until the following summer at 1939. It was never recorded. Satire is now acceptable. After Veda left the show I replaced her as the Fairy. As a result I was offered my first professional contracts as a solo comedienne.

"You are a new Gracie Fields."..

"a new Beatrice Lillie."..I was told.

"No, I am not" I answered.

"I am me."

Later in 1948 I saw the truly original Bea Lillie for the first time on stage. No one could possibly resemble her, the funniest comedienne ever.

So, for the next summer season I signed a contract to be a solo; sadly the political situation in Europe was uncertain, war was declared on September 1, 1939 and for now that was the end of any aspirations.

I was, like all single men and women over 18 years of age, conscripted for War service. I remained in London from 1939 to 1946. I evacuated London's children at first, returning from each journey. I taught those left behind in London in enormous classes, blackouts and bombing raids until peace was declared.

During 1939, after the declaration of War and until the raids became too heavy, Bill Owen and other Unity Theatre actors who were for the time being retained in London, created various forms of concert entertainment for shelters, Hospital wards or Church Halls. Theatres and schools were closed from September onwards. Invasion by the Germans was imminent. It was dangerous for buildings to be occupied. Some theatres re-opened in December and schools at Easter 1940.

Dame Myra Hess played her piano at lunch hour concerts in the National gallery. We performed our shows like strolling players in London and soon, to encourage normality, all entertainments were restored. Unity Theatre staged a revue called "Turn up the Lights" in which I sang a song written for me: "We are ladies all in uniform" which became a hit. I was in Army (A.T.S.) uniform.

Sadly the Unity building burned down in 1998. It had been the precursor to Joan Littlewood's work at Stratford-East. An original place in the Thirties, attempting to sweep away the conventional middle-class attitudes and bridging the gap between the Victorian Music Hall theatre and revolutionary theatre of the fifties and sixties. I am grateful for that experience when I was young, but am sad that I did not start a proper career as a solo comedienne. I had no fears and delighted in the magic of standing in a spotlight alone, rewarded with gales of laughter. It is a love affair with an audience that is intoxicating. I sang

great material to roars of laughter. I was invited by Leonard Sachs to
alternate with the then unknown Hattie Jacques at The Players Theatre
in Charing Cross. He asked me to come along to the theatre one
evening to see Hattie's performance. She was funny, a star in the
making. She was also a fine singer. I was somewhat concerned at having
to follow her. He required a singer and a comedienne. It was not to be, a
world war started and I was conscripted for war service.

Later Hattie was paired with Eric Sykes the marvellous clown. I had the
pleasure of rehearsing with them for two days. They invented the script
I was to play a third character if required. They prowled around with a
secretary to record their ideas and dialogue.

"Eunice, come in and be a customer, we're in Harrods."

Eric was playing an obsequiously polite salesman. A table served as the
counter covered with many props which he played with quite
succinctly. I was an upper class Lady...

"Madam may I help you?"

"Yes. I want an elephant."

and without batting an eye said: "Yes certainly Madam, what size?"

Absurd but amusing and fascinating to watch. Hattie was a talented
comedienne. She and Eric worked together like twin spirits, very inventive with an innate sense of the sanity of nonsense.

I went to an audition at Broadcasting House to replace Mrs. Dale on
radio, five minutes in a sound-proof booth with microphone. An
unseen voice instructed me to tell my name and what I intended to
recite. During the audition I had to do some dialogue with Mr. Dale.

The script was so banal that I wanted to make it farcical. Somehow I spoke seriously:

"Jim dear, something has gone wrong with our marriage...please pass me the dishcloth. Can we come together as we used to be." Hilarious.

Later at the reception desk, I told them I'd had an audition for Mrs. Dale and asked if I'd be able to do other work as well if I got the part.

"Absolutely not, you would be required to record every day, effectively you would become Mrs. Dale!"

I was horrified at this prospect. I immediately withdrew from the short-list.

Eventually, the delightful Jessie Matthews was hired and was a big hit. I heard back from the BBC that I had passed and that they would accept me on their list of actors for the permanent repertory company of radio plays.

* * *

Mime is internationally funny and thus Charlie Chaplin is known still everywhere. Some English friends do not find "way out" humour funny at all such as the Marx brothers or Spike Milligan. They lack logical thought, their humour is madly original and imaginative. I was in "A day in Hollywood / A Night in the Ukraine" by Dick Vosbrugh and Frank Lazarus. The second act was Chekov's "The Bear" acted with the bear played by Groucho Marx, the two Russian servants Harpo and Chico and Madame (my part) played by the stately English lady adored by Groucho. He called me his "Battleship Potemkin," wonderful. This musical play transferred to Broadway. The style, in London was "comedy up" – super normal. Joe Orton has written plays that needed this style of black humour, very serious deadpan acting of very ordinary

action of extraordinary life; a rare kind of play writing which the
director and the actors must be in tune with.

*   *   *

I had a part at the Shaftesbury Theatre in the musical "Our Man
Crighton" based on "The Admirable Crighton" by J.M. Barrie, starring
Kenneth More and Millicent Martin. During this time I was alternating
my work in the theatre with some teaching to make sure I always had an
income.

Towards the end of the run, I asked the management at the Shaftesbury
if my young students from the William Ellis Boys Grammar School in
Hampstead could attend a matinee at a reduced rate and occupy the
dress circle. I believe actors and drama teachers should encourage, in
this mechanical age, a love of live theatre and of the classics in particular.
The real theatre must never die.

At the final curtain, Kenneth bowed, Millie – a star for the first time –
bowed and then I stepped forward to wild applause from the dress
circle. Kenneth More muttered: "Your personal fan club in this afternoon Eunice?"

Later, as arranged, the lads came backstage, lined up in the street and
came through the stage door, Kenneth and Millie were marvellous,
signed each programme and asked each boy his interests. We descended
to the enormous stage. The boys gasped in wonder at it's size as the
Stage Manager explained the technical aspects. I reminded them:

"Now you understand why I teach you breathing, articulation and
projection; actors should never use microphones."

Years later I met some of these students who said: "We've never forgotten that visit to the Shaftesbury Theatre."

How nice.

＊ ＊ ＊

The strike was over and I returned to London from Berkshire. Commercial television executives agreed to an exact chart of payments for actors in commercials. The rates were much higher than those of the BBC which caused some of their technicians to move into the commercial sector at Thames Television and Redifusion. This also meant that very high BBC standards would now benefit the new commercial stations. Redifusion TV was in Wembley. The other, Thames TV, by the river at Teddington. There I worked hilariously with Benny Hill. I acted in "On The Buses" for commercial television, it ran for 5 years with the same comedy team led by Reg Varney. But most of my television comedy career was with the BBC.

The Wednesday plays directed by Ken Loach were avant-garde working class, left wing. One of his that was controversial at the time, an outstanding play, "Cathy Come Home." It told of a single mother overwhelmed by the decision to take her baby into care. When rehearsing with Ken Loach there were some blank pages on the script that were our cue for improvisation. This made for great naturalism and was great fun for the actors. The Director who enjoyed this method concentrated on plays about the working class in working class situations. We would ad-lib the crowd scenes. I loved this method too. One became a new character and invented imaginatively what you would say to others around you – great teamwork, five cameras filming – The Director would later select the most pertinent shots. Ken Loach is now very famous. He was an original. I am delighted I worked under his inspired directing.

It was advantageous for an actor to obtain a commercial as one is well paid for a short period of concentrated work, usually one day. With great joy I played Wagner's Brunnhilde. surprisingly in a commercial for "Minty Minto are a little bit stronger." The studio was located in Leicester Square. After lunch I was sent across the road to Clarksons (the costumier) – I was photogenic and had experience in comedy. I was often cast in the Brunnhilde mould with horns, helmet, long flaxen plaits and held a spear. I was formidable. I called a taxi and drove across Leicester Square and nobody looked surprised at the sight of this statuesque character in the back of a London taxi. It was hilarious. I waved my hand graciously like the Queen and pointed my spear out of the window.

At the studio they asked if I knew Wagner's "Ride of the Valkyries"?

"What are we advertising" I asked.

For the mint with a hole; I would raise my spear and make an O formation with my mouth…instead of Wagner's "Haloo."

I wonder who invents these exotic ideas for commercials. It was certainly great fun to perform as Wagner's heroine, if only for two hours in silence.

I much enjoyed the commercial for the new product from Schweppes "One-calorie" Diet. It was filmed one year just before Christmas, to sell the low-cal tonic for the Christmas parties. They were aiming their campaign at the young who wanted to keep slim. I was dressed in a white coat massaging the back of a beautiful, nearly naked! Model, in a studio filled with dry ice mist. The script was "One must suffer to be beautiful. She was pummeled by this dragon… "but no more because now I can have new One Cal Tonic." Our model was gorgeous but not an actress. She just couldn't remember her lines. That commercial was extremely well paid. I am called "two-take Eunice" at Pinewood

Studios. The technicians love me. In the theatre, I love rehearsals but in the film studio I want to film quickly, too many takes and get worse.

I imagine my most memorable commercial was made for French Television. I was to be a "blanchisseuse" at a French laundry competition. The product was a spray starch that you would use to stiffen collars. It was shot at Elstree studios. There was a handsome presenter of a competition between two of these ladies. One very tall, the other tiny. We each had an ironing board with a shirt on it. We would spray the starch while the host explained in French how this was a contest for the best blanchisseuse in France. We started rehearsals, first the camera on me the big one and then on to the small one. We were the finalists of this competition. It was 8:30am. The Director lay on the floor near me and instructed me to do everything that he said, facial expressions, the movement of the iron and the starching of the shirt. You must be experienced to do this, the concentration is total. We began. He said:

"Look fierce, quicker, slower, turn over the shirt, spray starch..."

Suddenly I realised that the ironing board was beginning to slip down to the floor. I waited to hear "cut" from the Director, the board descended lower and lower I was bending my knees to keep up and still following all those instructions from the Director until finally I was flat on the floor with the ironing board. The Director shouted: "CUT."

The studio filled with 20 crew burst into gales of laughter. The director was still rolling about on the floor laughing. It was quite a moment. I said: "Are we shooting that again?"

Fortunately the Director said it was one of the funniest takes he had ever shot... "Off to breakfast, it's so funny, I'm keeping it just as it is."

It can happen, my whole day's work over in ten minutes I received a nice large payment for that. It was shown throughout France.

I did a 45 minute commercial playing a Scottish farmer's wife sitting in her kitchen, advertising Scottish cheese which is bright orange and very tasty. We filmed at Pinewood. The set was that of a farmhouse kitchen. I sat at the head of a table with my broad-shouldered son standing next to me. I told him this cheese was wonderful, eat it. I would cut him a slice and then I would say:

"Hamish me lad, it builds you up."

"CUT!"

The restaurant at Pinewood is well known, beautiful and excellent; you could meet a Director or a casting director who could offer you some work. But, to my surprise I was told:

"Eat little at lunch, return at 2pm. You are going to fly."..

"To Scotland?" I queried.

"No, darling Eunice, on wires."..

"I'm not Peter Pan…why a Scottish housewife on wires?…I'm a tall and heavy lady!"…

"No problem, we'll use the Robert Morley wires. Well fit your waist with wires and a very strong belt with a couple of hooks and off you'll go up in the air. We'll put your costume overalls to hide the wires and that's that We'll have a practice of you flying through the air."

Apparently, when I told Hamish, my son, that the cheese would build him up, I would then be hoisted up on to the top of the kitchen sideboard, only my feet would be seen dangling in the shot. The effect should be hilarious. And so "flying" over this concrete floor, 12 feet up in the air, we concluded the task. I was ready to play Peter Pan. Unfortunately the wires crossed and I flew horizontally like a flying porpoise. I was left in the air, much laughter from the cast & crew. Eventually, my bottom was firmly fixed on to the top of the sideboard with my feet dangling: all for the viewer's amusement, Actors suffer not "to be beautiful" but for your entertainment. We must be mad, happily so.

My next commercial was shot at a school in Mill Hill in North-West London. It was located in the cricket pavilion. I played the wife of the club President They were launching a new lager and wished to appeal to a cross-section of people, avoiding class consciousness. There were very many extras merrily pretending to be drinking in the bar. I had expected to wear a sensible cocktail outfit. I was dressed in a Madame Pompadour outfit with an enormous flowing pink skirt. I wore long false eyelashes. Somebody took a photograph and commented that I looked like Barbara Cartland. I asked the director about this pink outfit. He told me, to my intense surprise, that I was playing Barbara Cartland!.

"But she would never be in this place drinking lager, it would be champagne out of a slipper for her." I said.

The advertisers were attempting to appeal to all ages and classes. Social conditioning at its worst.

These commercials were lucrative and helped to pay for my two mortgages on my houses in Holland Park. In those days the classic actors from the RSC avoided commercials, they were not considered dignified; things have certainly changed, the money/time factor is of course a strong consideration nowadays. These days the commercials are quite brilliant, satirical, original; with animals, babies and electronics which are used brilliantly. So that, often, the commercials are more entertaining than the actors.

I did a commercial for a new type of cocktail cheese, very plastic, alas. Lift a slice of this cheese put it between two slices of bread with some pickle. That would be your family lunch. Very convenient and tasty but not remotely as delicious as a traditional cheese. It was to be an upmarket commercial in appearance. The cheese sandwiches would be on a silver tray and offered by a butler in full uniform. The butler would come to me offering one of these canapés. I would inquire the name of the cheese, eat it, then say how lovely it was. Unfortunately, just before, I had been to a Health Farm in the country in an attempt to lose some weight and had come back especially to do the job. But had been warned by the people at the health farm not to eat anything. A little yogurt maybe, an apple. There were many rehearsal takes so I asked if I could mime the eating until the actual takes. To promote this product as suitable for children, some scenes were to be shot with children enjoying this lovely cheese. That was filmed in the early afternoon. The children are accompanied by a matron and must finish work by 4pm. This is to protect them from exploitation. During this time we rested and resumed work again after 4pm. The rehearsals must have been funnier than the actual film as I was continually spitting out this ghastly cheese at every take. When I returned to the health farm that evening. I hoped that an extra day's fasting would eliminate the calorie intake caused by this cheese. As I was slimming, I had to decline the invitation to a celebratory champagne supper after the shoot. I was away to resume my starvation diet; I never eat that cheese. I prefer Camembert and Stilton.

I made a commercial for Brook Bond Tea. The casting lady told me to wear the hat I was wearing when I auditioned. I have many hats and have always worn them. I'm told that I can wear virtually any shape being a "hat lady" with a strong boned, classic face (whatever that is?) I would always go to the Selfridge £1. hat sale. The commercial concerned me trying on many different hats, looking into the mirror with various reactions; puzzled, appalled, pleased; and the attendant would hand me a cup of this tea, so soothing after making such a difficult choice. I enjoyed that work – a sheer pleasure.

These days some of the commercials can be brilliant like those for British Airways, the more they insist on BA being the world's best airline, the more people believe it. Advertising does work. The toilet roll advertisement with the puppies is very effective. And the cat and dog commercials too. The visual tricks are so brilliant. They say never act with children or animals. How right. There's a shaggy dog who asks to be taken for a walk, is ignored, packs a suitcase and leaves home looking so sad. Absolutely wonderful.

I played the wife of a business man. It was a Sunday supplement offer where the wife could accompany her husband free of charge in an hotel for a weekend holiday. The inference was:

"Always take your little lady with you on your business trips"

I am six foot tall!

We are seen in a car going up Haverstock Hill, I am sitting in front wearing a huge hat with my tiny husband driving. As we arrive at the hotel I walk ahead, my small husband is left to carry mountains of luggage. Big powerful wife loving husband's business!

Tall lady has small husband, she gives him a little pat on the head…a comic visual like Benny Hill would pat Jack Wright on the head. My late husband was taller than me, so I never, but never tapped him on the head.

On my numerous trips to America I have had to sit through many a painful moment with their endless commercials. The concept of the BBC format of license paying is alien to them. Currently at £106. per year, it is good value considering the quality and variety of the programmes. And there are no commercials. How much longer can this last? On other British terrestrial channels, the commercials are at least at decent intervals. It is worrying however, that the present trend in Britain is to go the American way with an ever increasing number of satellite channels. More is not usually better and that applies to advertising as well.

Advertising has a huge effect on children and sadly it makes them more demanding and to expect so much more without effort. The parents are often not able to afford the amazing things that are shown on television, but as the children feel they must keep up with their friends, this can sometimes lead to crime, theft & all sorts of problems. There are so few examples of good moral well-being nowadays, about what is right and what is wrong. It is a dilemma that can only get worse.

I think the Internet and E. Mail systems are miraculous but terrifying, very fascinating to send immediate messages to friends or for business. To receive information within seconds can be very useful. But alas, some extremely dangerous ideas can also be sent on the Internet (children have access to evil ideas at the press of a button). Who controls the information so displayed? They are the new masters of thought – a terrifying prospect.

EUNICE BLACK – SOME HIGHLIGHTS

1961   A TASTE OF HONEY

1962   TALES OF MYSTERY
        SIX MORE FACES OF JIM

1963   ERIC SYKES SHOW

1964   MARTIN CHUZZLEWIT
        LANCE PERCIVAL SHOW

1965   WOMEN AREN'T ANGELS

1966   DROP DEAD DARLING

1970   ON THE BUSES (TV)

1971   ON THE BUSES (FILM)

1972   DICK EMERY SHOW
        DEREK NIMMO SHOW

1973   HOLIDAY ON THE BUSES
        THE TWO RONNIES

1974   THE BUNNY CAPER

LIFE TWO
THE 1937 TOUR OF FRANCE WITH BALLET RAMBERT

"a star danced and under it 'Rambert' was born"

Joanna had been studying classical ballet with Marie Rambert. Her company announced a forthcoming tour of France. I asked Joanna if I could come along. I am very experienced in the theatre I could help backstage. Madame Rambert asked if I could speak French, which I could. I was accepted as a member of the company. Without pay but my food and hotels were paid for and we travelled by 3rd class trains. Madame Rambert said I could assist where necessary. It was a great experience. We travelled around for 6 weeks and this was the first ever tour of France by a British based classical ballet Company

I had not realised the hard work and discipline necessary to be a professional ballet dancer, the blood, sweat and tears and the concentration involved. Ballet looks effortless. Talent and strict daily practice and dedication are imperative. Madame Rambert was an extraordinary lady, determined to get the very best out of the dancers and determined to show the world that English girls could be classical ballet dancers; and this was well before Ninette de Valois started the Sadler's Wells Royal Ballet. Madame Rambert started a ballet club and wanted to confound people by proving that English girls could be beautiful and talented in classical ballet.

We left London and travelled to Nice where I saw the brilliant blue

Mediterranean for the first time I was overwhelmed by the local culture, the French people and the atmosphere of the South of France, the outstanding beauty of the coastal mountains. French food was a revelation. I worked very hard. I watched class in the morning, fascinated by Madame Rambert and her little stick. As the dancers were practising at the bar, she would tap them on the shoulder, on the back, correcting the bad posture. Despite the very hot weather (there was no air conditioning then) they rehearsed five short ballets in the afternoon. We stayed for 2 weeks. I have found an original programme from that tour, part of British ballet history, from which is taken the translated introduction to this chapter. She also had vast knowledge and impeccable taste in classical music and introducing people to modern French composers which she used for her short ballets. The choreography was memorable for its elegance, wit and originality.

A former Tiller girl, a cockney lady, was the wardrobe mistress. Madame asked me to assist her with the enormous variety of costumes. They were transported in large baskets known as skips. I recognised all the costumes very quickly. I was able to help Mae put the correct costumes in the correct order in the correct dressing rooms. The dancers performed every evening from 9pm to 1:30 am. The costumes were cleaned and ironed every day. In the ballet "Les Sylphides" and in some scenes of "Swan Lake" the costumes are very intricate with many layers which require much attention and time to make them look good at each performance. My mornings were very busy washing and pressing. Drying was quick and easy in the hot sunshine. The ironing was difficult. Some locals helped; a selection of ancient old ladies who looked like refugees from the French Revolution. We washed and ironed madly.

Mae enjoyed a glass or two of wine. One day she collapsed under the pressure of the intense heat. She was immediately demoted and Madame Rambert announced that from thenceforth I was to be the Wardrobe mistress. I learned the ballets and the costumes very quickly. I would sit beside Madame with a pad and pencil taking notes of her comments. She had an eagle eye, observing for instance, the lovely lead dancer Maude Lloyd, she would say:

"The glove on her left hand has a button missing"…or

"That tunic needs shortening"…or

"That head-dress needs cleaning and repairing."

She had on eye for everything. Her standards were the highest, not only in dance but in every other department. Her professionalism was complete. Detail was all important.

A new ballet, "Pavane pour un enfant défunt" was being created for Maude Lloyd and Bentley Stone, a tall and handsome American dancer. It featured music unknown to me at the time by Ravel. Madame knew exactly which costume was needed and asked me to search for it. Made of heavy black brocade with many tiers, it was to be worn over a wire frame. It had wide hips as in a Valesquez painting. It was very heavy, I wondered how Maude could dance in such a costume. Madame explained a pavane is a slow, stately dance and Maude will rehearse in the actual costume. It required much repair and attention. When I eventually lifted it from the skip, it was worse than I imagined. It had been lying in moth-balls for ages. I examined the wire cage and pin-pointed all the places where it was broken. I asked Madame it I could spend a little money on a repair kit. She agreed but warned me not to spend too much! I spent about £1.50. of my own money, repaired the joints and made sure that they would not collapse under the weight of the costume. I then mended the fabric which I carefully washed and ironed. The finished dress was miraculously elegant. Maude looked lovely, with Bentley Stone in his Spanish outfit; they looked marvellous and theirs was a bewitching dance. When I told Madame how much I had spent, she cried: "How could you be so reckless with money."

I ignored her exasperation. I was having such a good time, helping in my humble capacity to create such a beautiful ballet.

On one occasion, as we were travelling in our 3rd class compartment, we pulled into a station in Southern France. Madame Rambert who was sitting in the corner by the window called out to a porter:

"De l'eau s'il vous plait"…some water.

It was very hot and we were perspiring. Madame took the jug and poured the water over herself! I was learning fast, our Madame Rambert was a true artiste and eccentric.

My first impression of a French theatre was the smell, a mixture of dust, garlic (provided by the breath of the stage hands), and of greasepaint. No Max Factor in those days. The sweat of elderly stage hands and of dancers who look so cool but whose costumes are wet after a strenuous solo. I would be in the wings to remove a shirt so that it could be washed as soon as possible. Backstage is not as romantic as the on-stage performance. The costumes must be washed every day to prevent rot Especially the silk shirts.

During rehearsals one afternoon, one of the male dancers performed a solo wearing knee-high leather boots. He should have been wearing soft leather ballet shoes. He was making a lot of noise. Madame Rambert rose up from her seat in the stalls. She screamed: "STOP, how dare you!"

She rushed out of her seat and chastised him backstage. She would not allow anybody to be funny or make jokes during rehearsals, ever. He did not misbehave again. I was inspired by her professionalism. The dancers never complained. In rehearsals for actors in comedy and farce, there is much laughter, that is, until rehearsals at a later stage become serious!

A stage hand about 50 years old, one evening in the wings started breathing over my shoulder:

"I love you."

Nobody had ever said that to me, then. He handed me what looked like a piece of lavatory paper on which he had scribbled, in English, I love your eyes blue, I love you, I love you. His name was Henri. I took the paper and threw it away. How well he knew me, my eyes are not blue, they are grey-green actually. That was my first ever love note. One remembers these moments in early life because they are firsts.

Tamara, one of the dancers, went onto the beach to sun-bathe. Next morning at class she was visibly darker. Madame cried in French and Russian: "How can you be a Sylphide in the moon-light when you are brown?"

She was ordered to put white make-up all over her body. She never transgressed again.

We travelled on to Séte, a small town on the Mediterranean with a tiny theatre where the prospect of a visiting classical ballet company was fascinating for the locals. They loved it. The stage, unfortunately, was riddled with bolts and nails – hazardous for dancers. A carpet covering was provided and the merry Frenchmen worked miracles with their hammers in an attempt to flatten the stage surface. Such are the hazards of touring in unusual territory. We travelled on to Biarritz and to Vichy. This town in central France where people go to take the waters, has a very big theatre indeed. It was a grand place. The people were quite unenthusiastic but quite amazed that these dancers were actually English. The back stage staff were not all that experienced. During a performance of "Les Sylphides," usually set in moonlight, the stage was flooded with brilliant orange sunlight. Madame Rambert was beside herself.

One day, as the dancers had not received their salaries, the leading dancer Walter Gore said: "Tonight we strike at midnight. We sit on the skips outside the theatre stage door." A very short but effective strike by ballet dancers, the first ever and the last, I hope, was a success! They were paid.

We went from Biarritz to La Baule in the north-west. Normandy is very beautiful. During this journey the company travelled in one carriage. Joanna and Eunice with all the costumes in skips were in another carriage. During the night the train divided into two sections. The dancers with Madame Rambert went westward to La Baule and we (with costumes) went east to Paris. I realised that we were unlikely to reach La Baule by the evening in time for the performance. We left the train with the skips, sat on the platform and were interrupted by the railway inspectors. They thought we were Spanish refugees. Fortunately I speak fluent French and pleaded with the Railway Authorities to get us to La Baule for the evening performance explaining that we were carrying the costumes for a travelling ballet company. There was much hilarity, much kissing and much French laughter and understanding. We were placed on the right Express train heading westwards. So we arrived in time. I later heard that Madame Rambert, when told I was with the others and the costumes, that she was confident that I would arrive on time and not let the company down. I was very pleased by that and felt quite honoured and very professional.

We were staying in a splendid hotel, not in the expensive rooms, but on the top floor and were told to use the back tradesmen's entrance at all times. We were not refugees but not considered smart enough to use the front entrance and the grand staircase. We were very amused by this and decided that I, being nearly six feet tall, would dress splendidly in a long purple cloak and would make a dramatic descent into the main foyer by the grand staircase. This I did, silencing the immediate wealthy entourage. As an actress I enjoyed every moment. It was great fun, even the hotel owners wondered who I was, I was so imposing! We felt it was our little protest against dancers being treated as third rate citizens, and not as the great artistes they were. Nowadays they would be received by the President himself…Once outside I ran to the back of the hotel, up the service lift to my room. Incidentally, as there was a shortage of beds, I slept in a bath! La Baule is a beautiful holiday seaside paradise. I recall looking out of my top floor window in the hotel at the miles of sandy beaches glittering in the moonlight. Two riders on white horses cantered along, the tails floating in the air, lovely.

So, as my scholastic term was approaching, I returned to London. So ended one of my lives, as a wardrobe mistress. It was a magical experience, especially to travel with Madame Rambert, a great artist.

LES BALLETS ANGLAIS DE MARIE RAMBERT

Translation from the original programme, 1937 tour of France

Adrian Stokes, Author of "Ce soir le Ballet" and "Ballets Russes" wrote in The Spectator: "When they write the History of English Ballet for our generation, the first chapter will undeniably be dedicated to Marie Rambert, her extraordinary personality and daring goals. She is the founder of the Ballet Club, the nursery of English Ballet.

It now remains for the French balletomanes to decide for themselves if these qualitatives may be ratified artistically. In any case these comments can be justified simply by the fact that Madame Rambert's troupe was the first to appear in London and throughout the country and that they will now be seen on their maiden tour of France both in Paris and in the Provinces, presented by Miss Daphne Deane, noted Impresario from the world of serious Dance and Theatre

When asked his opinion, Diaghilev stated that the English were now on a par with the Russians with regard to their potential dancing talent and indeed as we write there are three English Companies whose work is considered as serious and as important as that of any of their Russian contemporaries. Alas, Diaghilev died before he could witness the development of a School in England possessed with the distinct drive and unique qualities as his own. A school able to produce the highest standards in dance, choreography, designers and musicians. Those successful in English Ballet are not necessarily of English descent. For instance! Nadia Benois, leading designer with the Ballet Anglais is the niece of the celebrated Alexandre Benois and we note that quite often French composers are the inspiration for their works. English Ballet, like the school of Diaghilev has learned to benefit from and absorb the finer offerings available in foreign Art forms.

The "Dancing Time" the foremost publication on English Dance, recently published a retrospective account of the Rambert's oeuvre. They include: In 1928 during the "Sunshine Matinee" season presented by Mr. P.J.S. Richardson at the Apollo Theatre, Frederick Ashton's Ballet, "Leda and the Swan" was performed with costumes by William Chappel and starred Diana Gould, Frederick Ashton, Harold Turner, William Chappel, Prudence Hyman and Andree Howard. This in collaboration with acclaimed maestro Constant Lambert. From this performance was born one of the two great permanent London Ballet Companies.

In the spring of 1930, at the Lyric Theatre, and during a Matinee performance, Madame Rambert presented an afternoon of Ballet showing off the exclusive talent of her own Company. It was a memorable success; so much so that Sir Nigel Playfair offered his Theatre for a season of Ballet. After this, Marie Rambert and her husband Ashley Dukes decided to form a permanent Company in their own theatre in order to fill the huge abyss left by the death of Diaghilev. At first seasons were staged at the Lyric and at the New but eventually the "Ballet Club" was founded at the newly acquired Mercury Theatre in Notting Hill Gate.

And it was there, for many years, that Madame Rambert continued her relentless pursuit of excellence in Ballet, constantly linking new and established talent and thus creating the tradition of English Ballet. To this day, her former artistes re-assemble on a Sunday, at the Mercury, to dance, regardless of commitments elsewhere. They include dancers Pearl Argyle, Maude Lloyd, Elizabeth Schooling, William Chappel and Walter Gore; choreographers Frederick Ashton, Antony Tudor, Andree Howard and Susan Salaman; designers William Chappel, Sophie Fedorovitch, Hugh Stevenson, Nadia Benois and many more whose debut was with the Ballet Club and who are now in constant demand by the greatest Ballet Companies around the world.

.

LIFE THREE
As an Air Warden during the War
(1939-1946)

The start of the Blitz of 1939-1940, was a misfortune for me. I was in it. I was but a quarter of a mile from St. Paul's Cathedral, which was later to receive a direct hit which caused much damage. This first blitz by German bombers was directed on the docks and Liverpool Street Station. I was seated in a train waiting to go home to Woodford about six stations down the line. The train travelled in the black-out but suddenly came to a halt because of the Blitz. There were fires every-where. More and more bombers droned overhead. The train crawled to Highams Park Station. I lived ten minutes away opposite Epping Forest. The entire horizon was ablaze. The bombers flew overhead. I thought, sadly, that tomorrow London would be destroyed completely. I went indoors taking all the precautionary advice I had been given, placed a table across the fireplace making sure there was no fire in the chimney, placed a cushion inside the grate, positioned my body under the table, put my head on the cushion and hoped I would survive. I spent a sleepless night there. The next morning there was a great cloud of smoke covering London in the distance, that first blitz was over but the War had truly begun.

A rather terrifying time came in 1944 when the Americans arrived in vast numbers for the invasion of Europe. I was at my flat in Swiss Cottage, and knew that something was about to happen. You saw battalions of troops marching south towards the Kent coast who were to be the eventual reinforcements necessary for the invasion. Churchill, along with his team of experts, created the Mulberry Harbour, a huge concrete structure towed across the English Channel to lie off the French coast for the shipment of arms, food and men. It was a work of genius. Americans in huge numbers under the command of General Bradley and British troops under Field Marshall Montgomery had been mobilised for this greatest invasion in history. To land under fire from German artillery was heroic. Extremely brave mine-sweepers went ahead the night before D-day to clear the sea for the soldiers who were to follow. It was to be one of the great battles of all time, to re-capture the continent from the domination of the Germans who had been invincible in Europe. Their navy had sunk thousands of ships in the Atlantic with their submarine attacks. Several of my dear friends were on this first day of invasions. Commander Charles Hall, had been with the Commandos for many years landing unexpected invasions constantly surprising the Germans. His was one of the first ships to go in on D-day. The 5th Commandos were chosen to land by parachute before dawn behind their lines to confuse the Germans who were facing the sea; they expected the British and the Americans by sea, but not from above and inland. Alas, most of these brave men were killed as they landed. They were heroes.

I met Commander Charles Hall in Falmouth during the evacuations. At the week-ends, I would go to a small hotel to rest, have a good bath and go to the local Forces dance. I met him there and we became friends and lovers. He was like a hero from a marvellous story. I felt like we were Desdemona and Othello. I would listen to his Naval stories with eyes wide and a great deal of wonder. He had joined the Commandos at the request of Lord Louis Mountbatten. Charles was the Commander of a ship and he invited me to port and I was piped aboard. I fell in love with the men of the navy. They were brave and heroic and handsome in their uniforms!

On June 5th 1944, before the dawn on D-Day, in a mine sweeper,

Charles invaded France attempting to defeat Hitler's army. They cleared the mines to allow the safe passage of the invading armada to reach the Mulberry Harbour. Commander Hall dear Charles, followed to land the soldiers aboard his ship. The Fifth Commandos he had sent ashore the previous night to land by parachute were, to my great sorrow, killed as they descended. War destroys without mercy.

The forward attack lasted for months. The final battle in the Ardennes was won and the Allies marched on to Paris. When the time came to reclaim the French Capital, the Allies insisted that General de Gaulle led the French Battalion in glory back into Paris. The Germans still in Paris surrendered, many were imprisoned or shot. There was great jubilation among the French, but the War was not over, Armies had to fight eastward across the Rhine into Germany, to meet in Berlin with the Russians.

These were extraordinary times for us listening to reports on the radio. I am convinced that the more serious disasters were kept from us and we were informed mostly of the victories. Morale was all important.

* * *

In September 1939, I was told to arrive at Joseph Barrett School in Walthamstow, London E17 to collect a party of 60 children. It was very secretive. We did not know our destination. The children were with their shoe-boxes containing gas masks and their little cases, surrounded by very sad parents kissing them good-bye. They were marched onto a bus which took us to Paddington station. At that point I realised that we were heading west. It was a long journey, nearly 8 hours. We eventually arrived at Redruth in North Cornwall. We were going to the village of St. Stithians, 6 miles north of Falmouth, on the moors.

We were received in the Church Hall at 9pm and confronted with the prospect of many more hours completing forms and dealing with the formalities. My poor, stunned. crying and scruffy 60 children were sitting on the floor. I was told that each child would have to be seen separately and then assigned to various homes in the village. I would then make note of their location and report back to their parents in London with their precise address. I approached the lady in charge and asked if I could make a suggestion. The villagers, no doubt aware that no-one ever questioned the Lady of the Manor, were holding their breath...

"Ma'am," I said...

"Please forgive me but these children are exhausted and hungry; we've been travelling all day. Why not give them a cup of cocoa and a sandwich, a cuddle and put them to bed in the warm? We can return at 9am, happy and refreshed, to resume the paper work."

After a long pause, she said, to my great relief: "I think you are right Miss Holden"...

"Thank you...can a bed be found for me too?" I ventured...

"Of course, naturally."

The local Vicar's wife was very kind. She had been left with her two children and a huge Vicarage when her husband went away as a Padre in the Forces. She offered to take 6 children, which was marvellous. She made a dormitory for them. They were happy there.

The village Head-master was distraught and overwhelmed by these extra children to teach. My group of Londoners was not the only one, there were others from Southampton and Bristol. The school was tiny. There were not enough teachers, chairs or books. The original 50 or so pupils had now swelled to nearly 200. He begged the Cornish Authorities to allow me to stay on and teach at the school. Thank God. I was assigned the village hall with my 60 children and told to educate them. I appealed to my friend, the Vicar's wife for help. We had trestle tables, some benches and a blackboard with one stick of chalk. There was also a piano with some notes missing. I could invent my own timetable. As the weather was good, not the usual British summer gloom, we spent much time outdoors. The vicar's wife, bless her, eventually brought me 60 old-fashioned Bibles. I would spend the first hour of each day reading from this wonderful book. We read it all eventually. The children loved it and I read it with pleasure using my talent as an actress to make it even more dramatic. We would then go out and would enjoy the study of nature. My "nature" rambles were great fun…

"What's that Miss Holden?."..

"Grass" I would reply…

"Carrots…an oak tree…an apple tree…etc…"

with strict instructions not to touch or eat anything as these beautiful gardens belonged to the local farmer. I told them about the trees and the flowers. The Countryside was magic to the children who had come from the back streets of East London. In the afternoon the children would go into the field and kick a ball around. We would play cricket sometimes and on other occasions sing around the piano. Many of the children never went back to London, they fell in love with the countryside and the lovely people who had looked after them. Some of these children had come from tough homes with unkind parents. I had sadly to return to London, to continue my war work.

Before I returned to London from Cornwall, I walked along clifftops in north Cornwall and sat down to admire the views across the Bristol

Channel to Wales. To my horror I discovered that I was sitting on an ants' nest. They were crawling all over me! I brushed them off wildly, jumping up and down and must have looked quite ridiculous dancing on top of a cliff. When I returned to the village, I was promptly arrested as a probable German spy. Our Coast Guard had been on watch and thought that what they were witnessing through their telescopes was someone signalling to a ship in the Bristol Channel. The people who watched our coast-line were most vigilant. They soon discovered that I was indeed a teacher taking care of evacuated children from London.

Churchill had stated that we would never surrender. If the enemy landed by parachute, turn all the signposts in the wrong direction, especially those pointing towards London, a simple but extremely effective idea. Everyone must organize for the defence of their village or town.

Many years after the end of the war, a now classic television series was made called "DAD'S ARMY" This BBC series about civilian defence reminds us vividly of the people's response to Churchill's exhortation. A wonderfully funny interpretation of life in a small sea-side town taking heed of the recommended precautions. It starred the extremely talented Arthur Lowe and John le Mesurier with an equally talented supporting cast. It is without doubt my all time favourite television comedy program.

Eventually I returned to London, teaching in many blackboard jungles, helping the children of London to survive. My own survival routine was to spend Sunday afternoons with my two American friends who would call in for tea. They brought some wonderful records which we played on my record player. Brahms, Mozart, marvellous Operas. But mostly we enjoyed just sitting around and chatting. We would eat a tin of Spam or something fishy called Snook (horrible), which they brought with them. But never mind, it was food. On one memorable occasion they brought some steaks which I had not seen for years and we cooked them on a grill on my open fireplace. My first and last BBQ steak, or so I thought at the time. I listened to these young Americans ribbing each other mercilessly. They had European ancestry, spoke French, German, Polish, Russian & Italian fluently. They had University degrees, were very intelligent and witty, were quite different from their British counterparts who were in contrast, often stuffy and inhibited. At 4pm I would serve tea, Lady Bracknell style cucumber sandwiches, if I could obtain a cucumber that is. They loved my "tea ceremony," although I suspect they would have preferred coffee – but coffee was unobtainable.

At that time I met Frantisek Fubrobretin, a Czechoslovakian. He was Jewish from a wealthy Prague family. They had left their native city when the war broke out and now lived in Kensington. He joined the Czech Army as a Private. He took me to concerts. His uncle was a great composer not yet renowned in England. His name was Gustave Mahler. Frantisek had written a song for me. I still have it. I saw him at weekends. He did not wish to return to Prague to a luxury middle-class life as he believed in Socialism and in Marxism.

"I would live in a council house and work for my fellow countrymen."

I often wonder what happened to him. At least I have discovered Mahler's wonderful music, especially the Symphonies.

I met a Norwegian pilot, towards the end of the war whom I only saw briefly. He was terribly tall and handsome. He wrote to me when he returned to Norway. He had received the great honour of being chosen to fly King Haakon back to Bergen after the war. The King had been in exile in England.

Charles Hall sent a junior officer to see me one week-end. He was from Stornoway in Scotland, a Lieutenant in the Navy. He wished to take me out to dinner. My ration was so small, one week's covered one small plate. To be taken out to dinner at any time was indeed a pleasure. He had long black eyelashes and blue eyes, very sweet and charming. He confessed he was a virgin and felt so inhibited when listening to the sexual adventures of his fellow officers. In Stornoway, courtship was strict, couples were chaperoned before marriage, sexual intimacy forbidden. Dear Murdoch McLeod wished to lose his virginity...Moll Flanders obliged. I hope he returned safely to Scotland after the war.

One of the Americans, Richard Oliver, is one of the great loves of my life. He was from Columbia University in New-York. I fell in love with him. I was by then mature, no longer green in matters of the heart. I met him at Wigmore Hall at a Schubert concert. He had just arrived in London and was in counter-intelligence although I did not know that at the time. Not till he left the next year to join the French underground to restore Paris to the French. Amazing that young academics led such dangerous lives during the war. Richard, from an Italian background, was very witty and funny. I had never met any man like him. He turned my head. He loved Shakespeare. We went to the theatre and to concerts whenever possible. Most Sundays we would wander around book shops. We were twin souls. Had he asked me to marry him, I would have said yes. But he did not. In war time everything is temporary. You could be dead the next day, so you live for the moment. But after he left on the second front I was desolate, prayed that Richard would return one day, or I would go to him in America and marry him. This was the worse time of the war. Would the Allies defeat Hitler, or would the free world become a Nazi fascist State ruled by Germany? My heart had gone to France with Richard. I thought I would never see him or any of his unit again. One member, Robert Heitner, returned to London after the war and we have remained dearest friends to this day. I believed I would never love again and remained solitary for ages after Richard's departure until my friend Muriel insisted I accompany her to a dance at the Ritz Hotel...

Following the blitz of 1940, a great many homes had...been destroyed and many Londoners had been killed. The dome of St Paul's had been hit. Volunteers had put ladders up to places where they could climb out on to the outside of the dome and knock the fire bombs off into the street below to save the dome, There is a memorial chapel to the Americans at St. Paul's where the altar was hit.

The final 18 months of the war were plagued with non-stop V1 flying bombs (without pilots), a horrible invention of the Germans. They were terror machines. As they flew in over Kent, our pilots in their Spitfires and Hurricanes attempted to dive-bomb and destroy as many as possible but there were so many of them. We had had five years of blackouts, bombs and rationing and morale was very low at that time; stress and strain of losing people through death, and all the broken homes was beginning to take its toll. The men were fighting abroad and the women working in factories. The conscientious objectors went into the medical services. The land army girls as they were known became farmers. It was a very grim time. Even single young people like myself were exhausted.

I went to the theatre very rarely. My work was in the schools, the blackboard jungles where there were few teachers, classes of sixty or more, no shelters during daytime air raids. I would get so tired, all I wanted to do was go home with my head in my chimney as a mattress sandwich and go to sleep.

Looking back to 1939, I remember that Hitler had conquered the Rhine, Austria, Czechoslovakia and was now invading Poland. Our Prime Minister Neville Chamberlain went to Hitler to try and avert war, and did not succeed. Now war was imminent. I was having a brief holiday in France when it was reported on radio that all British persons abroad should return immediately. When I arrived in London I was conscripted and war was declared on 1 September 1939. My first assignment was to accompany children from London to their destination in the countryside as evacuees.

The big difference between this and the previous war of 1914-1918 was that this would be fought here as well as in continental Europe. Winston Churchill, who was, without doubt, the saviour of our Nation became Prime Minister. He had had a chequered career in the 30's, he was a maverick, once a Liberal, he was now a Conservative. He was head of the Admiralty because he was intelligent and very able. His arrival reminded me of that of Henry V at Agincourt. He was an instinctive leader and had a great command of the English language. Thank God that the radio had been invented since 1924, Churchill was able to communicate to the whole Nation on the BBC.

The invention of radar was a deciding factor in the air war. As well as the design and construction of the Spitfire and the Hurricane which were faster than the enemy bombers. Finding somewhere to be safe from the imminent bombs was difficult but eventually some people had shelters. Also, the London Underground was open at all times for people to seek safety. But it was not pleasant. We are often reminded of the bombing and destruction of Dresden and how horrible that was. But the Germans did not show any mercy with the bombing and destruction of London, the beautiful Wren churches and more importantly the countless homes and lives that were lost in London alone. London was being bombed non-stop and one bomber actually flew down The Mall and bombed Buckingham Palace. Her Majesty the Queen, now the Queen Mother, went shortly afterwards on a visit to the East End and said: "I too have been bombed, I am one of you."

The war was not only bravely fought by the British. The Polish, the Canadians and others from the Commonwealth were involved. In fact there is the Polish War Memorial on the A40 erected as a tribute to these brave fighters. I remember standing in my garden in Swiss Cottage looking up into the sky. I could actually see and hear the dive bombing above me in the blue sky. A street warden shouted that I should get back indoors as something could fall on my head.

The schools were in a terrible mess during the war because all the male teachers under 35 years of age had been conscripted to fight. I was assigned some terrible schools and made the best of what I could do. The classes grew larger & larger often as many as 60. I remember offering to take the whole school for the entire afternoon and give the teachers a break. They used the school stage, benches & chairs to arrange seating for a concert/sing-a-long. We put the piano in the centre of the hall. I would play standing up in order to see everybody. We wrote the words to the songs on the blackboard. We played and sang lullabies which they quickly learned. The afternoon soon went by. It was good for them to sing and forget the grimness of the wartime, living & sleeping in shelters or on the platforms of Underground stations or in Andersen shelters being frightened and bombed.

The flying bombs were a menace because you never knew where they fell. I remember being in yet another terrible school, trying to make the best of it, when the air-raid warning was sounded. There were no air shelters so the children were marched down under the school and sat in the corridors on benches. It was bleak, dark and very scary. We had no idea what was going on. We simply had to wait until someone came down to announce the all clear. It could happen at any time in the morning or afternoon. We were surrounded by electricity cables, water and gas pipes. I prayed there would be no direct hit as we would certainly die from one or other of these. The basement could also be flooded, a major worry for us. I made the best use of my big voice and told stories. We would sing, anything to forget this terrible situation we were in.

I believed that Churchill realised that Hitler could have won the war at that time. People were tired and exhausted. For this reason he hastened the Second Front, we must find where these flying bombs were coming from and destroy them. But the Germans invented another death horror…the rocket, the V2 which flew by itself. Straight up and straight down, destroying everything. They were very powerful and there was no warning siren. Churchill said that the destruction of the V1 & V2 sites were top priority. Fortunately, Montgomery's troops discovered the sites quickly and they were destroyed. There was great relief, in London particularly, which was battered and exhausted. The destruction of the V1 's and especially the V2's gave me new courage because after the first rocket had fallen so near to me I felt extremely depressed and fed up after five years of war. I had had enough.

The end came very quickly, it seemed. There was great rejoicing in London outside Buckingham Palace with the King & Queen and Princesses Elizabeth & Margaret and Prime Minister Churchill on the Palace balcony waving to the crowd of thousands around the Mall and Hyde Park.

After the war had ended, life tried to return to normal. I was no longer conscripted. I was teaching in a Grammar School as a specialist drama teacher. I was hoping that a particular gentleman friend of mine would return and we would get married and have children. So much changed for the young women during those 6 years of war. Many lost their intended husband. But also one had become aware of new experiences. Different types of men. Different nationalities, people you would never meet unless you travelled. We also discovered such things as courage and leadership. One could be attracted to older; intellectually and physically more interesting people. Expectations were very different after the war. For a time, the class system disappeared; working class, middle class, upper class, entrenched in our social life, had changed. People respected and admired each other as equals, so the British people voted for a Labour Government hoping it would build a new Britain, a new

Jerusalem. Before the war there had been many unemployed and the lowly miner would earn very little money and was looked down upon and not considered an equal. But the war changed all that. The poor man had proven himself to be a brave soldier, intelligent and should be treated better. The new Prime-Minister Clement Attlee promised to build a fairer and kinder and safer England; to re-build our Cities. It was to be a more Christian Britain.

Many houses had been destroyed. As a temporary measure, a bungalow type of building was introduced. They were very comfortable inside and so they became so popular that young couples wanted to keep them permanently. It was indeed an excellent way to house many people quickly.

* * *

Many years later I happened to be in Land's End. I was taking a long walk on the Moors and stopped at a Pub for a lager and a sandwich. Some soldiers in uniform entered. I told them that I had been in this area during the war taking care of some children evacuated from London. They too had been there during the war. I told them that I had known some men in the 5th Commandos and asked if they knew what had happened to them. Very sadly, they told me that they had been shot down on D-Day. They were great young men, they were heroes. It was strange to have met these men on a Cornish moor, because otherwise I would never have known for sure what had happened to my friends, especially Sergeants Kennedy and Tipton.

* * *

Like many young women whose careers had been halted or had been much delayed, I wanted to marry and have children or go back to the theatre. I went into a show at the Unity Theatre called "Winkles and

Champagne." I had worked there before the war and felt at home. To my great surprise we were asked by the BBC to appear on the new form of entertainment which was the talk of the age: television which they were inaugurating. It had been invented in the 30's, but suspended during the war. Now, in 1946, the BBC opened their first studio at Alexandra Palace. We were invited to perform a one-hour show there. I remember wearing red satin for the broadcast, but there was no colour alas. Eric Robinson conducted the orchestra and the stage was minute, there were 3 cameras and one microphone above.

We rehearsed in this giant conservatory that is Alexandra Palace. The 3 cameras, positioned in front and on either side would ensure the projection of the pictures through the air to the BBC centre in Oxford Circus. 15 miles away! and then to the people watching at home. Magic, a miracle...We found it difficult to perform without a live audience. Their reactions are always so important to us. The microphone was placed over our heads on a long stick. There was a great battery of lights above us. Very thick make-up was required especially around the eyes.

My gentleman friend at the time was a Naval Officer and I arranged a ticket for him to watch the show at Broadcasting House. I wanted him to tell me what he thought of the show when I met him for supper.

This was 1947. I have photographs of us performing "Sporting Girls," during my first television broadcast. I also sang a number called "Yes You Are" which was addressed to the men in the audience (or at least those in television land). I am very proud to have discovered "Sporting Girls" whilst perusing through books of Victorian music & lyrics at the British Museum. I sang it as a solo for TV. There were 3 "Sporting Girls," the hunter in tweeds; the tennis player in bloomers and another lady playing cricket. It was a hit.

Later when I met my boyfriend he said I looked stunning, no colour but marvellous to see the close-ups.

"I'm not sure I like this medium, television"; I said.

"There's no audience."

"Television will not last." How wrong I was!

At the end of the evening he said: "You look so marvellous dear Lady, will you marry me?"

And of course, I said: "Yes."

And that was that.

Laurence Olivier in *Romeo and Juliet*, Old Vic Theatre

Edith Evans as the Nurse in *Romeo and Juliet*, Old Vic Theatre

Personally autographed photograph of Bentley Stone - Ballet Rambert

**For Unity
Theatre at St
Pancras Town
Hall - 1947**

Turn Up the
Lights **- Unity
Theatre**

Winkles & Champagne -
**Unity Theatre production
for the BBC
at Alexandra Palace
(right: in rehearsal)**

Unity Theatre production

Inherit the Wind - St. Martin's Theatre, 1960

As Lady Bracknell on tour

The Student Prince - Cambridge Theatre

As Rose McCaulay

**As Madame
Arcati in *Blythe
Spirit* on tour**

**Entry photograph in
*Spotlight***

Glamour pose circa 1950

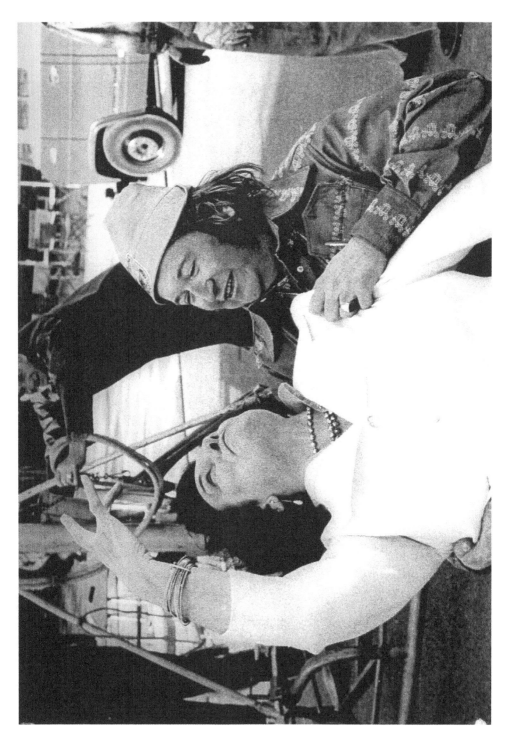

In *On the Buses* with Brian Izzard

In *Operation Bullshine* with Donald Sinden

The Admirable Crighton -
Shaftesbury Theatre 1964

Advert for Trust House Hotels

It's no rest for Eunice

WHEN "Our Man Crichton" ends at Shaftesbury Theatre tomorrow week, former Walthamstow High School girl Eunice Black—formerly Holden—who has the rôle of Lady Brockenhurst, will still be busy. Eunice is now acting with Kenneth More, Millicent Martin and David Kernan in the musical.

She has just recorded a Whitehall farce for B.B.C. television, with Brian Rix and Terry Scott.

Explained Eunice—she was formerly a lecturer at Homerton College, Cambridge—"I have a wonderfully funny part of Ruby Bandle in 'Women Aren't Angels.' " The play will be shown at peak viewing time at Christmas.

In *Chitty, Chitty, Bang Bang* with Dick Van Dyke and Sally Ann Howes

See How They Run rehearsals and as Miss Skillon, 1979

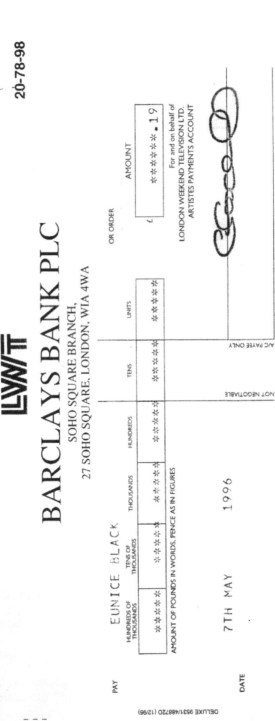

Who'd be an actor?

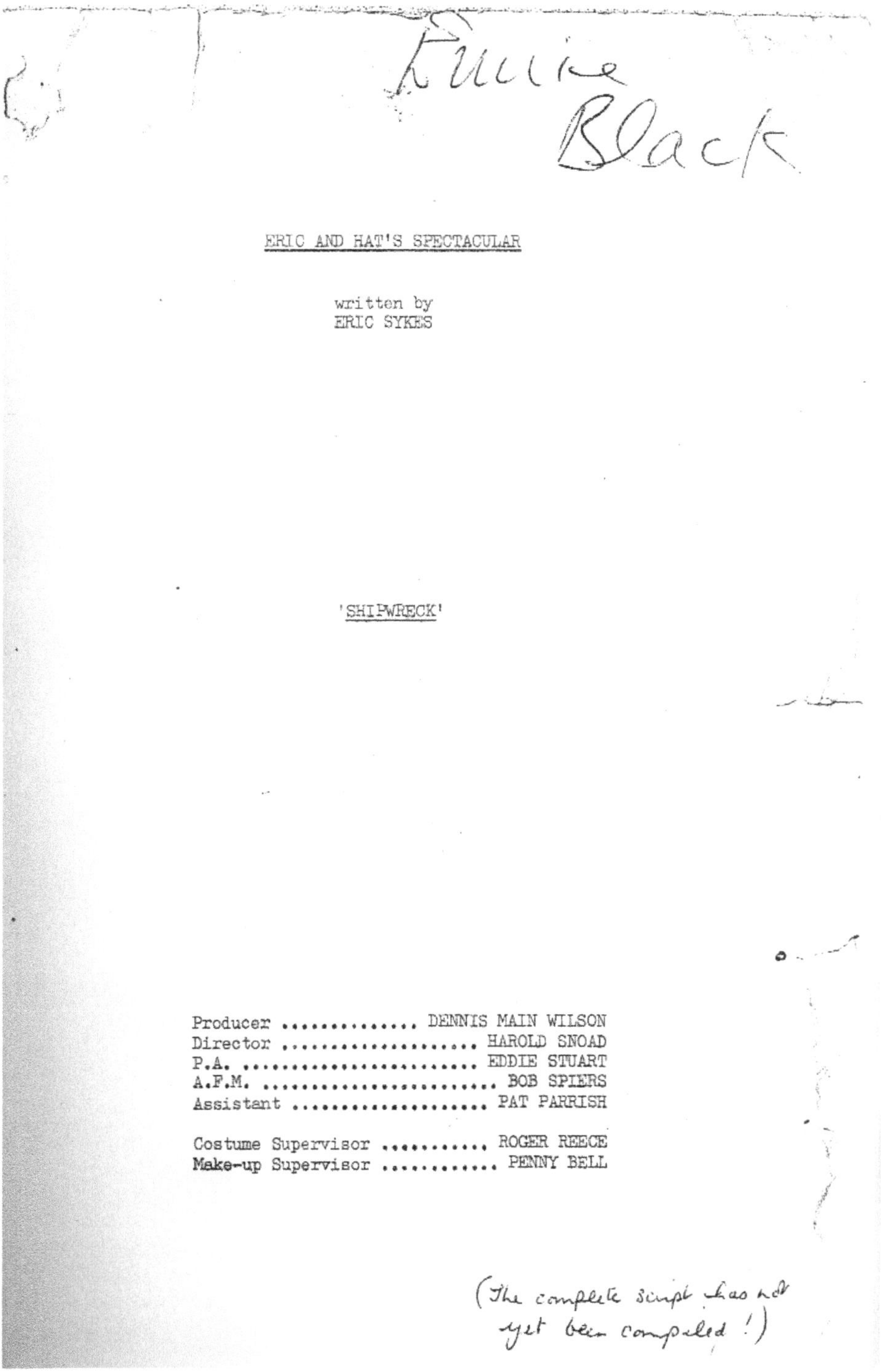

Eddie
Black

ERIC AND HAT'S SPECTACULAR

written by
ERIC SYKES

'SHIPWRECK'

Producer .... DENNIS MAIN WILSON
Director .... HAROLD SNOAD
P.A. .... EDDIE STUART
A.F.M. .... BOB SPIERS
Assistant .... PAT PARRISH

Costume Supervisor .... ROGER REECE
Make-up Supervisor .... PENNY BELL

*(The complete script has not
yet been compiled!)*

Working script with Hattie Jacques & Eric Sykes

<u>ACTION</u>   <u>SOUND</u>

<u>SCENE 4: "HARRODS" SET.</u>

(CUT TO ERIC BEHIND
COUNTER IN HARRODS.
BACK TO CAM.)

HAT:
(V.O.) Excuse me.

ERIC:
(TURNS) Good morning madame,

what can I do for you?

HAT:
Well, I know this is silly

and it's not for me, actually

a friend of mine said you

could get them here, and to prove

once and for all I decided, I mean,

well, I mean, he makes these

statements - he said Alan

Whicker did it in Kew Gardens.

ERIC:
Did he. There's a lot of

it going on, you know, there

was a case -

HAT:
No, it's all right and

somewhere, someone has to

draw the line. Well do you

supply er -

Hattie
Do You Supps
Lady
Good Morning

ACTION

(LADY COMES TO COUNTER)

HAT: (cont'd...)

No, that's all right, I'm

in no hurry, please serve the

lady first.

LADY:
(Thank you.) Is my elephant

ready?

ERIC:
Almost, they're just giving

him a test run round the block.

LADY:
It was his left tusk, wasn't

it?

ERIC:
Yes my lady, and his right.

As a matter of fact we had

to replace the right one, we've

given him a plastic one.

LADY:
A plastic one, but it's -

ERIC:
You won't be able to tell

the difference, Madam, you'll

still be able to hang your

hat on it.

Eric ~~continued~~ → 2 of confidence.

ACTION
my ~~not a joke.~~   SOUND

LADY:
And the manicure?

ERIC:
Yes Madam, although strictly
speaking it's not really
included in the five thousand
mile service.

LADY:
I see. Now I'd like to get
something for my noace.

ERIC:
Ah yes, how about a water
buffalo?

LADY:
No she had one of those
for Easter.

ERIC:
Of course. I packed it myself.
I'll tell you what, how about a
pair of white rhino?

LADY:
Are they house trained?

ERIC:
One moment. (HE GOES BEHIND,
COMES BACK FLOPPING HIS HANDS)
No. But you don't have to have
them in the house.

CAMS   ACTION   SOUND

LADY:
I thought they would look

rather splendid on either

side of the fireplace.

ERIC:
What a delightful picture.

(F/X ELEPHANT TRUMPETING)

ERIC:
Excuse me, I think that's

your elephant. (HE GOES ROUND

BACK)

HAT:
I've come for some crocodiles.

LADY:
Oh yes, what kind?

HAT:
Oh half a dozen assorted.

LADY:
You can get some rather

splendid baby ones about that

long, they go very well with

chips.

(F/X TIGER GROWLING)

[Handwritten annotations in left margin:]
I don't know,
is this your first.
Yes
Take my advice and
start with a baby one ... this size
Well I was thinking ...
trying a very big one like ...
Ah, you're having guests

look a
advice
start with
a baby one
... you're having guests

[Handwritten annotations over dialogue:]
that ... is ... you first
Yes. I tried ...
... once

ACTION   SOUND

ERIC:
I've just had an idea,
would you like to have atiger
along with the elephant?

LADY:
Certainly not.

ERIC:
I'll have to separate 'em
now. (HE TAKES A CHAIR AND
EXITS)

LADY:
Oh dear. I hope Bimbo will
be all right, I haven't insured
him against tigers.

HAT:
Well they are traditional
enemies.

LADY:
Yes, but not at this store.
I mean you can expect it in a
supermarket.

(F/X ELEPHANT GUN FIRES.
ERIC STAGGERS OUT)

LADY:
Oh dear, bad news again?

CAMS   ACTION   SOUND

ERIC:
I'm afraid so. (HE TAKES
A PIECE OF PAPER AND A PENCIL)
I'm afraid Bimbo took musk, it's
very prevalent at this time of
year, especially with a plastic
tusk. We had to put him down.

LADY:
Ah the law of the jungle.

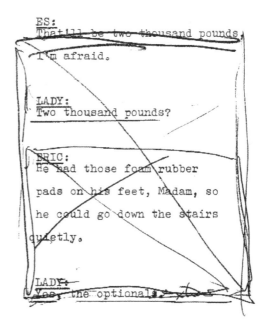

ES:
That'll be two thousand pounds,
I'm afraid.

LADY:
Two thousand pounds?

ERIC:
He had those foam rubber
pads on his feet, Madam, so
he could go down the stairs
quietly.

LADY:
Yes, the optional

ERIC:
Then there's the tiger.

LADY:
The tiger?

CAMS   ACTION   SOUND

ERIC:
Unfortunately Bimbo fell
on him. I'm afraid he's completely
useless, even for a rug, but
we'll not count the pig.

LADY:
I didn't order a pig.

ERIC:
Inside the tiger, my lady –
bait.

LADY:
~~Eight thousand pounds ten~~
~~shillings and sixpence. What's~~
~~the ten and six?~~

ERIC:
My suit, my lady. *I caught it*
in – fast.

LADY: *Thank you.*
I see (SIGNS A CHEQUE)
2 = Good Morning

ERIC:
~~Can I interest you in a forest~~
~~bred lion or a Thomson gazelle?~~

LADY:
~~Do they go together?~~

ERIC:
~~Not for long. Ha ha. In case~~
~~he gets peckish on the journey.~~
(Makes face)
Fade 20 – Not today thank

CAMS

ACTION   SOUND

LADY:
(HANDS OVER CHEQUE) ~~Not today~~
~~thank you, good-bye.~~ Good
morning

ERIC:
Goodbye. (PICKS UP HOUSE
PHONE) Lady Pontefract's
been in again. Eight thousand
pounds. Thank you, sir.
Well it keeps her happy.
Now, Madam?

HAT:
I'd like to see some crocodiles.

ERIC:
Wouldn't we all. You're in
the wrong department, Madam, this
is Babywear.

Daily Express, 23 October 1964, my birthday!

The Rambert Ballet tour of France, programme

DAPHNE DEANE

PRÉSENTE

LES BALLETS ANGLAIS

DE

MARIE RAMBERT

MARIE RAMBERT

RÉPERTOIRE

...er de Danse	Musique de Lord Berners	Suite des airs	Musique de Purcell
Façade	» William Walton	Dark elegies	» Gustav Mahler
Bar aux Folies Bergère	» Chabrier	Jardin aux lilas	» Chausson
...jeune fille et la Mort	» Schubert	Les planètes	» Gustav Holst
...Sirène	» Ravel	Lysistrata	» Prokofiev
L... descente d'Hébé	» Ernest Bloch	La muse s'amuse	» Déodat de Sévérac
...rting sketches { Le Boxing	» Lord Berners	L'enlèvement de la boucle	» Haydn
{ Le Rugby	» Poulenc	Cendrillon	» Weber
{ Le Cricket	» Arthur Benjamin	Le Jongleur de Notre-Dame	» Respighi
L... pavane passionnée	» John Dowland	Lac des Cygnes	» Tchaïkovsky
Valses nobles et sentimentales	» Ravel	Le mariage d'Aurore	» »
Méphisto Valse	» Liszt	Les Sylphides	» Chopin
...Masques	» Poulenc	Le spectre de la rose	» Weber
...priol suite	» Peter Warlock	L'après-midi d'un faune	» Debussy
Tableau florentin	» Corelli	Carnaval	» Schumann
Mars et Vénus	» Scarlatti	Le lutteur	» Lora Aborne

BALLETS ANGLAIS
MARIE RAMBERT

Adrian Stokes, auteur de « *Ce Soir, le Ballet* » et « *Ballets Russes* », écrit dans son article au « Spectator » de Londres : « Lorsqu'on écrira l'histoire du ballet anglais de notre génération presque tout le premier chapitre sera consacré à la personnalité et les buts de Marie Rambert, fondatrice du Ballet Club, la pépinière du ballet anglais ».

Il reste au public français de juger si cette opinion peut être justifiée au point de vue artistique. Mais elle est juste en tous les cas si ce n'est parce que le Ballet Rambert fut la première troupe anglaise qui parût à Londres et dans les provinces anglaises, et qui paraîtra pour la première fois aux spectateurs en France, hors Paris, en qualité de Ballet Anglais sous la direction de Mlle Daphne Deane, Impresario du Ballet et du Théâtre Intellectuel.

Lorsqu'on demanda à Diaghilev quels sont les pays qui produisent les meilleurs danseurs, il a mis les Anglais au même niveau que les Russes; et, à notre époque il existe en effet trois troupes anglaise dont l'œuvre attire une attention aussi sérieuse que celle qu'on accorde aux Russes. Diaghilev est mort sans voir le développement en Angleterre d'une école de ballet aussi individuelle que la sienne, et qui réussit à former non seulement ses danseurs, mais aussi ses chorégraphes, musiciens et dessinateurs. Ils ne sont pas tous nécessairement des Anglais; Nadia Benois, l'une des dessinatrices du ballet anglais, est nièce du célèbre Alexandre Benois, et l'on remarque que le Ballet Rambert s'inspire souvent des musiciens français. Le ballet anglais a appris, comme celui de Diaghilev, à s'attirer et à absorber tout ce qu'il y a de meilleurs dans l'art des autres pays.

Le « Dancing Times » revue prééminente de la danse en Angleterre, a publié dernièrement un résumé de l'œuvre des Ballets Rambert : « En 1928, la « *Sunshine Matinée* » organisée par Mr. P. J. S. Richardson au Théâtre Apollo fut l'occasion d'une représentation de « *Leda and the Swan* », ballet de Frédérick Ashton, avec des costumes dessinés par William Chappel, et dans lequel parurent Diana Gould, Frédérick Ashton, Harold Turner, William Chappel, Prudence Hyman, Andrée Howar et en collaboration avec Constant Lambert le célèbre chef d'orchestre. De cette représentation naquit l'une des deux grandes troupes permanentes du ballet de Londres.

« Au printemps de 1930, Madame Rambert donna au Lyric Théâtre en matinée un spectacle composé entièrement de sa propre troupe. Le succès en fut tel que Sir Nigel Playfair leur offrit son théâtre pour une « Saison de Ballet », et par suite de cette saison, Marie Rambert et son mari, Ashley Dukes, decidérent de former une troupe permanente dans son propre théâtre, pour rendre à Londres les saisons régulières de ballet qui avaient été interrompues par la mort de Diaghilev. D'autres saisons suivirent au Lyric et au New Théâtre, mais pendant ce temps le « Ballet Club » s'établit dans les Mercury Théâtre qu'il avait acquis au Notting Hill Gate.

Et c'est là que ,pendant de longues années, Madame Rambert à continué son œuvre de former et réunir les talents, et a fondé une tradition du ballet anglais; et c'est à ce théâtre que viennent toujours danser le dimanche ses propres artistes, quels que soient leurs engagements dans d'autres spectacles. Parmi les danseurs se trouvent : Pearl Argyle, Maude Lloyd, Elisabeth Schooling, William Chappel and Walter Gore; les chorégraphes : Frédérick Ashton, Antony Tudor, Andree Howard, and Susan Salaman; les dessinateurs : William Chappel, Sophie Fedorovitch, Hugh Stevenson, Nadia Benois ;et d'autres encore qui ont fait leurs débuts au Ballet Club et dont la collaboration est constamment sollicitée par les meilleures troupes du monde.

ENSEMBLE DU BALLET MERMAID (LA SIRÈNE)

PROGRAMMES

des

BALLETS ANGLAIS DE MARIE RAMBERT

FOYER DE DANSE (d'après DEGAS)

Ballet de Frederick ASHTON — Musique de Lord BERNERS

L'étoile	MAUDE LLYOD
Le maître de ballet	WALTER GORE
Les coryphées	Mmes SCHOOLING, MORFIELD, SVETLOVA, GEE, FRANKS, SAREL, SCOTT, STEPPHEN.
Un abonné	JOHN ANDREWES.

LA DESCENTE D'HÉBÉ

Ballet de Antony TUDOR — Musique d'Ernest BLOCH — Décor et Costumes de Nadia BENOIS

Hébé	ELISABETH SCHOOLING.
Mercure	LEO KERSLEY.
La nuit	MAUDE LLYOD.
Hercule	FRANK STAFF.
Nymphes d'Hébé	Mmes MORFIELD, GEE, SAREL, ELLISON, SCOTT, TRUSCOTT.
Nymphes de la nuit	Mmes SVETLOVA, FRANKS, BARRETT, BROWN, WATT.

1) Hébé en servant le nectar aux dieux renverse la coupe. Mercure lui annonce qu'elle est chassée de l'Olympe.

2) La nuit doit emporter Hébé, qui résiste jusqu'à ce qu'on lui montre une vision d'Hercule qu'elle rencontrera sur la terre.

3) Hébé, nouvellement arrivée sur la terre, rencontre Hercule.

4) Apothéose.

SPORTING SKETCHES. Ballet de Susan SALAMAN

1) LE CRICKET — Musique d'Arthur BENJAMIN.

Fielders	Mmes GEE, SVETLOVA ou BROWN, SCOTT.
Batsman	FRANK STAFF.
Bowler	LEO KERSLEY.
Umpire	JOHN ANDREWES.

2) LE RUGBY — Musique de POULENC.

Le joueur de Rugby	WALTER GORE.
Ses admiratrices	MAUDE LLOYD, ELISABETH SCHOOLING, CELIA FRANKS.

3) LE BOXING — Musique de Lord BERNERS.

La jeune fille sportive	CELIA FRANKS ou ANN GEE.
L'entraîneur	LEO KERSLEY
La vamp de luxe	PRUDENCE HYMAN
Le champion anglais	WALTER GORE
Le champion américain	FRANK STAFF

BAR AUX FOLIES-BERGÈRE (d'après le tableau de MANET)

Ballet de Ninette de VALOIS

Musique de CHABRIER — Costumes et Décor de William CHAPPELL

L'étoile du can-can	MAUDE LLOYD
La fille au bar	ELISABETH SCHOOLING
Grille d'égout	TAMARA SVETLOVA
Hirondelle	ANN GEE
Nini patte en l'air	CELIA FRANKS
La Môme Fromage	HEATHER BROWN
Valentin, garçon	WALTER GORE
Adolphe, habitué du bar	JOHN ANDREWES
Gustave — —	LEO KERSLEY
Le vieux marcheur	FRANK STAFF
La servante	SUSETTE MORFIELD

LE LAC DES CYGNES

Poéme chorégraphique en un acte d'après PETIPAS

Musique de TCHAIKOVSKY

La princesse Cygne	PRUDENCE HYMAN ou MAUDE LLOYD.
Le prince	BENTLEY STONE ou FRANK STAFF.
L'ami du prince	JOHN ANDREWES
Pas de trois	ELISABETH SCHOOLING, CELIA FRANKS, LEO KERSLEY.
Quatuor des cygnes	Mmes SCHOOLING, FRANKS, GEE, SCOTT.
Les cygnes	Mmes MORFIELD, SVETLOVA, SAREL, BARETT, BROWN, ELLISON, STEPHENS, WATT.

Un jeune prince, accompagné de ses amis, vient chasser au bord d'un lac. Il voit apparaître des cygnes qui, sous l'aspect de jeunes filles, dansent au clair de lune. Epris de la Princesse des Cygnes, le Prince interdit la chasse et prend part à leurs jeux. Mais voici l'aube, et les Princesses enchantées auxquelles le Mauvais Génie fait reprendre la forme de cygnes, s'envolent. Le Prince veut les suivre, mais le Mauvais Génie lui barre le chemin. Impuissant de vaincre sa magie, le Prince s'affaisse et succombe.

FAÇADE

Esquisses ironiques du Music-Hall anglais de Frederick ASHTON

Musique de William WALTON — Costumes et Décor de John ARMSTRONG

Rhapsodie écossaise	CELIA FRANKS, MARY SCOTT, LEO KERSLEY
Yodelling Song :	
La laitière	SUSETTE MORFIELD
Les yodelleurs	WALTER GORE, FRANK STAFF, JOHN ANDREWES.
Polka	MAUDE LLOYD
Chanson populaire	WALTER GORE, FRANK STAFF.
Valse	Mmes SVETLOVA, FRANKS, GEE et BROWN.
Tango, Passodoble	ELISABETH SCHOOLING, WALTER GORE
Tarantella sevillana	ENSEMBLE.

WILLIAM CHAPPEL et WALTER GORE

SUSETTE MARFIELD

FOYER DE DANSE, (D'APRÈS DEGAS)

DAPHNE DEANE
qui présente pour la première fois en Europe
le Ballet Anglais de Marie RAMBERT

AU STUDIO
LA COMPAGNIE DU BALLET RAMBERT A SES DÉBUTS

Édité par NICOLAS
Éditions Artistiques
Paris

Les photos de ce programme
sont du Studio DOGGART et ROGERS
Londres

Imprimé par
V. LEBENSON
Édit. Paris

PRUDENCE HYMAN et WALTER GORE

ANDRÉE HOWARD

MAUD LLOYD

PANELA FOSTER

FRANK STAFF

LA MUSE S'AMUSE

MAUD LLOYD — WALTER GORE

ELISABETH SCHOOLING

BAR AUX FOLIES BERGÈRES
(d'après le tableau de Manet)

WALTER GORE

LA DESCENTE DE HÉBÉ

Commander Charles Hall

**Lieutenant
McLeod**

**Frantisek Fubrobretine,
Gustave Mahler's nephew**

**My last holiday before the War
- Monte Carlo**

Sergeants Kennedy & Tipton

In Switzerland, 1948

GREEK THEATRE
GIRLS' HIGH SCHOOL
WALTHAMSTOW

The Cast wish to offer their sincere thanks to:

Miss M. Norris for her kind permission to use the Greek Theatre.

Mr. J. S. Arthur and Messrs. R. R. Davis, D. S. Easson, J. Spinner, C. A. Taylor, W. Thompson and T. Woolf for arranging the lighting effects.

Mr. L. C. Belchambers for organising and directing the Orchestra.

Mr. E. G. Bull for arranging the sound amplification.

Miss Ethel Eaton and Mr. N. A. C. Bignell for accompanying at rehearsals.

Members of the O.G.A. and O.M. Operatic Society for the song "You spotted snakes".

Miss V. E. Allen and Mr. F. J. Trevers for their co-operation in the business of the play.

The ladies and gentlemen who have acted as programme sellers and stewards.

Greek Theatre production of *A Midsummer Night's Dream*

OLD GIRLS' DRAMATIC CLUB " OLD MONOVIANS' DRAMATIC SOCIETY

PRESENT

"A Midsummer Night's Dream"

by

WILLIAM SHAKESPEARE
With Mendelssohn's Music

Characters in order of appearance:—

Theseus, Duke of Athens ...	Ronald Dubock
Hippolyta, Queen of the Amazons, betrothed to Theseus	Gladys Phillips
Egeus, Father to Hermia ...	Roy Davidson
Hermia, Daughter to Egeus, in love with Lysander	Eileen Standen
Lysander, } In love with Hermia	{Douglas Coates
Demetrius, }	{Jack Allen
Philostrate, Master of the Revels to Theseus	Peter McDermott
Helena, in love with Demetrius ...	Jeanne King
Quince, a carpenter ...	Alfred Bishop
Snug, a joiner ...	Bill Allen
Bottom, a weaver ...	Sidney Parks
Flute, a bellows mender ...	John Payling
Snout, a tinker ...	Norman Barnes
Starveling, a tailor ...	Roy Houseman
A Fairy ...	Ruth Parker
Puck ...	Ken Pettegree
Oberon, King of the Fairies ...	Eunice Holden
Titania, Queen of the Fairies ...	Mary King

Attendants, Courtiers—Joyce Atwood, Sylvia Curtis, Adele Enders, Hilda Kirk, Ione Melville, Betty Monk, R. D. Barry, J. Cater, D. J. Chittock, P. Ellis, D. Pettegree, B. Sorenson, R. Whitcomb, W. White.

Fairies—Joan Barratt, Elsie Bignell, Ethel Goddard, Dorothy Griffiths, Margaret Heaps, Gladys Methven, Winifred Moore, Eileen Preston, Grace Putnam, Linda Sheppherd, Ruby White.

THE PLAY PRODUCED BY EUNICE HOLDEN.

Scene: Athens, and a Wood near Athens.

The Play will be presented in two acts, with an interval of Fifteen Minutes

Lighting by	Mr. J. S. Arthur
Orchestra directed by ...	Mr. L. C. Belchambers, Mus. Bac.
Sound Amplification by ...	Mr. E. G. Bull
Costumes designed by	Edna Wilsdon
Dances arranged by	Joan Barratt
Business Manager	Jack Allen
Box Office Managers ...	Vera Prior and Stanley G. Holdsworth
Chief Steward	H. Berry

Members of the Orchestra

1st Violins
H. F. Handcock
Miss M. Roebuck
J. F. Manning
H. J. Watson
R. C. Jennings
N. S. Lempriere

2nd Violins
K. Paton
E. H. Boult
O. Reed

Violas
Miss E. M. Houchen
S. F. Pritchard
E. R. Scammen

Violoncellos
G. H. Bower
Miss D. Nash
E. R. Gulliford

Flute
G. Lawn

Oboe
Mrs. L. C. Belchambers

Clarinets
A. S. Lucas
P. Bennett

Bassoon
W. S. Bennett

Trumpet
R. H. Watson

Horn
R. Allen

Accompanists
N. A. C. Bignell
G. H. Bramhall

UNITY THEATRE
has the honour to present

"WINKLES & CHAMPAGNE"

AN EXTRAVAGANT ENTERTAINMENT

comprising

All the Arts of the Drama—most faithfully presented, and a Musical Feast to bring tears and laughter to the eyes of all beholders

FIRSTLY

Direct from its presentation at the Theatre Royal, Drury Lane

A SOUL STIRRING AND MORAL DRAMA

in Eight Glorious Scenes entitled

"TEMPTATION"
or
VIRTUE IS ITS OWN REWARD
by Mr. John Brougham

DRAMATIS PERSONAE

Mr. Granite (A Wealthy Merchant)	Mr. WARD
Sterling (A Faithful Clerk)	Mr. CHANEY
Tom Bobalink (A Truckman)	Mr. LEVINE
Polly Bobalink (Tom's Better Half)	Miss BURTON
O'Bryan (An Irish Labourer)	Mr. OXENBOULD
Henry Travers	Mr. WARREN
Mary Travers	Miss RANDALL
Mrs. Grimgriskin	Miss HOLDEN
Williams (A Clerk)	Mr. PRYCE

SCENES

I	GRANITE'S OFFICE	V	GRANITE'S OFFICE
II	TOM BOBALINK'S HOME	VI	TOM BOBALINK'S ROOM
III	THE TRAVERS' HOME	VII	GRANITE'S OFFICE
IV	A STREET	VIII	THE TRAVERS' HOME

SECONDLY

Miss Katherine Loveday, the well-known Operatic Mezzo-Soprano, after her recent successful appearances at the Eagle Tavern and several other High Class Places of Amusement

WILL SING

items from her repertoire

THIRDLY

contrived at GREAT EXPENSE and with a Wealth of Detail we humbly offer

A REPRESENTATION OF

"THE CROWN & CUSHION"

where friends may meet and drink and sing and a Good Time will, we trust, be had by all the present company.

There follows an **Interval of Fifteen Minutes** during which, should any of our Patrons so desire or crave, **Refreshments** will be available in the Bar, and we would re-assure any Lady who may desire to partake of same that, this being a **Highly Moral Establishment**, she need have no fears for her **Personal Safety** within its precincts.

FOURTHLY AND FINALLY

We bring our **PRESENTATION** to a close with an Up-to-Date and, may we venture to say, Modern, Representation of

THE MUSIC HALL

In the Chair, Mr. Joseph Levine.

who will expatiate on the Virtues of, and Introduce the Artistes whom, at Great Expense, we have engaged for this **Monumental, Moving, Magnificent and Much Awaited**

MUSIC HALL

ARTISTES AND SINGERS

Mr. Christopher Ball	Mr. Paul Diamond	Mr. Harry Newton
Mr. William Bird	Miss Katherine Edwards	Mr. John Oxenboold
Miss June Burton	Miss Ann Fishburn	Miss Barbara Perry
Mr. Mark Chaney	Mr. George Harvey	Mr. Edward Pryce
Miss Elsie Chisnall	Miss Eunice Holden	Miss Joy Raffe
Mr. Jack Colclough	Miss Celia Lang	Miss Margaret Randall
Miss Wendy Corum	Miss Doris Levenson	Miss Tess Richman
Mr. Aubrey Cutler	Mr. Joseph Levine	Miss Karen Rock
Miss Patricia Daly	Miss Beryl Lund	Mr. William Ward
Miss Doreen Davis	Miss Kay Mollinari	Mr. Charles Warren

Musical Arrangements under the Direction of Mr. Benjamin Norris and Mr. Stanley Edwards

The Orchestra led by Mr. Jacques Godwin

Piccolo and Flute Obbligato by Mr. Bertram Fiddeman

Winkles & Champagne - Unity Theatre

OH! Sir James - Plymouth 1979

LIFE FOUR
My academic life:
Homerton College Cambridge

I left Walthamstow High School in 1934 and went to Homerton College, Cambridge as an apprentice teacher. It was an all women's College and very strict. We London girls were not used to the regimentations of a boarding school and expected to go to the theatres on our own and be independent. Not there. We were shut in at 6pm and all the windows and doors on the ground floor of this enormous building were locked. We would then retire to our bed-sitters until 8:30, at which time we descended for supper, followed by bed-time at 9:30. It was like a Nunnery. I found it funny and frustrating to be locked in at 6pm. I refused to do any home-work in my room in protest. I worked after supper. The Lady Principal Miss Allen, a formidable lady, was in her last year prior to retirement. She was the very model of a Victorian Head Mistress, strict on discipline, and resembled Florence Nightingale. I found it very restrictive after the freedom of London and a friendly High School atmosphere. But I filled in and was delighted to have a room of my own at last, on the top floor If you wanted to go out in the evening or at week-ends you had to get special permission stating where you were going and with whom. I do understand that they were duty bound to keep control of us in the absence of our parents. But we were 18-19 years old and it did seem very petty to me at the time. This went on for a year until the Head retired. Her replacement, Miss Skillicorn was 37 years old and was far more liberal. Slowly she changed these restrictions, bright colours could now be seen, bowls of flowers and a 10pm curfew. It was better and we were treated like adults. We were once told in a formidable lecture by Miss Allen, in her strong Scottish accent, that there were thirty thousand young men nearby in the University and insisted that our behaviour be nothing less than impeccable at all times. Dates or friendships were out of the question.

The one new lecture I found fascinating was psychology because it gave one an insight to the human condition, which enabled me to look at my fellow human being with a changed perspective. In the grounds of Homerton there was a nursery school where the local parents brought their small children. We were taken there to watch the children, having had lectures on babies and under fives. They were lovely little children. We looked at them with a more scientific eye rather than simply comment on how beautiful and funny they were. My study of the Human Race lasted two years and was utterly fascinating especially as I had had no younger brothers or sisters to watch. Perhaps all secondary students, boys and girls, should be instructed in this area; they would make better parents later.

There was plenty of marvellous food. I had always been hungry at home except when mother made plum duffs and puddings, but here there were three full meals every day. In the morning a great clanging bell rang over Cambridge. We hurried out of our rooms and into the dining hall by 8am when the bells stopped. We were seated in our places, bowing our head over our breakfast and saying the morning prayer. There was a high table at one end in this great vaulted Victorian hall where the Head Mistress and teachers would sit. At 9am we went to lectures. I found some of them positively elementary compared with the very high standard the A level teachers had taught us at Walthamstow High School. But now I was here to learn the skills required to be a good teacher. Some of the lecturers had never taught in London or in a tough big city school: the secondary moderns with less able pupils.

Even in the secondary school some children could not read or write and came from extremely poor backgrounds. These middle-class girls had been to Cheltenham Ladies' College, light years away from the real world of teaching in a State school and were really lecturing about something they didn't know. For many this was undoubtedly their first teaching assignment. They were lecturing by numbers, by the book, without real feeling or knowledge of their subject. In my view some of the training was useless really. I do sincerely hope that all training college lecturers now acquire the relevant experience before attempting to inspire other prospective teachers. They must be aware of all inner-city difficulties, more so now than ever before with the growing number of ethnic minorities who do not speak English. The pupils return home after class to vastly different customs, religion & culture and their parents are unable to help their children with the language.

Future teachers should receive at least three years training. Students in the 6th form who express a desire to be teachers should be sent to a secondary, junior or infant school first and learn about teaching. This way so much time and money would be saved when it becomes quite clear which of the students have no talent or liking for the profession. Surely this could be organized and the benefits would be enormous. Many students, after their three year degree course do not go on to teaching but to a different profession. This, in my view should not be allowed and they should teach for at least three years to repay their grants. We did and thought it no hardship to do the work for which we had been trained.

The prominent experience of your first year was to do one month's practical teaching at a given school where the Lecturers would sit at the back of your class and give you a critique and some advice afterwards. You would go on your bike, the basket on the front containing your books, and cycle to the appointed school. Just before I was due to commence my month of training, disaster struck.

My sister Lucy who was 24 years old had travelled to France and Spain. A rather daring trip for us in those days. During her travels, somehow she contracted typhoid. We think it must have been the local water and Lucy had not been inoculated. The symptoms became apparent three weeks after her return. The doctor's original diagnosis of chronic diarrhoea led to an extremely tragic series of events. My mother who was nursing Lucy, unaware of her actual condition also fell victim to this highly contagious disease. My mother died. I was in College and was given permission to leave immediately, they'd had a message that my mother was ill. As I travelled to London many thoughts raced through my head. They would not be sending me home unless she was gravely ill. I imagined that she must already be dead. An inner spirit told me that I was going home to mother's funeral. When I arrived, it was dreadful to find George, Fred and Lucy in a very distressed state. She had passed on. I was right. I was too late. For the moment, they were unaware of the cause of her death. We were quite devastated.

Lucy was miserable, her hair had fallen out, she was emaciated, typhoid was still not diagnosed. Three weeks later I returned to College and now I was ill. I had contracted the disease from my sister. I was taken to Addenbrooke's Hospital. George, now my legal guardian, was contacted as his permission was needed to proceed with an emergency operation. "Do anything necessary" were his words.

He arrived in Cambridge within hours, but after the unnecessary removal of my appendix. This was not the cause of my malaise.

George told the Hospital staff and doctors that following a coroner's examination he had just received the news that his mother had died from and his sister was still gravely affected by typhoid. TYPHOID! they were shocked. There was no cure available at that time. I had been in a ward and in the operating theatre. Immediate steps had to be taken to prevent an outbreak and I was taken to an isolation area. I remained on the verge of death for a week I remember feeling hot and semi-conscious not knowing where I was. Typhoid was dreadful. As I was young and strong the one possible treatment was starvation. I was given some liquid every two hours to keep me alive. Later I heard that my fellow students, the Lecturers and the Principal had said prayers for my survival.

After three weeks the crisis had passed, I had survived my ordeal. I was told to go home for a long convalescence, thus unable to complete the first term at Homerton.

My former Head Mistress and teachers had heard what had happened to me and offered a place on the south coast for the prescribed rest period allowing me to recover, gain some weight and return to College. I thought that was very kind. Feeling weak and painfully thin I was taken in a coach to a home for "distressed gentle women." I was lifted out of the coach, saw the sign and had a good laugh. I was there for two weeks, near Brighton. The invigorating sea air, the love and attention of many refined elderly ladies – my new found friends, good food and plenty of rest contributed to a speedy recovery and I was soon back on my feet returning to College in the middle of spring term. Miss Allen said I would have to stay an extra year. This I could not afford and thankfully it was agreed that this would not be necessary if I did extra work in the summer vacation.

During that summer, Miss Park, my former English Mistress at Walthamstow invited me to direct Shakespeare at the Greek Theatre. An ideal and productive way of enjoying life in the summer despite having to catch up with college studies.

In January of my second year the ILEA (Inner London Education Authority) inspectors came to the College and outlined which teaching posts were available to "A" students and I was offered a job. I wrote to

George that I would soon be earning my own money; thanking him for making it all possible. I passed my exams and was off.

I continued over the next few years directing four Shakespearean comedies at Walthamstow. I enjoyed these productions with a fine company of actors, a beautiful theatre and the magic of William Shakespeare omni-present.

My time at Homerton was wonderful and I made many friends. Hylda Mandy and I had acquired a couple of rusty old bicycles and had a good time discovering Cambridge and the surrounding countryside, Ely and its beautiful Cathedral, the Gogmagog hills and villages. Breakfast at 5am in a punt on the Cam was so exciting in those heady days. At my first attempt at punting, I stood on the back and grasped the 16 foot pole. I had to throw it in the air, as it came down vertically, I dropped it into the water and then pushed away and the punt went forward like jet propulsion. But the first time I held the pole too long it stuck in the mud vertically. The punt went away under me and I was left clinging onto an upright pole in the middle of the river. Inevitably I went down with the pole into the muddy river. I swam to the shore and climbed into the adjacent field. After that disastrous first attempt I became quite competent. It is a delightful, slow, stately and graceful way to pass a pleasant summer's day.

I truly believe that two years at Cambridge, a wonderful experience, has had a lasting and positive effect on my whole life. It is my opinion that Cambridge being near the freezing North Sea and enveloped in clouds and damp winds makes their humour imaginative and rather dotty. The comic talents that have emerged from there have served us well.

My first post as a teacher was in Walthamstow at Wood Street Secondary Modern School. The Head Mistress placed me with a group of children having difficulties with rudimentary reading and writing. I was to teach them on a daily basis. When they could read and write more fluently and felt more confident, they would re-join their various classes. I, who was brought up with books abounding, felt a duty to help them. I taught them for a term. In retrospect the most fruitful three months teaching of my career. They looked solemn and dull at the beginning. By Christmas they could read. My method was to teach them by voice to learn parts in a play. After several weeks, we opened the books and they read their parts. They were amazed, they could actually read.

During the holiday season everybody participated in a short play to entertain the rest of the school as part of the seasonal celebrations. There was a party and we decorated a beautiful tree. My students had felt left out because they could not read. This year would be different.

"You will be able to read by Christmas and act a play" I told them.

"And I will find you some great costumes."

It was through drama that I managed to teach them to read. They did learn, they did perform that Christmas in lovely costumes and I was overjoyed with pride.

Today in the year 2000, alas, this great love of reading is being diminished by the easier, visual entertainments of video games and television. A great pity.

Institutions survive the individuals and Homerton is no exception to the fate laid out by more modern times. They now allow both men and women students with the inevitable consequences. Well...no comment...

On a summers' day in 1951 I returned for a day so happy Cambridge had not been altered or destroyed during the war. Quite by chance I met Miss Skillicorn, the Principal of Homerton, in the grounds. She invited me in for a drink. She asked for details of my life in London and I was happy and proud to recount what had happened to me since we had first met. I told her about my wartime experiences, my marriage and my acting career. She was thrilled to hear about my part in the Unity Theatre production "Winkles and Champagne" which had subsequently been broadcast by BBC Television in 1947. I told her of my studies at the Royal College of Music, my L.R.A.M. diploma for all things theatrical. My study of stage direction under Michel Saint-Denis at his London Theatre Studio in Islington, and my further directorial studies under professional directors at the British Drama League. She was most interested to hear that I had been awarded their diploma, the A.D.B. – Associate of the Drama Board, given only to 5 men and myself. I had also attended a LABAN course in mime; ballet dancers from Sadler's Wells attended these classes. Laban, from Vienna invented his own dance movement notation. He directed us to piano accompaniment to express an event or story in group mime. A wonderful and imaginative experience.

I explained to Miss Skillicorn that after a very long war service, my husband in the Navy and myself in London, we both wished to travel worldwide. He would sketch and I would write our adventures. With my varied qualifications I could get work in theatres or drama schools. He could work as a teacher. After a year we would return to the domesticity of a house, mortgage and children. But, as Robbie Burns has said: "The best laid plans of mice and men…

And so it proved.

Miss Skillicorn. to my amazement, then said: "As you are so experienced and qualified I can offer you the post of junior lecturer in Drama starting in September."

I accepted this post with great pleasure.

I decided that my lectures in the early part of the day until lunchtime would be on the history of the theatre, dramatic literature and poetry. Secondly, the value and use of speech training and acting in schools. Above all I wished to direct both my male and female students from Sidney Sussex College in Shakespeare productions. My last was "As you like it" for May week in 1953. It was to be performed in the Master's garden, but the weather became wintry and we played very happily in the main dining room. The dining tables carpeted formed the stage under the charming balcony on each side of the door; very Elizabethan Globe Theatre. On the walls were portraits of the Masters of the College, later including my old school friend, Dr. David Thomson, historian, but above all Oliver Cromwell complete with a wart on his chin.

My Rosalind hoped to be a teacher of Drama. She was beautiful, an excellent actress, but her Orlando was handsome but with no passion or charisma. Two weeks before the first night he resigned. He was due to swim against Oxford to achieve his swimming accolade. I, desperately searching, found a professional actor, such pleasure for me. The audience thrilled at watching such a delightful duo.

My girl students were highly intelligent, hand picked from thousands of applicants. During a month of practical teaching, I sat at the back of a class where the student gave a prepared lesson. I had been in that position myself and knew how difficult it could be for the student. It was similar in tension and nerves as an actress at an audition in an empty theatre. I allowed for nerves in my criticism later. But one recognised at once students with teaching ability, flair, personality and the immediate response of the class. Some students, like some aspiring actors in front of an audience, have no rapport with a class of teenagers and should never teach. The invention of the tape recorder at that time was invaluable. When I recorded a students' voice and played it back, the faults in the speech shocked the students. Chiefly monotony, mumbling, incoherence, very poor articulation. If a student had a good musical ear, I could transform his or her voice production. Great discussions ensued with students with northern or other native accents. I love regional accents. These students did not wish me to impose a BBC "southern" accent. So I explained that my intention, as a teacher was for them to communicate and be understood. I would help them be splendidly articulate and understood by all. Therefore they should be able to soften strong accents but always be articulate. These lessons in 2000 A.D. are more than ever necessary but are sadly neglected. As Bernard Shaw said in Pygmalion: "Why can't the Englishman speak his own language?"

Those days were idyllic. I was in Cambridge during the week, my husband and his friend Henry Moore in Little Hadham and Much Hadham respectively and at week-ends we'd return to our London flat in Hampstead where we enjoyed going to concerts and to the theatre. A more wonderful existence combining work and play was difficult to imagine. We travelled in our SSII Jaguar of 1934, a red sports car with magnificent leather upholsterery and chrome fittings. Roman bought it in Hampstead for £200. Recently at a Christies' auction a car of that year was sold for £65,000.

Cambridge is, I hope, still a country town. The Backs, the river Cam meandering by King's College Chapel, Trinity, Clare and Queens Colleges are a splendid view at all seasons, in Spring and Autumn especially. I wished to stay forever...

But the BBC Television asked me to join them in London. The temptation to work in such a new medium was great. I sacked myself from Homerton to start my exciting and fascinating career No.3 in television.

On arrival, I hinted that I was a classical actress. They said: "No, comedy for you;" and I started rehearsals with Jimmy Edwards, Arthur Hayes, the young Ronnie Barker and June Whitfield; with Frank Muir and Dennis Norden as script writers.

✳   ✳   ✳

Quite a few years later I had met a charming young man who was helping out on one of the Hellenic Cruises who invited me to attend a function at Emmanuel College – Cambridge. It turned out to be a rather Pythonesque evening!

I was to be Guest of Honour at the annual dinner of the dramatic society of Emmanuel College. I dressed to kill in a skin tight purple evening dress, wore a mile long feather boa and glittered with sparklers. Along with my false eye lashes, the look was quite over the top! I was greeted by two lines of students all bowing as I descended from my taxi. To my dismay I was ushered into the presence of the Master and senior Lecturers for cocktails. They looked so serious and I felt over dressed.

We thankfully adjourned to the dining room upstairs magnificently lit by candlelight to enjoy a sumptuous banquet with fine wines. I had been asked to make an hilarious speech and needed to be deliciously lugubrious. My feather boa was moulting a snowstorm of white feathers. My neighbour, an elderly gentleman, removed snowflakes from his soup. I asked: "Are you a guest?"

"Yes," he grunted...

"What to you do?" I said; then came the surprise answer: "I play the silent piano!!!!!!!!"

"At the Wigmore Hall," I said.

"Yes, the audiences are very attentive…"

"Do they pay?"

"Oh yes," he said…Well you can see the type of absurd conversation this was.

This exchange put me well in the mood and at that moment for no apparent reason. I burst into song.

The students expected to escort me back to my hotel but were astonished to hear that I was staying with the Master at Sidney Sussex College, my old school friend Dr. Thomson. They delivered me to the porter expecting him to refuse me entrance, as they thought I was joking. Well…

"Good evening Mrs. Black" he said.

"The Master is awaiting you in his study."

The students were dumbfounded.

LIFE FIVE
THE POLISH IDYLL
(My husband, adventures in Spain and elsewhere)
A life transformed by a meeting with Henry Moore and Feliks Topolski

The war was over when I met Roman Blachowsky at a Forces dance held regularly in a hall behind the Ritz Hotel in Piccadilly. We went there for many of our subsequent dates. A complete gentleman, he enquired why I had not danced with him as he was as tall as I was. He had noticed that all my dancing partners were short! Somehow I always seemed to end up dancing with short men. Later on I accidentally met him at Piccadilly tube station. We were both going to Swiss Cottage. He shared a studio there with other Polish painters in Fellows Road. He was wearing a British Naval Uniform. He was on leave and spent his time with other Polish friends serving in the British Forces. He particularly enjoyed going to the studio of Pacewitz in South Kensington who for many years had a studio in Paris for Polish painters, where he was acquainted with and a great admirer of Bonnard. Roman carried on that tradition.

He invited me to visit his studio; I was delighted. He then made a charcoal drawing of me. I was amazed that so near to my home existed this bohemian looking, very Parisian studio. He always arrived home from leave with beautiful gifts from overseas, earrings and yards of exotic materials from foreign lands – so wonderful at a time of strict clothes rationing.

Roman had come to England in 1938 to do research at Queen's College,

Cambridge. His degrees were in Geology. He lectured in his subject at Poznan University in Poland where his father Professor Blachowski was Chancellor. He was a philosopher. Madame Blachowska was a painter and ceramic artist.

On his return from one particular leave, he told me that his father was in London but that sadly his mother had been denied a passport to travel with him and to see, at last, her only son Roman. How sad that the Iron Curtain had separated the families of Communist Russia and those of the democratic Western World. The British Government invited twelve Polish Professors to visit four British Universities to collect classical books to take back with them. Roman said how delighted he would be for me to meet his father. The Professor later commented on how generous the British Universities had been donating their books. Before his departure he asked if he could store some books donated by the Universities in my flat in Swiss cottage. Of course I agreed. Later huge lorries collected them, so in my small way I helped re-stock the Polish Libraries.

The Germans had destroyed so much in his home-land. Poland was now Communist with a Prime Minister approved by Moscow, the country subjected to Marxist doctrine. All University students had to spend one year studying Marxism. The Professor was still permitted to remain Chancellor of Poznan University as he was quite old and would retire shortly. Roman would not be permitted to lecture in Poland as he had worked with the enemy, the British. And he would not be accepted as a Lecturer of Geology at the University as he would most certainly be followed by the secret police.

In the summer of 1939 Roman was told not to return home. Hitler had repossessed the Rhine Land, Austria and Czechoslovakia and now Poland. Roman joined the Polish Army in London as a Lieutenant. He was sent to Paris then to the Maginot line, the French defence on its long eastern frontier. Alas, Hitler, having conquered Poland marched westwards to Paris. Roman's French, English and Polish forces were swept into the sea at Dunkirk. He was drowning, his head on fire, but was saved by British people who sailed out from the coast in a variety of boats to rescue those still alive. He recovered in Scotland, returned to Cambridge to lecture. Later, he volunteered for the Air force and Navy as England was losing the war. He was accepted by the Merchant Navy and remained in that service until 1949.

The formalization of the Iron Curtain was a real tragedy for Europe, dividing the Continent from North to South. Communism/Democracy. The Russians had wanted to occupy Berlin but did not succeed. It was divided into four sections: English, French, American & Russian and split by the Berlin Wall. The Russians had such animosity against the Western democracies because they thought that the West was keeping the secret of the atomic bomb from them. They did not want people to return with Democratic ideology. It was impossible for ordinary Russians to travel to the West, as obtaining a passport was difficult indeed. Eventually they founded "Intourist," the Russian Tourist Organisation which at least made Russia more accessible for us if not actually helping their citizens much. But you were constantly followed by a guide on any trip within the USSR and other Communist Countries.

Before Professor Blachowsky went home, he expressed the desire to attend a performance at the Opera and we went to Puccini's "La Boheme." Perhaps, inspired by this, he said he hoped Roman would stay in England and we would marry... He told me that his son loved me very much and I said that my love for his son was equally enthusiastic. But I did insist that he leave the Navy and concentrate on expressing his natural talents.

Our wedding was planned for Saturday April 23rd 1949 at Caxton Hall

Registry Office, Shakespeare's birthday, England's National Day and on the same day Roman's parents had married. On the Thursday prior, Roman telephoned, still at sea, to tell me that there was a strike at London Docks so he would not be able to arrive by Saturday. He was off the coast of Holland and would do his very best to try to arrive but it was doubtful. He did however tell me that he was now sporting a beard and I was horrified. I ordered him to shave it off before we next saw each other! At the eleventh hour he arrived and the ceremony went ahead as planned. It was a post-war marriage, very subdued and humble with a small cake, my very closest friends and family at our flat in Hampstead. But it was wonderful and I loved it. We hadn't made any plans for a honeymoon and so pretended to guests when asked about it. One of Roman's friends quietly suggested Rye in Sussex, so we eventually called a taxi and asked the driver: "Where is Rye?"

"It's a beautiful preserved medieval town near Hastings," he said.

He took us to Victoria Station for our train journey to Hastings. It was perfect. On arrival, a short bus ride followed and we spent our first night at The Mermaid Inn in Rye. We had a lovely four poster bed which managed to survive the night. We came back after two days because how ever nice and romantic, it was expensive for us. It was a wonderful and memorable honeymoon...all you need is the person you love.

My husband attended Art School and during that first year he was their star pupil much praised for his originality. He eventually applied for a position at Little Hadham in Hertfordshire. The Education Directors for Hertfordshire loved the Arts and Architecture. Henry Moore lived in Much Hadham, nearby. My husband became the Arts teacher at the delightful Hadham Hall School. His classes of twelve students only, were unusual and pleasing. Roman could have returned to Queen's College Cambridge as a lecturer in Geology. I wondered if he should follow a career as an artist and art teacher. One winter's day, with a few of Roman's pictures rolled up under my arm and some watercolours and a sketch book, I headed for the home of the great Henry Moore. I wanted to receive an expert's point of view; was my husband a talented painter? Should he make a career as a painter? It was a big step. I went by Green Line bus (a service provided for destinations outside the greater London area) from Hampstead to Much Hadham in the bleak winter and walked in the snow until I reached his house, at least one mile away uphill. A brief stop at the local pub for a drink and further directions and I arrived. I knocked and to my amazement, the great man answered the door himself. I introduced myself and asked if I could have his opinion on my husband's work. He invited me in for a cup of tea, which was most appreciated on that cold day. He did not know me but welcomed me as a friend. We sat in front of an open fire. He asked me what had I brought for him. I explained that my husband born in Poland was now British and had served in the Navy. He looked through the sketch book and all the paintings. He then asked me if I would like to see some of his work. He opened his famous sketch book with the drawings of the people sleeping in the Underground during the war. He said that he thought my husband's paintings were good and that he should indeed pursue a painter's career. He mentioned that he was shortly to be a guest sculptor at The Slade School and suggested that Roman come by and say hello. As I was leaving he asked if I would like to see his present work. A memorable experience. I remember the high roof of the studio with frosted windows and the winter light coming through. There, in the middle of the studio was a huge plaster sculpture of a mother and father seated on a bench holding a child. It is one of his most famous works and I saw it during its creation, a moment I will never forget.

I went back through the snow to catch my Green Line back to London, my thoughts swimming. If Henry Moore was of the opinion that Roman had talent, than indeed he should paint. Creative ability is so rare. If the urge to work full-time is there it should be encouraged.

Roman and I felt that for our first holiday we should go south to the Mediterranean. I was teaching, Roman would go ahead and we would meet later. He and a naval friend had bought the hull of an old fishing boat in Cornwall called "Our Girls" which they were re-fitting. They expected to sail to the Mediterranean. I would arrive by train and we would meet in Nice on an appointed date. Then we would sail around the Greek Islands...at least that was the plan.

Eventually the boat was finished and he sailed (alone in the end) south-ward. A week later, on Sunday, I was sun-bathing in the garden. I answered the front door, a Daily Mail reporter, delightedly taking photographs of me in my bikini, stood on my step and informed me that my husband was dead! Reporters are ruthless, taking photos of you when you are distressed. Naturally, I wanted news, more details. Lloyds of London had reported that his ship had sunk off Gibraltar but later telephoned to report that he had in fact been picked up by a Spanish fishing boat after his boat had sunk. He was so lucky and I so relieved. His passport and a roll of his paintings were the only things he saved. They were in a water-proof container when he landed from the Spanish fishing boat. The Authorities wanted to see his papers immediately. He told them that he was a former British Naval Officer. They immediately contacted the British Authorities who welcomed and spoiled him after his ordeal, giving him fresh clothing and money. They sent him off on his way to Nice for his rendezvous with his new wife. Meanwhile, I was speeding to Nice thinking that I would find him half dead. I told my distressing story to other passengers on the train who were most sympa-thetic. When the train, finally, pulled in at Nice after what had seemed an interminable journey, there he was on the platform in immaculate Naval clothing clutching a bouquet of red roses. My fellow passengers applauded us from the open windows. It was marvellous and so wonderful that he was alive and well and we were together again.

We were happily re-united and stayed the night in a small hotel when Roman told me that a friend of his had invited us on board his yacht for a two week cruise. We left the next day – I was going to help with the cooking and other chores. We sailed due south for a day. During the course of the night Roman cried: "Get under your bunk and don't come out, don't ask why."

I could hear from above machine gun fire and then silence. The night passed. We sailed another couple of days and eventually returned to Nice. When ashore he told me that we had been on a mission helping the French Police. It seems unbelievable, by today's standards, that such dramatic action could be taken for the smuggling of cigarettes and wine, but in the early 50's this was a big deal. We sailed out pretending to be tourists on holiday (which I thought we were!) ending up in hot pursuit of wanted criminals and their arrest. All the others on board were Police Customs Officers. So although I did not know it at the time, I had just been an undercover policewoman on anti-smuggling duty!

After those moments of excitement we enjoyed a wonderful holiday along the glorious Cote d'Azur. We went inland over the mountains to EZE which overlooks the sea. It has now become a paradise for the rich and famous, but does retain its beauty. Further along the coast we met the man who first proposed marriage to me. He was a French-American. In the German-Italian invasion during the war, he had been arrested and taken into custody in Germany. He married a Dutch woman who was also in the prison camp. They had now returned to Cavalière to live in his villa. We stayed a few days with his wife and two children. So Charles Moskon & Roman Black met, the man I might have married, the man I did marry. We all liked each other. It was fun and heart warming that we could live our new post-war lives.

Later we meandered up the Rhône Valley to Arles where Van Gogh had lived and painted. The place seemed unchanged. The elements of the paintings are still there, the house and the railway bridge. You could almost see him walking along. We went to the outskirts of the town on a blustery hot summer's day. The sun was enormous, dark red and it filled the sky. The corn in a field was bending over, it was just the scene that Van Gogh had painted and quite uncanny. We made our way along the valley to Avignon and slowly back to Paris, where we stayed on the banks of the Seine just beside the Basilica of Notre-Dame in a tiny street called "La Rue du Chat qui pêche.".the fishing cat... They say that if you sit long enough on the streets of Paris outside the cafés of the Place Saint-Michel, you are sure eventually to see someone go by that you know.

* * *

Whilst we were living in Little Hadham, my husband received a letter from Commander Greer asking if he would join him on a voyage around the world sailing his new yacht as his navigator. They would leave from Malta and sail through the Mediterranean, Gibraltar, the Panama Canal and the Pacific. I agreed this was a wonderful opportunity, "But I must come as well."

I could write a book, Roman could sketch and illustrate during any free time. We'd make a wonderful adventure of it

The prospect of freedom to travel making up for lost time after the long war years was exciting for Roman and myself, we both loved the dangerous unknown. We planned to be away for a year. The flat was let to Ronnie Barker. We arranged to have what little money we had sent to various places in the Caribbean. We assumed that this would be THE big adventure of our lives before settling down. We went by train to southern Italy and then by boat to Malta. The schooner was gorgeous, very slimline. We met Commander and Mrs. Greer and the two young Frenchmen crew. We were to be in Malta for three weeks fitting out and I made regular trips by water taxi to do the shopping assuring all necessary provisions. It was very hard work but enjoyable, all part of the excitement related to our forthcoming journey. The British Council invited me to lecture on the Theatre and Roman to exhibit some of his works. All together it was an idyllic few weeks in Malta.

One morning we were asked into Commander Greer's cabin and bluntly told that we would have to return home. We were devastated and dumb struck. What was going on? We had made arrangements in England to be away for a year. He explained that Commander and Mrs. Jones had expressed a desire to accompany the voyage and were offering a substantial sum for the privilege, whilst we, although not being paid were offering nothing. He had reluctantly changed his plans and seemed genuinely saddened for us but he now realised that the voyage was impossible without an injection of cash. Nevertheless I was furious and extremely disappointed, so unfair. We left immediately that afternoon and went to the shipping office to book on an available ship to take us to Sicily. The Captain of our ship told us that we could stay on the deck overnight but when we arrived in the evening we were offered dinner with him and a beautiful cabin for the night. He knew what had happened to us, thought it very cruel and had obviously decided to show us some decent human courtesy. A good and kind man. We never heard how our lost journey went…

But I now believe that God was protecting us because two months later when we would have been in the mid-Atlantic, I became very ill and was rushed into hospital for emergency surgery. Had I been on the high-seas without access to proper medical attention. I would most certainly have died.

We did get another chance at our "last big adventure" when Roman was offered a teaching post in Australia.

* * *

From "THE TIMES" of MALTA – Wednesday April 11, 1951

by a Staff Reporter

RARE CULTURAL EVENT
Husband and wife to appear before two Institutes.

It is a rare event in Malta's cultural life that a husband and wife should, quite independently, appear before the members of two Institutes at the same time.

This evening Mrs. Eunice Black A.D.B., L.R.A.M., will lecture to members of the British Institute in Valetta on "The story of the Old Vic and the Tradition of Acting Shakespeare." And while Mrs. Black tells her audience of the inspired work of Lilian Bayliss in creating the Old Vic and Sadler's Wells theatres, her husband Mr. Ian Black, will open an exhibition of his water colours of Spanish scenes at the Hotel Phoenicia and under the auspices of the Malta Cultural Institute.

STAGE EXPERIENCE

Mrs. Black has had considerable experience of the stage and has studied under Michel St. Denis of the Young Vic and at the Royal Academy of Music, London. She toured France with Madame Rambert's ballet Company before the War, and since then has appeared in various television productions.

The water colours being exhibited by Mr. Black at the Hotel Phoenicia themselves have a story. In 1947 Mr. Black bought the hull of a Cornish fishing boat and converted and rigged it as a ketch. Sailing from Falmouth Mr Black visited various ports in Southern Spain. Here he painted a series of water colours which included scenes of Cadiz, Cordoba, Seville, Toledo, Avila, Segovia, Alicante and Valencia. Shortly after leaving Gibraltar Mr. Black's ketch started shipping water and sank. Mr. Black swam around for same time until he was picked up by a Spanish trawler. All that he had with him was a water tight packet containing his passport and the collection of paintings which is now to be exhibited under the auspices of the Malta Cultural Institute.

Mr. Black has exhibited at the Royal Academy and at the Royal British Artists and Redfern Galleries and has had one man shows in Spain, at Corunna and Madrid. Formerly he was a University lecturer in Geography and did research at Edinburgh and Cambridge Universities. Forsaking the quiet of an academic career Mr. Black joined the Merchant Navy in 1942, first as a galley boy and then in 1944 as an Officer. But before this he had served in 1939-40 with the Army in France and was invalided out. Mr. Black started painting in 1946 and has studied under distinguished pupils of both Bonnard and Vuillard.

ARTISTS IN SPAIN (written in 1951)
WATERCOLOURS AND IMPRESSIONS

INTRODUCTION

"Give me civilisation, Miss Fleming, you can keep your progress."
Christopher Fry
"Venus Observed"

When we cross the Pyrenees at Canfrano to enter Spain, we feel that a stage curtain has lifted to reveal the vast plains of eternity. The cushioned loveliness of France is left behind and, to the south, the high burnt sierras stretch as if to the moon under a metallic sky. Modernity is left behind. There is nothing but the primeval earth, the air and the sky and man is insignificant.

Here John Donne could stand and challenge:

"At the round earth's imagined corners, blow
Your trumpets, Angels, and arise, arise
From death you multitudinous infinities
Of souls, and to your bodies go.
All whom war, death, age, agues, tyrannies
Despair, law, chance, hath slain."

For here is a living cemetery of history, layer on layer, that, unlike other western countries, shows the austerity of a tale of suffering not softened by the superficial comforts of the twentieth century.

We stand under the stars outside the old walls of Avila or on the barren moon mountains of Guadix and feel that we are alone in an unpeopled world. The landscape is always dramatic, like the open air studio of an architect Colossus who has built his towers and ramparts, his cathedrals and aqueducts and left them to crumble into golden ruins on the wide roof of the world. Spain is a country where grandeur flaunts its decay, but is never decadent. The past dominates the present. As one looks from the train window, on the long journey across the plateaux of Extremadura and Castille, the endless burnt plains are a lake of rock from which, at rare intervals, rises a tiny village, with its square rust coloured houses gripping the earth, blindly staring in the sun. Above it, like the periscope to God, stands an immense church tower. For hours one has seen nothing – only a goatherd, his black goats nibbling at the stubble, or a donkey, blindfolded, patiently circling a well. Time has stood still.

Out on the Atlantic, we have sailed in our small boat far from land, and if the ship is good and the wind kind, we can feel that the sea is a friend and there is a deep contentment. But an ocean of land seems pitiless, and these immense Spanish plains are rocky and bare. The afternoon heat of summer is an oven blast and there is nothing hospitable to man.

This is the land that has made the ironic, anarchic and fatalistic spirit of the Spaniards. There is no place for sentimentality, but instead a vigour, a directness and a resignation in their attitude to life which the sentimental Nordic peoples find hard to understand. It is a land of the spirit, proud and ancient. The people have courtesy, simplicity, and innate elegance. For me, the Spanish woman is the most beautiful of any race.

> "Grace was in all her steps, heaven in her eye
> In every gesture dignity and love"
> The Spaniard, with his more rugged Picasso face,
> deep scars of thunder had entrenched, and care sat on his
> faded cheek, but under brows of dauntless courage, and
> considerate pride waiting revenge."

The bullfight, in itself a pageant of death and courage, is Spain. It is all light and colour, dignity and splendour, it is brave, gay, tragic, and inevitable.

JACA

"And the fleas that tease in the High Pyrenees,
And the wine that tasted of the tar?
And the cheers and the jeers of the young muleteers
Under the vine of the dark verandah?"

We cross the Pyrenees at Canfranc and follow the river Aragon to Jaca. We have left the luxurious green of the French valleys and come instead to these steep wild mountains of Spain. Old Canfranc is a burned ruin, a sad crumbling village that was destroyed in 1944.

"Only the high peaks hoar:
And Aragon a torrent at the door.
No sound
In the walls of the Halls where falls
The tread
Of the feet of the dead to the ground"

So we journey to Jaca, in the centre of a small plain surrounded by mountains. We watch a long mule train with soldiers cross the plain and go up the rough zig-zag cart track into the hills. We eat churros freshly cooked in the street. A machine, at the turn of a handle, squeezes out a corrugated sausage of dough which is dropped into hot fat. A sharp sizzling, and the churros are pulled out, dusted with sugar and eaten hot.

We find a good wine bar in the Calle de la Salud, used mainly by the soldiers from the barracks. It is crowded in the evening with men who eat enormous ham sandwiches, narrow loaves cut in half longways with no butter, and drink the local white wines and a marsala-like sherry. Seven glasses of this and a bowl of tripe cost three shillings. The noise in this low-ceilinged room is like the blast of trumpets. The voices are lusty, full of good wine, and harsh like the hot summer landscape. They pass the communal wine bottle, tilting their heads back, the spear of wine quite six inches long between the neck of the porron and their own mouths. They sing passionately and with vigour. They sing Juan Simon, our favourite. Fingers click and snap and soon one man after another dances and everybody cries "OLE" and stamps their feet. The local singer bursts into a jota. At the height of the clamour a blind man walks straight through the dancing singing men, tapping his stick and offering lottery tickets. No one stops or takes any notice. Indeed, "There is little friendship in the world, and least of all between equals."

AVILA in Old Castile

"The blue,
Bared its eternal bosom, and the dew
Of summer nights collected still to make
The morning precious"

Avila is a painters' town. To a painter who loves weathered churches and pure light and colour, Avila is a town of enchantment. It stands high on the hill plains of Castile, surrounded by a waste of rock and boulders, the town of beloved St. Theresa the Virgin of Ecstasy, a town of churches, so many, that the cathedral itself is buried in the bones of the ancient wall and small churches overspill outside the city. It is a town of church bells, of mysticism and nobility in decay. Undulating in careless magnificence over the barren hills, the Romanesque walls encircle the old town completely, the towers solid and like toy soldiers in their ordered perfection. A thousand years ago, Alfondo VI brought craftsmen and builders from the north, and these men, with Moorish prisoners, built the wall as a fortification. The stones are mellow, gold and huge.

On market day, the friendly people pass through the Puerta del Alcazar on their panniered donkeys, the women gay in flannel skirts swirling low, the men dignified in broad black conical hats, brown capes and light breeches. Green water melons lie in heaps on the stones. Panniers are packed with tomatoes, peaches, greengages and grapes, the sweet white muscatels covered with sacking. Oxen draw the rumbling carts, the old water carrier chides his donkey to pull the heavy jars more smoothly.

It is best to walk around the city walls early in the morning before the heat of the day, while the street cleaners are spraying jets of water over the sandy earth. From the high terrace the blue sky on the wide horizons has an electric brilliance against which the blue-green cypresses stand like spears from the burnt sienna fields. The rough streets descend sharply in wide shallow steps to the river and to the wild foothills of the mountains of the Sierra de Gredos.

There, across the parallel old and modern bridges, we drink in the wine store of Senor Maximo Velaxos. Each of his big day vats, in cobwebby dust, hold eight hundred litres of good wine. They are made in a nearby village and cost, empty, five pounds each. But the golden wine is only a penny a glass. The cabras, the goatskins, hold a hundred litres each, and there they stand, looking like obscene stuffed pigs sitting up to beg, decapitated. The lovely sixteen litre bottles of red wine – all heaven for ten shillings – stand row on row in their straw containers. The local wines, the blanco, the tinto and muscatel are in great demand and we drink a glass of wine from each barrel, but in the end decide that the dolce, a marsala like wine from South Tarragona, is the best of all…

Our host, the seller of these wholesale wines, refuses any payment.

"What are a few glasses of wine among friends? Those who are buying it wholesale in my fine leather skin containers are paying for your drinks," a remark that annoys a man who is loading his cart with wine. With a stick and a heave-ho, he hauls the skins onto his tumbril, prods his oxen and starts off to the mountains. In the dried river bed the goats skip over the sandbanks: there is the sound of bells everywhere.

We follow the sweep of the old bridge up and left through the ancient gate and find the oldest quarter tumbling in decay towards the setting sun. The squat houses are only nine feet high and seem to have been carved out of the earth itself. There is no traffic, only donkeys, mules and horses.

Through the Puerta de San Vincente we go outside the walls again to the oldest and smallest church in Avila, the church of San Segundo. There on the parapet, we sit overlooking the river, admiring the tiny golden sandstone church in its churchyard wild with grass and pecking chickens, its dramatic huge burial crosses slanting in the sun. It is asymmetrical, with a pink tiled roof and a superb Romanesque porch. Inside are two Roman arches and a gallery with delicate railings on the pillars stretching the whole width of the church like an Elizabethan setting for Twelfth Night. The simple altar decorations are two pots decorated with blue bulls and flowers.

Only a few minutes' walk is our other favourite church, the church of Virgen de las Vacas. It faces a cobbled square with a fountain and a pump where the women come for water and a chat. Over its door is a roof on rustic pillars, and in the high bell tower is a stork's nest. It is a fairy tale church, ancient and simple. Children swarm around us, come sitting in the foreground hoping to be sketched into the picture. They make comments in deep hoarse voices. They wear alpargatas, and are thin and slow-eyed. The little girls, like bonbons or French gateaux, are enchanting in frocks with frilled epaulettes, the boys have short pants, dose cropped hair, big smiles and bony brown legs. As we sit on a wooden bench drinking wine, a sleepy dog droops along the gutter, the quiet women stretch their washing on the ground to dry, old women in black carry pails to the fountain, and the yellow houses glow in the blazing sun. The breadseller's donkey drinks at the well, walking elegantly over the rough stones.

SEGOVIA in Old Castile

"A tower'd citadel, a pendant rock,
A forked mountain, or blue promontory
With trees upon't, that nod unto the world
And mock our eyes with air:"

There is only one way to see the castle of Segovia. Descend the motor road, the ronda de Santa Lucia, to the north of the town and look, look up to the high towers and the dramatic wall plunging into the rocky chasm. It sails, immense and fantastic, like the prow of a ship, over the waving poplars.

Although it is now a military museum, against a thunderous grey sky it is the castle of medieval knights, the castle of the wicked ogre of our nightmares and fairy tales, the castle of Otranto. The cliff edges to the valley are burnt sand and granite, the river Eresma an encircling cicatrice of rocks and tall trees.

High up on the plateau of the town is the cathedral, the last Gothic church built in Spain, with its soaring columns and "pillared shade high overarched, and echoing walls between".

Segovia is a town of churches, their turrets and spires of all shapes – San Esteban, san Andres, San Lorenzo, San Martin de los Caballeros, San

Clemente, Santo Tomas, and the church of Vera Cruz, home of the Knights Templar, with a curious twelve sided ground plan – their names, like their towers and porches, magnificent, golden and mellow. We dine on roast whole piglet, a delicacy of the region, and drink rioja the wine of Logrono in Old Castile, an excellent white wine, delicious with the goat's cheese of La Mancha.

Toward the east of the town, crossing the Plaza Azoguejo, is the Roman aqueduct, a giant striding from hill to hill eight hundred and forty yards long, one hundred and sixty-five arches rising in a double tier to nearly a hundred feet; a colossus of granite blocks not joined by mortar.

Beautiful, dramatic Segovia,

> *"at whose sight all the stars*
> *Hide their diminished heads."*

TOLEDO in New Castile

> *"With antique pillars massy proof*
> *And stored windows richly dight*
> *Casting a dim religious light,"*

The cathedral of Toledo dominates the hill, at the foot of which curls the Tagus river. With its lovely choir stalls and screens, its tremendous soaring nave and its unique double ambulatory and glowing stained glass rose windows, it is the most superb of all Spanish Gothic churches. The narrow, oriental, crooked streets twist round and up steeply from the Alcantara bridge. Goldsmiths hammer the delicate earrings, swords and daggers inlaid with wire gold thread, and panniered donkeys go by, their double baskets filled with gay blue pots from Talavera de la Reina and wine jars.

But Toledo, for the painter, is the home of El Greco. His "Twelve Apostles" is in the cathedral sacristy, and "The Burial of Conde Orgas" is in the Church of Santa Tome. His house is cool and dignified, with an inner courtyard and garden, and glazed tiles and ceramics from Talavera. In his studio and beyond the hall are a magnificent collection of his pictures, one of which is a striking landscape of Toledo as it was in the late sixteenth century.

Here, in 1580, until his death in 1614, the Cretan, Domenico Theotocopouli lived and painted. His extraordinary paintings, with their long, twisted fingers and heads, their undulating vertical lines, and their strong blacks, greys and purples, have the ecstatic fervour of a visionary, and the dynamic inevitability that bring the Christ to us more vividly than any other painter has done.

To the east of the town is the ruined Alcazar now a memorial to the courage of a group of Franco's men who held out against attack until they were relieved. This stark monument, built in 1538, was once the most elegant palace in Toledo.

The Alcazar is a shattered ruin symbolic of the twentieth century, but in Toledo there are buildings of all styles and periods that link the past with the present. The Gothic cloisters of San Juan de los Reyes are the most graceful and delicate in Spain, the interiors of Santa Maria La Blanca, the churches of Cristo de la Luz and Las Tornerias are completely Moorish, the great encircling defence walls are Roman, and the Hospice of Santa Cruz is the first building in Renaissance style to be completed in Spain. But under a burning sky, parched on its rocky hill, Toledo, the chief religious centre of the country, has a golden harmony.

ANDALUCIA

CORDOBA

"Proud and godly kings had built her long ago
With her towers and tombs and statues all arow
With her fair and floral air and the love that lingers there
And the streets where the great men go."

We come to Cordoba across the plains of La Mancha. through vine-yards and vast olive orchards, passing windmills on hillocks that remind us of pictures by Goya haunted by the ghost of Don Quixote. It is strange that in our crowded carriage is a Spaniard like Sancho Panza who talks with great vivacity on the greatness of Spanish painting and the decadence of all modern painters.

The heat is intense. Now we are in Andalucia. The Guadalquivir flows sluggishly by, cattle graze on the river bed. On her banks Cordoba lies, wrapped in an eighteenth century calm, like a moated village. We cross the bridge to the great mosque, the loveliest Moorish church in all Spain, with its huge brown walls ridged at the top like a vast rectangular fortress, in complete contrast to the delicacy of the interior. We sit outside in the courtyard of orange trees, grateful for the coolness of the four fountains. From the brazen sunshine we walk into the deep shadows of the pillared mosque with its pools of cream light, grey light and vivid stained glass reflected on the dark floor like a flower on velvet. Long ago, in 755, the Moors who had conquered southern Spain elected a wise ruler, Abdurrahman the First, to be the King of Spain. He was a great builder, with a taste for beautiful gardens, and in Andalucia he repaired the ravages of war and neglect. He brought new plants, the date palm, the banana, the saffron and mulberry trees, the sugar cane, ginger, myrrh, and the cotton plant. But he is renowned as the builder of the Mosque in Cordoba, the construction of which was continued for many centuries. He actually worked at it with his own hands for an hour each day. The Mosque had nineteen doors, from each of which extended an avenue of pillars in the direction of Mecca. He built one thousand and ninety three pillars, each a single stone brought from Nimes, Narbonne, Carthage and from Roman ruins in Spain. Overhead was a wooden roof of odoriferous woods which supported a dome crowned by a gold pomegranate. Four thousand six hundred lamps hung on silver chains. The walls were lined with white marble inlaid with gold and encrusted with crystal. It was the Mecca of the West, and pilgrims walked round each column chanting a verse from the Koran.

Today, this decoration has gone. In the centre is the Christian temple, ornate, overdecorated and ugly. But it is the great singing loveliness of the thousand Arab pillars in the "deep but dazzling darkness" that envelop the spirit. The mass begins. The priests in jade green and gold vestments, the little boys in fluttering white-sleeved cassocks, which are constantly slipping from their shoulders or being used as fans to keep them cool, walk in procession through the Arab pillars. Pigeons fly across the Christian dome. The incense rises in a soft cloud. It is a friendly service. People come and go, small children enter with deep seriousness and sit quietly. The acolyte holding the gilded cross has a long, bony face of great beauty, like an El Greco painting.

Cordoba is the town of the painter of gypsies Julio Romero de Torres, whose paintings are found in the Museo de Bellas Artes. He died in 1931 aged forty-five. We spend one evening in this house as the guests of his brother and sister. We sit in the little cobbled square by the museum and drink wine, the evening sky turns from pink to indigo, a horse drawn carriage goes by in which a lady with a mantilla is fanning herself, a guitar plays nearby, and dim lights glow behind the iron grilled windows. We go into the courtyard and soon the upper balcony is filled with people: we order wine and olives for all, and while the dignified patron pads to and fro with glasses and bottles. Our friend, a local engineer, arrives with his guitar, and we all sing, and snap our fingers, and the guitar is passed from player to player as the evening dies away. We wander home through the little square des Capuchinos with its drunken lanterns lighting the Christ crucified. No traffic, no noise, no twentieth century; but wine, music, sweet courtesy, and soft Andalucian air.

GRANADA

"All but the wakeful nightingale;
She all night long her amorous descant sung.
Silence was pleas'd; now glowed the firmament
With living sapphires."

Under the wild peaks of the Sierra Nevada stands the Alhambra, the palace of Moorish Kings who lived there seven hundred years ago. We walk up the winding approach under the elm trees to the sound of water and of birds, and wander through the cool gardens, the patios and shady courtyards of a fairy tale palace from the Arabian nights. But at night, with a crescent moon "dwindled and thinned to a fringe of a finger nail held to a candle" and under a sky of velvet, the spell is like the enchantment of the Sleeping Beauty's hundred-year vigil. As we look across from the balcony of the Alhambra, the gypsy hill of Sacromonte sparkles like a hanging carpet of diamonds. Castanets snap far away, a group of children play ring-a-ring of roses, and the talk of women at the doorways rises up to the stillness and shadowy quiet of the empty palace, fountains, rivulets, cascades of water murmur all around. Single jets purr or spurt or wave softly in gentle arcs, waterfalls and streams curl and patter. The air is filled with the scent of bougainvillea under the elegant dark cypresses,

"where a candy-coloured, where a gluegold-brown

Marbled river, boisterously beautiful, between
Roots and rocks is danced and dandled, all in froth and
water-blowballs, down"

Very early one morning, in the cool of the day, we walk up the ravine of the Darro river; looking back at the Vega, the wide plain of Granada, all pink and dove gray, shimmering in the distance. The white painted tile lintels of the gypsy houses stand out against the pale mustard yellow of the foothills. We enter a house with "Arab Baths" on a small notice over the door. Inside are superb "Turkish" baths, two hundred years older than those in the Alhambra, with fine graceful columns supporting a roof of holes like a metal fancy cake dish, holes which were, long ago, filled with coloured glass.

We pass the little church of Nuestra Senora del Rosario de Fatima, with its simple wooden beamed ceiling. Fatima is a Portuguese name. Our Lady appeared in the village of Fatima in Portugal, and this church is built in her honour. One Madonna, lighted, has a look of anguish. On the altar are inlaid the weapons of the Crucifixion. A lovely cross stands in the entrance courtyard. Above are the burnt sienna cliffs of the Alhambra, below, the gorge with its bridges and donkeys.

As we go further up the valley, the gypsies come out to talk to us. The children, dirty and ragged, beg for pesetas and cigarettes, but are reprimanded by their mothers. They are fascinated when we sit down to draw and to write. A beautiful young girl says her cave is cool in the summer and warm in winter. It is spotlessly clean, has electric light, and a little chimney that juts out on the slope of the hillside. The walls and roof are solid rock. Her door is covered with sack-cloth and has a two foot square window above.

Outside, the prickly pear with its spotted lemon-like fruit, grows in profusion. A huge pig lies almost gracefully on its side in an alcove, and below, in the rocky ditch, two women climb down to wash their clothes, and fill pails of water with a tin canister. At night, all dress in their finery, their long frilled spotted dresses, their earrings, and roses in the hair, and dance passionately to the sound of guitars and castanets – alas, an entertainment now highly commercialised.

Another day we visit the Aladdin's Cave of the tapestry works of Senor J. Lopez Sancho. He is a stout, middle-aged Spaniard with a delicious ironical humour. He draws for us, with ease and precision, many weaving patterns on checked paper, all most delicate and complicated, declaring that he is only a business man and not an artist. He shows us, with obvious enjoyment, the hand woven cloth whose unusual and original colours he most admires – one in stripes of beige, grey, off white, deep brown and lime green glimmers and shines like satin. His workpeople sit at large looms making cloth up to two metres wide. The man stands, leaning his seat against a long tilted plank, his feet marching in a slow walk on the pedals, his hand pulling and flicking the crude string that moves the shuttles at lightning speed in a wooden slot across the material. The women are making carpets at vertical looms. A thick shiny needle is placed across the threads and the cross threads are woven dexterously by hand round the needle and through the vertical threads to make both pile and pattern.

Senor Sancho also dyes the wool. "We are performers of all crafts" says he, "but masters of none." But this is not true, for his carpets and cloths and cushions are superb masterpieces.

We visit the small ceramic works near the Plaza de Toros.

Three potters sit, each in a hole in the floor, and turn, with their feet, a heavy wheel. The local clay is fine, wet and pliable and a rich burnt sienna colour. The potter makes three or more pots from one lump. To finish the bottom of open bowls, he makes a lump of clay roughly the size and shape of the inside of the bowl, smacks the bowl down onto it, and finishes the bottom with a turning tool. This is done the same day. For pots, he makes an open cylinder and places the pot upside down into it, so that he can turn the bottom. Huge stacked bundles of juniper are used for heating the kiln, which reaches the temperature of 1500°C. The juniper is expensive and is brought from the mountains. One popular dish and pattern is the pomegranate – the symbol of Granada. Another local industry is the manufacture of horchata drink. It is made from chufa nuts which look like shelled walnuts. Our friend, the owner, is immaculate at night in white jacket and bow tie, when he sells lemonade and horchata drinks at his stall. But when we visit his small workshop in the morning, all is different. He greets us in faded but very clean working pyjamas and alpargatas. With two other men and a boy they start the day's production.

There is a machine like a large coffee grinder, four pails, three flat metal pans, a sieve, three vats, and one press for getting the liquid from the remains of the chufa kernels, and two cylindrical tins with a spout at the base for draining purposes. The method is simple. First the chufa are soaked overnight. Then he pours the chufa into the top of the machine and starts the electric grinder. A jet of water runs constantly through at half pressure. Horchata, a milky liquid, comes out at the bottom in the flat pans and is mixed with the husks of the kernels. This is passed through a sieve over a bath. The husks are squeezed out by hand and thrown into a pail ready to be pressed and made into animal cake. The horchata is poured into big vats which are surrounded with ice and cork. Sugar is added, and although this drink will last eight days, it is sold as soon as possible.

A lovely drink – almost as good as the local wine.

We spend another day travelling in a tiny bus to within five hundred feet of the very top of the Sierra Nevada, to the tremendous peaks of

Mulhacen and Veleta. Over ragged gorges, and barren depths we twist and turn through the wild mountains, a terrifying and magnificent journey. We climb, on foot, for four hours, and stand on the razor edge of the peak. To the south the vast ridge descends in a perpendicular cliff to a naked valley of rocks. The wind howls in a vast uprush. Far, far away, over the coastal ridge, glimmers the Mediterranean. We turn away in fear and look down instead to Granada below, graceful, elegant and peaceful.

ALMERIA

"A dark
Illimitable ocean without bound,
Without dimension, where length, breadth, and highth
And time and place are lost."

Almeria, a fishing port, where steamers leave for Spanish Morocco, lies to the south of the most desolate and barren wilderness in all Spain.

It looks ancient and sublime from a ship, the setting sun turning the sea to pink shot silk, ultramarine and purple, above which glows the sandy gold of the Moorish Alcazar on the hill.

The shadows hide the suffering and poverty in its alleys and streets. On the hill, too, is a huge statue of Christ. He stands with arms raised in benediction. From Him, a precipitous flight of steps end suddenly in a jagged drop separating His grandeur from the jumble of filthy slums that lie below. This is the most sordid poverty we have seen in Spain, the poverty of hopelessness. The steps to God are broken as if heaven itself has disowned the wretched human beings below. These poor are ugly and pitiful, and nothing romantic can disguise the Goya-like horror of their lives.

But at night, under the moon, these poor hovels have a medieval beauty, with their curved porticos, twisting alleys and stepped cobbled lanes. Some of the fishermen have climbed up to the terrace to breathe the fresh Mediterranean air. A mother lights her candle at the base of the Christ and shields it with her fan. As she goes away, she turns and kneels on the stones to pray. A child runs back and kneels with her.

In daytime we descend once more and come unexpectedly to the colonnaded square its centre completely filled with shrubs and trees. A few steps more and we are in the cathedral square. A serious small boy appears from nowhere and conducts us proudly through the cathedral which has the bastions and towers of a fortress. Its garden has a fountain and goldfish. Inside, there is overdecoration, but the fine pillars soar splendidly into a vaulted roof.

We take a bus to watch the fishermen at work. It is 7:30 a.m. Six men launch a small boat and row out in a wide arc dragging one line. A cork buoy marks it about a quarter of a mile from the shore. This is repeated until a line of buoys make a wide semi-circle. The net is like a long, finely woven stocking with a bag at one end. The boat returns to the shore, the men jump out and start to haul. After an hour's pulling, everybody bent double, excitement grows for the bag is almost in: at last it is on the beach, and out tumble octopus, squid, and a handful of tiny fish. The men stamp on the octopi. They are put into a separate basket, for they are a favourite delicacy of Spain. There is a sea hedgehog, a sea horse, a starfish and a stingray, a revolting sea slug and a Portuguese man-of-war. The fish are quickly placed in baskets and the older children ride off on bicycles to market, while the men start to tow out once more far a second haul. They earn only five shillings a day.

The fish bars of Almeria are a great delight. The fish are freshly cooked in an open kitchen – a model of shining saucepans and heated slabs over the wood fire ovens The chef, in his white cap, tosses the gambas, crabs, calamares and small fish with expert skill. Toasted gambas with the local dolce (white) wine are delicious and the feast costs only a shilling. Our "patron" places wicker chairs for us in the street gutter facing the hotel entrance. There is no motor traffic. We look with affection at a little column, on which stands a figure of Christ. It is surrounded with a railing and has four rectangular wrought-iron lanterns. Blind people stumble by, gaunt and hungry. There are so many in Spain, but here in Almeria there are so many more thus afflicted, because they work in the local esparto grass industry the dust from which affects the eyes causing disease and blindness. A little girl begs for a peseta. She grabs the money and rushes to the churro stall, buys a handful in paper and stuffs them into her mouth ravenously.

In contrast to the humble lives of the workpeople stands the Moorish Alcazar with its castellated walls clambering over the hills and enclosing a mound of stone slabs. The first forecourt is transformed from a desert into a terraced garden with tobacco plants, geraniums, azaleas, roses, fountains, streams and wells. An open-air stage has been built on the highest level where dances are performed at fiesta times.

From the second court, where the Moorish garrisons once lived, we can see the coastal plain, and the African-looking settlements of white flat-topped houses. A girl is breaking sticks. She raises a stone above her head and brings it down on a stick stretched across a hole in the ground. Only after many attempts is the stick broken. A woman brings out a bucket with holes, fills it with lighted charcoal and cooks her meal in a frying pan held over it. Another woman scrubs her child at a public fountain, which stands on an unshaded rock, where the sun beats down all day. Others are sweeping the cobbles, but to keep cool and clean in Almeria is like one of the labours of Hercules.

In complete contrast, at fiesta time, Almeria is an enchanted town.

The horse-drawn carriages parade in the twilight along the ramblas, the women entrancing in their shawls, roses, mantillas and earrings, the men, smoking cigars, superb in flat round hats, and the jackets and tight trousers of Andalucia. The bullfights are tremendous, everybody leans from balconies or parades in the streets. The children, like small imitations of their parents, are dressed immaculately. The Ortegas are the matadors and kill their bulls with the greatest courage and finesse. Down by the port is the fairground; fairy lights hang everywhere in fantastic designs. Almeria is "en fete" and her misery is forgotten.

"Like a rich jewel in a Ethiope's ear"

she shines and glitters on the edge of that dark hinterland northwards which shuts her in upon herself. An extraordinary land, the deserts of the moon, stretching towards Murcia and Guadix, high mountains with jagged parched valleys, canyons with flat-topped sides as if some mad giant has slashed the earth with a scimitar. No plants, no birds, no life. Under a bank of grey cloud, in the twilight, it is the land of the lost, the land of the dead.

ALICANTE in Levante

"Groves whose rich trees wept odorous gums and balm,
Others whose fruit burnished with golden rind
Hung amiable."

Over the grisly mountains of eastern Andalucia, sleeping like a herd of elephants covered with a grey tarpaulin, we turn and twist and come to Sorbas, a burnt-up town built precipitously across two razor-like ravines, and then, as if entering the Promised Land, we descend to Lorca and the pleasant irrigated plains of the Mediterranean seaboard. The grapes are large, sweet muscatels. Orange groves scent the air. Little boys sell jasmine buttonholes, the intoxicating white flowers pinned as a bouquet on the top of a stick. Elche, like a plumed duchess, waves its thousand palms into the blaring sun.

Below us, on the sea, is Alicante, a big port and a fashionable holiday town. Up the hill, with its twisted crooked alleys we call on our old friend Senor Martinez, a seller of wholesale wines in the Street of a Hundred Fires. We drink from each barrel and take a glass of one of the oldest wines in Spain. As we have brought him a present all the way from England, he refuses payment, and instead, gives us a bottle of wine as a gift.

On the hilltop is the ancient castle of Santa Barbara. With an official permit, we climb through its layered courtyards which remind us of all the invaders who through the centuries, have tried to conquer this coast – Hannibal in 231 BC, the Greeks, and the Moors in the Middle Ages.

To our great surprise, we find the castle ruins inhabited by a friendly crowd of beggars, sent there from the streets while waiting to be restored to their own villages. They jokingly refer to their stay in the castle as their summer holiday, and tell us to admire the magnificent views along the coastline, especially at sunset. They do not beg from us, but with true Spanish gallantry dust an old chair for me to sit on and offer us a slice of their melon. We return later, with wine and cigarettes, and enjoy a merry Beggars' Opera party under the stars.

"All politicians are bad" one old man remarks. "We fight and rebel, but whoever wins, the poor are always poor, and the rich men richer. Let us live in peace and be content with what we have." In Alicante, glowing and prosperous, that seems to be easiest and wisest.

TARRAGONA in Catalonia

"This castle has a pleasant seat; the air
Nimbly and sweetly recommends itself
Unto our gentle senses"

We sit on the Roman walls at sunset and look westwards over the mountains. Cypresses spear the sky. The ilex, pine and juniper are black against the golden, sun-baked hills. Tarragona is the most theatrically magnificent of all Catalan towns, the Cathedral and the ancient walls crowning a summit of rock that descends as a cliff into the wide blue way.

The main avenue on the hilltop runs directly to the sea, and here in the evening is delightful animation. We sit for hours, sipping wine, watching the crowds of men, women and children stroll pleasantly up and down, the men in dark suits, the women sparkling, elegant and beautiful, with superb gleaming black hair, fine pale skins and graceful walk, the children demure and serious; we have never seen such exotic and chic hair styles for small girls – bows, top knots, plaits, ribbons, fringes, all shiny black against their pristine flowered dresses. By English standards, they seem too quiet and well-behaved, but they are certainly not unhappy.

Like her people, Tarragona is a proud and dignified city. The cyclopean masonry of the walls was probably erected by the Iberians fifteen centuries before the birth of Christ. The turrets and gates are Roman, the great Julius Caesar himself once gave his name to the city. There are the remains of an amphitheatre, where the audience sat long ago on the tiered seats facing the stage and the sea, surely one of the most beautiful situations in the world to watch a play. But the Cathedral, for me the most attractive in Spain, is the loveliest building of medieval Tarragona. It faces a little square, a flight of steps leads to its facade carved in 1278 by Master Bartolomeo The cloisters are delicately carved and surround a central fountain sweet with the light and shadow of shrubs and orange trees. The Romanesque porches and towers, with tiled apses, crowd in an irregular group of honey coloured stone.

TOSSA DE MAR on the Costa Brava

"Look at the stars! Look, look up at the skies!
O look at all the fire-folk sitting in the air!
The bright boroughs, the circle-citadels there!"

From Port Bou to Blanes stretches the rocky wild land of the Costa Brava, with its pine-covered hills, valleys and ledges, its promontories a deep orange red, plunging into a purple blue sea. Into these bays sailed the Greeks, the Romans and the Phoenicians, the Carthaginians and the Moors, and on the headland of Tossa was built in medieval times a walled city to protect the fisherfolk from the pirates. Winding with grace and strength, turreted against the sea and sky, the wall encloses the Villa Bella on the hill, a maze of steps and pathways, gardens and archways. Through the empty porticos we look down on the crescent bay, the boats in lines on the beach or at night when the fishermen float out to hunt for lobsters the lamps on the boats shine like glow-worms over the dark sea.

Some evenings, in the town square, to the sound of the brass band, everybody dances the sardana in a big circle. This ancient Catalan dance, with its undulating intricate glides and hops, is very popular, and is often danced to the accompaniment of coplas – the music of the flag-eolet and tambourine.

Tossa is now, in the summer, more English than St Ives, and it is rumoured that the Spanish government wishes to ask for the return, not of Gibraltar, but of Tossato Spain. Other coastal villages look with envy at the prosperity of the Spaniards of Tossa.

But the Costa Brava is long and unspoiled. The coast road runs high over ravines and mountains, there are hundreds of footpaths and tracks down valleys and rocks, to secret bays and hamlets as gay and as lovely as any more populated town, and far more unspoilt for the artist. Here on remote beaches, the poet, the painter and the writer can find the peace and beauty of an earthly paradise.

ACKNOWLEDGEMENT OF QUOTATIONS FOR SPANISH SECTION

"Grace was in all her steps"
PARADISE LOST – BOOK 5 – 488   MILTON

"deep scars of thunder had entrenched"
PARADISE LOST – BOOK 1 – 600   MILTON

"And the fleas that tease in the High Pyrenees"
"Only the high peaks hoar:
TARANTELLA   HILAIRE BELLOC

"The blue,
Bared its eternal bosom"
SLEEP AND POETRY   JOHN KEATS

"There is little friendship in the world"   FRANCIS BACON

"A tower'd citadel, a pendant rock"
ANTHONY & CLEOPATRA   WILLIAM SHAKESPEARE

"Pillared shade"
PARADISE LOST 1   MILTON

"at whose sight all the stars"
PARADISE LOST – BOOK 4   MILTON

"With antique pillars massy proof"
IL PENSOROSO   MILTON

"proud and godly kings had built her long ago"
THE DYING PATRIOT"   JAMES ELROY FLECKER

"all but the wakeful nightingale;"
PARADISE LOST – 4 598   MILTON

"deep but dazzling darkness"
SILEX SCINTALLANS. THE NIGHT. 1.49   HENRY VAUGHAN

"dwindled and thinned to the fringe of a finger nail"
MOONRISE   GERARD MANLEY HOPKINS

"where a candy-coloured"
EPTIHALAMION   GERARD MANLEY HOPKINS

"A dark, illimitable ocean without bound,"
PARADISE LOST – 1   891   MILTON

"Like a rich jewel in an Ethiope's ear,"
ROMEO AND JULIET   WILLIAM SHAKESPEARE

"Groves whose rich trees wept odorous gums"
PARADISE LOST – 4   248   MILTON

"This castle has a pleasant seat?"   WILLIAM SHAKESPEARE

"Look at the stars! Look, look up at the skies!"
THE STARLIGHT NIGHT   GERARD MANLEY HOPKINS

I sailed to Australia during January and February of 1952 and reached Adelaide, the Cheltenham of the southern Australian coast. The climate was such that we wore summer clothes by day but it could be very cold in the evenings even whilst wrapped in fur. The wind blew in from the Antarctic. We returned there later in the year to study the art, culture and history at the aboriginals, the original inhabitants of Australia.

When we were in Sydney we saw the Aboriginals who had come to the city, the lucky few that had not become ill with diseases. Some drank a lot, and were very pathetic. Not knowing what to do, the authorities placed them in a large compound outside Sydney. It was sad and tragic. Toy boomerangs were made and sold to the tourists. I do hope that the question of the future of this aboriginal race has now been addressed and solved.

The more fortunate Aboriginals stayed in the outback on farms, and were very good workers, of great use to the farm owners. Sometimes they would like to go off on walk-abouts to the Northern Territories beyond Alice Springs, the town in the central outback of Australia. They would disappear for a couple of months and later return to their farms. They still painted extraordinarily fine paintings and their drawings on the walls of caves were unique. Their special design was to paint fish with its bone structure visible as if translucent seen through its skin. They also painted kangaroos in the same manner, to propitiate a "God" who would send them good hunting.

I remember hearing of an artist named Namatiera who lived in Alice Springs and who was well known throughout Australia and considered brilliant, he was however, alas, taught to paint western style, his own heritage neglected. Various pottery firms used the Aboriginal art designs to make plates and such for the tourists. I have two still in my possession.

We wished to write a book about them and do research in the Northern

Territories, but found that it was very far away and more importantly the Government did not allow visitors or tourists. Instead, much Aboriginal art had been collected during a Government expedition and was in a Museum in Adelaide. We went there and met with a Professor who was most generous who offered us a portfolio of photographs that he had gathered. These had served as the base for the Australian Museum of Aboriginal art. We were without doubt fascinated by the subject of the Aboriginals and we did eventually complete the book. It's called "Aboriginal Art Old and New," published by Angus Robertson, and is an acknowledgement of Aboriginal primitive culture, especially their painting, nomadic way of life, their "DreamTime" religion, their corroberry dancing and their extraordinary invention of the boomerang.

It would be wonderful to be able to return to Australia one day and have the opportunity to re-visit this very fine museum.

After that we went to Melbourne which prided itself on being completely English. There is a first class Art Museum and my husband was introduced to Mr. Sydney Nolan who was a well known Australian painter. I felt that the people of Melbourne wanted to be English and have BBC radio accents, a pity! Be yourselves... Australian, such a marvellous people with your own voice and culture. Now they have their own identity and will host the Games, no doubt with great style.

My husband had gone on ahead of me from England to obtain details of his school and to find lodgings for us. He hoped to find a flat to rent, but there were none. So finally we shared a large house with other tenants. There was one kitchen with one large refrigerator, we were allocated one shelf. We filled ours with food but sadly, overnight, everything vanished. Communal living was a simultaneously memorable and horrendous expedience.

We took a bus inland from Melbourne some 100 miles to the North, a hilly wooded countryside. Our immigrant friend there was originally English. He loved gardening. The ubiquitous gum trees are not deciduous and have leaves throughout the year. The big tall main stem is cream and peeling and so decorative. My husband loved to draw them. Our friend had planted several English varieties of trees, oak, elm and ash...and many English flowering plants. He created an English country garden...he was a "Capability Brown" the second!

I had one introduction, arranged from London, to a top radio presenter who immediately invited me to work on radio. I declined as this was not the reason I had come to Australia. I was on an adventure with my husband and a media career demanded dedication. I told him that I had worked in television for the BBC. Australia had just discovered television and so he promptly offered me work in television. Again I declined. My life as a theatre and television actor was in England and would be resumed at a later date. So, I survived the temptation of joining Australian radio and to be involved at the start of their television industry. I wanted to observe their education system at close hand, the schools and the students; and was also interested to see their theatres and meet their actors.

Meanwhile my husband was un-happy teaching in Melbourne. He had been spoiled in England with a marvellous art studio at Hadham Hall in Hertfordshire. His classes there were small and everything was provided. They did pottery, stone and wood carving with painting as a priority and weaving was a special interest. In Spain he bought chequered paper and printed on to this the designs the peasant women were using weaving on their looms. He re-created these designs on English looms, which made lovely patterned materials. He taught the children any skill they would like to try. Within two years at Hadham Hall School, all the children were producing beautiful arts and crafts exhibitions for him. He sent some of their works to the Annual Exhibition at the Royal Academy of children's art and several were chosen. The boys loved wood carving, the girls enjoyed weaving. Activities they would not have known about had he not been their teacher. He was very skilled and accomplished at so many crafts, and loved teaching.

In Australia nothing was provided in the State schools and the classes were large. They had desks, nothing else, no apparatus. He had to ask them to bring their own materials and few did, which led to the problem of how to occupy the students. After three months he had enough, saddened by the situation, we moved to Sydney.

The public houses in those days in Australia closed at 6pm. Most men finished work at 4pm or 5pm and proceeded immediately to the pub to get themselves completely drunk. You would then observe a quasi Dickensian scene. A woman holding a baby to her breast outside a pub sitting on the ground and pleading with her husband to come home and not spend his money on beer. It was quite unbelievable! Women gathered at one end of the pub and men at the other. They did not converse – a working class ritual, men were men and the women knew their place. I was fascinated by what, to me, seemed a Victorian attitude. How things have changed.

In Sydney we stayed across the bay from where the Opera House now stands. It is a stunningly beautiful harbour, as glorious as San Francisco with inlets and wonderful houses overlooking the deep blue sea. The small boats in the harbour were used like buses. Our first week there coincided with particularly hot weather and one of the many new immigrants (from Italy & Greece) had dived into the harbour and was eaten by a shark! After this incident we were quite certain to remain on one of the beautiful (and safe) beaches for our aquatic pursuits. Bondi beach now extremely commercial, I am told, was then exquisite along the coast facing the Pacific ocean. We remained in Sydney for three months and loved the city, its people, their vitality; so lively and full of fun.

With such an influx of European immigrants, it was considered a disgrace for the local girls who had boyfriends of foreign extraction. I'm sure that all have now intermingled to their great advantage. The Italians went north mostly, direct to Brisbane and beyond to the semi-tropical climate; to grow oranges and tropical fruit. During our visit to that part of the country they told us that they made a good living able to earn in a week what they made in a month in the old country. They were happy to be in Australia. They could send money home to Italy so that their relations could eventually join them in their new country.

While we were in Sydney, my husband and I both fell ill briefly and needed medical treatment and penicillin. There was no free National Health Service. We soon found that all my husband's income was spent on the medical bills. I had to find employment.

I went to the Town Hall clutching my diplomas and CV and asked if I could teach or lecture. The Education Committee was meeting that very morning. What luck! They met on the 3rd floor I was shown in immediately. There was a semi-circle table with a Chairman sitting in the centre. They were so warm and charming. They asked questions about London: "How's Trafalgar Square?"

'What are you doing with the pigeons?'

A marked difference from a similar interview in England!

I told them that I was hoping to find a position as a teacher. They asked: "Do you wish to teach in a College? or a University?"

I said: "I would like to work in a normal school, I want to meet teenagers."

"You can start tomorrow" was their reply.

I went on: "I can teach English and Drama, my special subjects, but also Art, Music and History."

So I was to begin teaching Drama and English in an Australian state school.

The next morning I arrived punctually at the appointed school. The Head Mistress placed me as a replacement in a class where the teacher was absent, ill. It was a science class. I was given this huge book of her College lectures on various scientific subjects.

"What do I do?" I asked.

"Write on the huge blackboard from page 36...the class will copy it down."

So I wrote it as clearly as I could, told the class to copy it and learn it. So they quietly proceeded to do just that. They had their own books and pencils. Eventually I asked them what it meant? They looked blank. What an extraordinary way to expect young adults to learn. Perhaps they didn't want to discuss it as I was the replacement teacher. The bell rang, they closed their books and went to the next lesson. I wonder if that method still continues to be used? I was told that in the State Education system, all schools conformed, the same lessons being taught on the same day. I wondered, how do they know if all the children have understood what they were copying, was there no discussion? At the end of the year they are examined and are required to have learned it by heart and attain a mark of 50%+. If they do not, they must repeat the subject in the following year and the teachers are not promoted and do not get an increase in salary. A very strange procedure.

Some of the teachers later asked me if they could watch one of my drama classes as they did not have the subject in their current curriculum. I began my Master Class in Drama in the schools central hall. Both, teachers and pupils, were enthralled, they loved the new subject and leaped into action; thrilled with their reaction, I was elated. I had clearly been a hit at that school because when we left Australia on our return voyage to England, many of the teachers and students came down to the docks to wave me goodbye. I was very touched by this gesture.

A while later we decided to take a short holiday to see the Great Barrier Reef. We went by train as to allow us to see the countryside, but hour after hour of outback was boring. At one point the train came to a halt. From the distance some men on horseback appeared. They reached the train which was now stationary and were handed fruit, vegetables, newspapers and magazines. It was like I imagined the American far west to have been years ago. The train arrived at Brisbane where we stayed only briefly. It can be very hot there. The people sat on their door steps, wore big Stetson hats with corks around to keep the flies away. The men wore khaki trousers down to their knees with thick woollen socks to ward off the mosquitoes and big thick boots. It might have been a movie scene from a western set long ago; but it was reality. I wonder if the English would be like this if they did not have such a damp, wet and cold climate. They sat there in their thick boots and their hats on the back of their heads with a can of beer in their hands. Brisbane people were very easy-going and friendly. I loved them.

From Brisbane we ventured North to view the barrier reef of corals which stretches hundreds of miles along the Northeast coast of Australia. We were headed for South Molle Island where we planned to stay for a while. We reached this small island by boat. The Hotel had been built by ex-Germans. It had a large communal dining room and the food was excellent. The corrugated iron roof was most attractive.

Along the coral beach there were separate cabins on stilts. The weather was warm, the ocean Mediterranean blue. Unusually at that time of year they were experiencing tropical rainstorms, which neither of us had ever seen before. The water descended like waterfalls. The cabins were designed in such a way that the rain went right through them. That is why they are built on stilts. It was a very lovely holiday. We swam in the nude from nearby tiny islands.

We were greeted as we arrived by people who had been there all winter, elderly and probably wealthy Australians. They wanted to know if we played bridge, they immediately wanted us to make up a foursome. How happy they were to live in this lovely climate during the winter months, especially if they came from Melbourne or Adelaide.

We went in a glass-bottomed boat, told to wear thick rubber solid shoes because we would actually stand on the coral reef, there is about six inches of water above the reef. We realised why we needed heavy footwear; there were deadly poisonous creatures living on the coral and you could easily be stung. Our view from the inside of the boat was stunning. You could see the amazing reefs descending for miles into the ocean, great cliffs of brilliant coral. I hope the pollution created by modern life has not destroyed this wonderland. The danger will come from the development of the coast as a holiday paradise, I imagine that is well under way. Already there was the beautiful Hayman Island Hotel popular with honeymooners. Inevitably many more would be constructed.

Two weeks after our arrival, suddenly the heavens opened and we experienced endless tropical rain for several days and nights. We could not leave or return to the mainland. Two rivers had become one, the land between them now flooded. We would have to wait until the water subsided and the land re-appeared.

I learned to water-ski! I climbed down a small ladder at the back of the

speedboat and put the skis on my feet and knelt. Wires were un-wound!
I floated 50 yards away at speed. When commanded I would attempt to
stand up. With any luck I would...and I did. The speed increased. I did
not fall over on my first attempt. I pressed to the right, pressed to the
left; I whizzed in a semi-circle over the blue waters. I felt like a
champion. It was exhilarating. The deep aquamarine warm sea and the
glorious un-spoiled coastline complimented this memorable day beautifully. A garden of Eden...no hotels, nothing. My husband, ever fond of
practical jokes, suddenly shouted...SHARKS... alarmed I looked left
and right and promptly fell off my skis. The captain said there might be
some sharks but there was enough good food around them in the sea to
avoid humans. The motorboat returned and scooped me in a net out of
the water and I crawled along a platform on to the boat. It was so
exciting to learn how to water-ski in such perfect, ideal surroundings.

We returned to Sydney and sailed home to London via India, the Red
Sea and the Mediterranean. I was so pleased to see my students one last
time, they wanted me to stay and open a drama school. That would have
been marvellous: appearing on Australian television too...but circumstances were such that we had to return home to England very quickly,
a journey of at least five weeks.

On that return voyage I met a lovely lady, Em. Sanderson, she was a
New-Zealand Maori. In London I helped her find a flat in Hampstead
and she became a hostess in Leicester Square at an establishment next to
the Alhambra Theatre, now an Odeon Cinema. She was the manageress
of a restaurant which had a regular clientele, she enjoyed that. She has
now, sadly, passed away. Her brother was a Maori Bishop. She loved
England, the Royal Family, our history and culture. She was patriotic,
generous and kindly. She came for a year to see the mother country and
stayed ten years before returning home to Auckland.

* * *

The Polish idyll, what happened?

During September 1955 we had planned a Sunday outing in our red sports car with our shaggy dog Sally. We were going to Suffolk driving around the countryside admiring the wonderful little villages. I was deliriously happy and very much looking forward to it. Just as we were leaving the telephone rang. A voice said: "Would Mr. Black come immediately to the hospital, his child will be born today?"

I said: "I'm sorry Madam, you have the wrong number."

At that moment Roman took the receiver from me and spoke: "Yes, I'll come right away."

And my whole world fell apart in an instant. I couldn't believe what I was hearing at all. I lived in misery for many weeks alone, it was a terrible shock. I loved him dearly. I knew he loved me. It was unbelievable.

Anyhow, we had to come to terms with it and obviously his affection for me was still as great as ever. It was all a big mistake, etc. Would I forgive him? But I said: "You are now the father of a little boy, I want you to be happy with him, go, be a father."

After 18 months, I stated: "We must come to a decision. I, alas, cannot have children. You should go away and be a good father somewhere and have more children and I will be an actress full time, an academic sometimes and a writer occasionally."

And that very painful decision was made with love. I said: "The most important thing is for you to legitimise this child, so I will instigate divorce proceedings."

A divorce of love, is it possible to comprehend that? It was a decision made by two artists whose ambitions had been much delayed by a long war service. It can be done between two artistic people who understand and love each other. He wanted to paint, like his mother: and I wanted to act. Shakespeare if possible. And act full time.

Forever afterwards I often saw him in the front row wherever I was working in the theatre. I was in a long West End run of the "The Student Prince" when after a Saturday matinee the stage-door keeper informed me that there was a Mr. Black and two children who wished to see me. I told him to send them up. They arrived at my dressing room. The boy, just getting quite tall, about 14 years old, the image of his father, very handsome. And a bright dark haired girl of about 10. Delightful children. I sent them off to get their programmes signed by the rest of the cast Roman looked at me and I at him. I said: "Are you painting, what are you painting?"

"I have won the gold medal of the Paris Salon for an English landscape."

"Good, go ahead" I said. He looked at me and said: "Those two children should have been ours."

"Don't say that, it's wrong. But I'm glad you're a father and I hope you are a good one."

Long gaps past thereafter, except for spotting him in the audiences, watching me act...in Manchester, in Newcastle. We always kept in touch, remotely. I hoped he would one day be successful and sell his paintings and perhaps even be in the Tate Gallery. My love for him never changed and I'm sure he felt the same way. So it is possible to have a friendly loving divorce. Naturally I would have preferred if we had stayed together, but this situation was very moving for us both.

He collapsed from a cerebral haemorrhage whilst painting in his studio at the Chelsea pottery. The door was open and the potters heard the noise. He was taken to St. Stephen's Hospital in the Fulham Road where he was placed on a life support system. It was me that the Hospital telephoned. They explained the situation, that he was dying, and that I could not see him in intensive care unit. If he survived, he would be a cripple in a wheelchair for the rest of his life. I prayed to God that he be taken.

He died, a proud Pole to the end but English in his heart. Extraordinarily, the previous week he had telephoned me every day. He had never done that before. How could he ever have thought that within a few days he would be dead. God moves in a mysterious way sometimes.

He had never been back to Poland because of the wretched Stalinist regime and had only seen his parents once. My great sorrow is that we never made it there together. He would have loved to show me his great country and its remarkable people.

LIFE SIX

A Landlady

(And how I unexpectedly started the restoration of Holland Park)

"how beauteous mankind is,
Oh brave new world that has such people in it"
said Miranda in "The Tempest.."..
Agreed: from the sublime to the ridiculous

I have been a customer at my Bank in Swiss Cottage since 1942. The reason I have remained there is because the Manager at the time was the only person who would lend me the money to buy 77 Lansdowne Road. At first he refused to lend money to a single woman for an old property like those in Holland Park. He asked if I was planning to re-marry as they preferred to lend to a husband in regular employment. Loans to women were not available. I had 3 months to vacate the flat in Hampstead and I wanted to retain my independence. It was time I bought a house and I needed a mortgage. I went back to the Bank in desperation, told the Manager that this would be my final request for help and again he refused. At that point I became very angry: "I'm at my wits' end, I have to move. I must buy a house. I am confident that I can repay the loan. You must help me."

I thumped my fist on the desk. He recoiled. I then gave a speech that rivalled Henry V's at Aingcourt: "Lend me the money, I won the war, my husband was in the Navy, everyone said the women of London were the most brave and courageous in the world during the war, we acted and worked like the men. We did a wonderful job. But now you will not lend me a few thousand pounds in order to secure a roof over

177

my head. Move into the 20th century National Westminster Bank…!"
I thundered at him. He cowered under his desk, I rushed out of the
room apologizing madly. The next morning he telephoned. I thought
this is notice, please leave my Bank and never come back. But no, to my
utter surprise he said: "Mrs. Black I will lend you the money. Buy the
house today. I was very moved by what you said to me yesterday. I will
lend you the money and pay for the restoration. Here are the repayment
schedules at 7%."

(Little did he know that I had nearly hit him and thrown him out of the
window!)

So, I was able to buy the house that day. I was then recommended an
excellent builder, Mr. Willett from Camden Town. My friend told me
that he was surrounded by an excellent team of workmen and
craftsmen. I told him that I wanted the house restored to its original
splendour no matter how long it took. He gave me an estimate which
was satisfactory. The team were professional and worked every day
from 8am to 5pm.

The Bank Manager supported me completely reminding me that should
I miss one payment, the house would be re-possessed…

"The payments will be made, I promised."

The workmen completed the restoration in one year. The 7 year loan
was unusual. I repaid the Bank in six. I was the owner of a superbly
restored Victorian house, 77 Lansdowne Road, Holland Park, London
W11.

After moving in to my new home in Holland Park I worked, firstly as a
Lecturer and Director of Shakespearean plays at Cambridge and then
for BBC Television. I did supply teaching for which there was always

work. It gave me an insight into the education system throughout London, from Chiswick to Golders Green. I was never unemployed and repaid the Bank loan, but not without personal sacrifice.

The finished house, a corner property, looked like the Taj-Mahal on a moonlit night, gloriously white with the immaculately repaired stucco, the beautifully trimmed garden, the ornate gate and tubs of flowers. I made the top two floors into apartments to let. The income would be essential in order to meet the hefty commitments associated with owning such a property; the mortgage, the builders and the rates.

They were self-contained flats which I furnished and equipped with some new furniture and some from the auctions which were always full of bargains. Viewing was on Thursday afternoons with the bidding on Friday. There was every kind of furniture. I had marked mid-Victorian book cases & bureau desks which nobody wanted at that time. Dealers wanted 18th and early 19th century, but not Victorian. I bought a lovely chest of drawers and other pieces, some Art Nouveau too. Modern furniture was cheap. I noticed some beautiful art books which I managed to acquire for a very modest sum. The programme said "assorted books." I assumed that that referred to the books on show. But no, I collected acres of books, most of which I did not want! It took four trips in my mini car to transport these books which I stacked in the basement of a property I had acquired at 119 Elgin Crescent. A pile 27 feet long and 3-4 feet high. I decided that I would spend one week-end, a very happy time discovering what treasures I had acquired. I enjoyed myself very much. I decided on examination that they were from an old rectory because there were many Bibles and Prayer books. What I was amused to find hidden among the popular novels and favourite light reading titles, were some beautiful French books in very good condition, of the type you would see for sale on the book stalls along the Seine in Paris. I also found some Victorian travel books about India. But I found three first edition Dickens which werc single stories each in one

tiny book, each printed separately in 1845. They were real treasure. One
was in good condition and the other two not so good. I gave most of the
novels away to the local Hospital, kept some of the travel books and
naturally the Dickens' novels, forever – my special treasures.

I was able to furnish the house very well with nice pieces, now
valuable...irony of fate. Victorian furniture is considered antique and is
much admired. I chose the pieces because they were appropriate for a
Holland Park period house built in 1850. They seemed at home there.

Holland Park has a rich and wonderful history. When I arrived in this
area in 1954-5, I went to the Kensington Library to read the history of
Lord Holland.

The district, mainly the homes of faded gentility when I arrived, is now
extremely fashionable and has become very expensive. I loved the
atmosphere and the neighbours and was always very happy at No. 77. I
do hope that my spirit lives on there after 43 years...I did not want to
leave...

I discovered the entire area west of Notting Hill Gate on foot and fell in
love with it. You could imagine the open coaches passing by with
footmen and servants, children playing in Montpelier Gardens with their
nannies pushing babes in large bassinet prams. The area had also been
well planned with the Church on the hill in Ladbroke Grove. Away to
the West are curved crescents. The designer of the whole district was
Charles Allum, an architect and artist. He had been given the entire area
in 1840-50, open country at the time with a racecourse and potteries
owned by Gypsies. The area extended to Portland Road and Clarendon
Road and through to Shepherd's Bush. I find it strange that this man has
not been honoured with a monument or something, he had great imagination and vision having designed one of the most beautiful areas in
London, a model for architects of the future, urban living at as best.

The Gypsies lived in an area within the racecourse now called Pottery Lane. It is surrounded by small lanes because the richer people on the hill did not want them to stray into the area of greater prosperity, such as Lansdowne Road. These big houses were for the new middle classes of the Victorian era; properties in Mayfair and Belgravia were too expensive, few were available. They instructed Mr Allum to create a beautiful neighbourhood for their families.

When I moved to Notting Hill, people were astonished that I lived north of the Park. I loved it. The area is artistic and eccentric (still, but maybe not for long). Near Holland Park Avenue are single houses for professionals, hard working artists, doctors, teachers & musicians. To the north there is a real cockney market, Portobello Road. If you are in central W.11 such as Elgin Crescent you enjoy both areas, walking around, shopping and chatting to locals. It is so peaceful and quiet away from the heavy traffic and crowds. The private gardens are quite magnificent. Birds; sparrows, black birds, robins & blue tits, can be seen. And squirrels too. The middle of the country but with the added attraction that it's near the West End. Many of the locals are in the Arts. People are courteous and civilized but not snobbish. When the BBC built the television centre in 1958, this area became popular with television personnel. I was working for the BBC at the time, I could reach the centre for rehearsals in 10 minutes. Others who also worked at the BBC admired my house and realised that restoration made these properties desirable once again. Within 3 years, Lansdowne Road was entirely renovated. An architectural marvel!

When my house was finally finished, I moved in, acquired a dog from the Battersea Dogs' home. My lovely shaggy dog Sally that had cost me only £1. She and I walked around the communal garden then and Mrs. Anderson came out, she was the self-appointed Head Mistress of the gardens. She had lived there a long time.

"Oh you have a dog, do not make a mess, who are you?" she asked, she continued: "We have very strict rules in the garden, no rubbish, no noise."

I agreed wholeheartedly and we became good friends. I hope the tradition continues. It is a communal garden, extremely charming and delightful with lovely trees and rose beds, a village of pleasant neighbours.

We formed a garden committee and we built a children's playground at one end, with ladders and swings. Everybody contributed and it was the first of its kind within a communal garden. We decided to hold a summer party on Midsummer's Night. They were very enjoyable indeed. Those evenings were usually warm and dry but we raised a tent in case the rains came. We hired a steel band that created an atmosphere conducive to much merriment. In the afternoon we had a children's sports day with lemonade and doughnuts and prizes. There were old fashioned games that the children loved: an egg and spoon race, a sack race, a 3-legged race and a memorable tug-of-war between Lansdowne Road and Elgin Crescent and I was used as "anchor person" for the Lansdowne Road team. It was immense fun, very well organized. Later the children were put to bed and we would then entertain friends to dinner and eventually wander out to the garden and dance until midnight. It was friendly like a village fête, very amiable and pleasant. In those days we could leave our windows and doors open without danger. It was usual for friends to call in after dinner and so I used to leave my gate open. One year, I had become friendly with a gentleman who was a Chief Inspector at the local Station. He had come to the party and his men kept watch. That occasion, although the others did not know, was the most protected party of the year. I did however find a young lady sitting in my drawing room. She had not been invited by anybody and had walked through my open door and helped herself to a drink. She was a German tourist and thought the English were so hospitable to have parties where all are welcome and the doors are left open. Although she was harmless, the police suggested I should keep the door closed in future. These days, alas, open doors are impossible. Now there is tight security whenever there is a garden function, what a pity.

I live in Holland Park to this day. In 1985 I moved to my other property at 119 Elgin Crescent. The big house was too expensive to maintain. So it had to be sold.

In 1960, I was working in television nearby and could go home to give Sally a run in the garden before getting back to the BBC for a quick sandwich and work at 2pm. A young lady was playing with my dog. I told her that I really liked those smaller houses in Elgin Crescent and would buy one, should one become available. My intention at the time was to have a place for my brothers and sisters to live when they retired. She told me No. 119 was for sale. It belonged to her mother-in-law who wanted to move to the country. At 1:15pm I spoke to the charming French lady who owned the house and I said I would make an offer. I went back to work that day. We stopped rehearsals with Jimmy Edwards at 4pm. Unexpectedly I had enough time to go to the Solicitors and formalize the offer.

Their offices were in Victoria Street. Two days later my offer was accepted and I would soon own 119 Elgin Crescent. I had no money! Some of the loan for No 77 was still outstanding but I still decided to approach my Bank Manager. In for a penny... To my great joy and astonishment he agreed immediately to lend me 50% of the funds to acquire a second property (I had not let him down and I believe he had faith in me)... The balance would come from The Sun Life Insurance Company. So now, I had two mortgages that truly felt like albatrosses round my neck. This meant no holidays, no new clothes, no drinks or smokes but a very sedate life for the immediate future. These are the sacrifices of which I spoke.

I went immediately for my first inspection and the owner refused to let me see the basement, which I found most curious. What was she hiding?...dead bodies! Refugees?...We went into the sitting room. It was very shabby. The while paint had turned black and the atmosphere was medieval! There was a marvellous Broadwood grand piano in the corner that appeared to be in very good condition... apart from the two legs which had pierced through the floor boards. No doubt the place was riddled with dry rot. The piano, at a precarious angle was supported with two chairs. Three stags' heads with impressive antlers adorned the wall – Daddy, Mummy and Baby. Immediately in front of them was a marvellous old Art Nouveau lamp-shade made of black and orange silk. It had tassels hanging from it. There was a Victorian fire-guard and a screen wobbling about on very pretty legs. It was very eccentric, not without charm. I told her that I was going to purchase the house. She was pleased that it was me and confident that I would restore it as a period house of 1820. Her daughter-in-law had lived on the top floor, the bathroom was used to keep coal because there was a real fire up there. It was hard to believe that coal was actually kept in the bath tub.

When I completed the transaction and owned the house, I immediately descended to the basement to see what disaster awaited me. The stair-case reminded me of the stairs in Robert Louis Stevenson's "Kidnapped"; rotten & old. These were the original steps which had been there since the house was built in 1820. With a torch I saw cobwebs, rats, rusty iron beds and a water logged floor. My heart sank. It was like a medieval dungeon. The floor was rotten, there were two old rusty fireplaces in one long room. The wall in between had been taken down and an RSJ put across the ceiling. There was an outside lavatory in a shed in the small garden. You could see many mice scuttling in every direction on the rotten damp floor. Two small windows provided the only glimmer of outside light at the front and back. They were boarded up with nails at every inch and the wood was rotten. This basement had not been inhabited for many years. That was clear. Formerly a servants' kitchen but now derelict.

I decided to undertake the renovations myself and began with the floor. I soon realised that the entire basement would require a damp course treatment. I set out to acquire the relevant advice and purchase the right materials. Whiteley's was a wonderful Department Store in Bayswater. Victorian and old-fashioned. The staff always courteous with old world charm. They had a house craft department in the basement and it was there I sought advice. The salesman sold me rolls of white paper, paint and paste and explained that I could technically do this job myself and wished me good luck, convinced that as a woman I would never get the job done!

I spent 3 years without a single holiday, working 7 days a week and every spare minute up a ladder painting and decorating. The whole house was rebuilt, an enormous task. The grand piano had been left behind by the previous owner, I inherited it along with the extraordinary stags' heads which I thought were hilarious, belonging more to a stately home than my humble sitting room in Elgin Crescent.

I proceeded to clean the basement thoroughly, apply the roll, let it dry and painted it (Many years later we were told that this paper was highly inflammable...) I installed a permanent continental stove which would provide heat for the whole house. I had been to an auction and bid for electrical and gas appliances; and some carpets. I bought a lovely brass stove with glass doors just as I had wanted and rolls of carpets. I replaced the old, tiny, windows with larger modern ones. I had bid for 3 lots of carpets and was very lucky ending up with enough to cover the whole space. It was transformed into a studio. The basement had become a romantic elegant artist's home. Among the rolls of carpet, I found four beautiful Kilims which I loved – Persian and Turkish – quite valuable. People are so much more aware these days of antiques, that I doubt if these types of bargains are still available. The Victorian period is now in fashion. In 1960 I also bought a beautiful needlework box on a triangular stand and several lovely chests of drawers. One piece of furniture, my builder told me to burn immediately because it had wood worms. I had heard of such creatures. I was fast becoming wise in dealing with every facet of the art of renovating old houses. When one restores successfully, one is left with a great sense of achievement...an old house has been given new life.

These houses have rooms with such lovely proportions and the original cornices are charming. Because I am tall, I particularly enjoy the high ceilings, elegant with walls on which to hang your pictures. I extended the ground floor balcony off the sitting room by 7 feet (thus creating extra space below, now with sliding glass doors on to a diminished, but still lovely patio garden). I was the first to do this but since many have copied my idea. Balcony views over Montpelier Garden are a joy.

As a landlady I made many mistakes at the beginning. The top floor of 77 Lansdowne Road was a self contained 2 room, kitchen and bathroom flat with an entrance hall. My first tenant there was an American music student. I thought he would be very pleasant and charged him little, what I thought he could afford. I went away to work in Northampton. The first floor tenant was a widowed Irish lady and her son. When I returned she told me that the gentleman on the top floor was having all-night parties. I went in, the place was a shambles; two short weeks, everything was upside down including the furniture, clothing scattered everywhere. I had no choice but to ask him to leave and ask the builder to restore everything. The Irish lady was pleasant and stayed for several years always keeping her flat immaculate. I let one room to a gentleman who was a travelling salesman and was looking for a small pied-a-terre. He was middle aged and handsome and charming. His business card looked legitimate. His first monthly cheque was fine but the second bounced. For three weeks he disappeared, when he re-appeared he was profuse with apologies and excuses…but the next cheque bounced too. It took several more weeks to trace him and after that I insisted that all further rent payments be made in cash, I also gave him his notice to quit. A year later the police came to see me. They told me he was an experienced con. man and had finally been caught in Hull. His victims were insecure middle-aged ladies. One lost her life savings to him, one agreed to marry him. I was learning fast – all tenants are not angels.

Another tenant in the top flat was a gentleman of about 50, who was always very quiet. One day I invited him in for a drink. He was apparently quite wealthy and did not need to work. I asked: "What are your pastimes?"

"Stag hunting" he replied.

I was speechless. I decided that my Mr. X was a little peculiar. He eventually gave me notice, said he was buying a house in West London. After his departure I discovered several dozen plastic bags with small pins inside. They were wrappings from new shirts. I also found several pairs of Y fronts. He never washed his underwear, just bought new ones. The duvet cover had been burned or cut and there were feathers, like snow, everywhere.

I have swiftly learned that dealing with friends can be a nightmare. I let a flat to a young actress for a mutually agreed 3 years. Soon after I was leaving for three months to work in repertory. On my return she announced she was leaving! I was aghast. I later found out that the moment she arrived and my back was turned, she moved in her actor boy friend who also happened to be a part-time carpenter. The flat had been totally re-decorated in neutral colours prior to her arrival. What they had done in three short months was quite unexpected and horrific. The lounge had been turned into the bedroom with a huge iron four poster bed, the bookshelves on either side of the fireplace had been torn down, the former bedroom was now a living room. He had ripped out the fitted electric heaters, a storage heater near a power point had been moved into the hall where there was no electricity supply. The fitted wardrobes had been pulled out to create a dining alcove. The entire floor space was completely covered with every type of litter imaginable. The curtains had been pulled down in every room. It would be an understatement to say I was very happy to see them leave. The builders moved in yet again and restored the flat to its original state. Hallelujah! I was still learning the joys of being a landlady.

In the Elgin Crescent house, I had installed wash basins in every bedroom as to simplify the morning bathroom problems and subsequently let the house to three girls from Bangkok and one Indian girl. One was studying Music, two were secretaries and the Indian girl was a mystery. At that time I was living in the studio below and had assumed that these four tiny young girls would be quiet. No such luck...they sounded like herds of elephants up and down the stairs. They wore wooden clogs. I had already forbidden the music student from having a piano in the house. Piano practice is very noisy and disturbs other tenants and the neighbours. But while I was out she installed a piano (badly damaging the staircase). I remember her attempting the "Moonlight Sonata." She played the wrong notes, I was below cursing every sound. With alarming regularity they would receive several guests at a time. On one occasion I went upstairs to see what was going on. A dozen men from the far-east sat in a circle each with a bowl of rice. There was a heavy smell of oriental spices. They arrived by taxi and each carried a bag of food. I stood by the door and greeted each one. They each bowed low to me saying: "Mr Wong."

"Mr. Woo."..
"Mr. Ting."

and so on. The last tiny man's greeting was: "I am little Pee!"

I retreated to my studio leaving the Bangkok four to their merriment on the top floor.

After a year, thank God, the three girls returned to Bangkok. The Indian girl announced that she was moving in with an English gentleman as his housekeeper...!, so ended my "Bangkok experience"

I had a group of Australian journalists. They had not shared a house before. Although they were very charming, they inevitably had very late parties most nights. They would arrive very late and cause a riot in the street which is always very quiet. I was worried that the neighbours would start to complain. I pleaded with them to be more careful and they tried to reform. They did no cleaning and so I told them that they must employ a cleaner. But soon afterwards they returned to Paris and then to Australia. Before their departure they gave me a lovely farewell gift. They said: "We have been bloody awful, we don't know how you have put up with us."

We had a good laugh and I said: "Thank God I have worked a lot and was not often here, otherwise life would have been truly unbearable." Not one to generalize, I vowed however never to have Thai or Australian tenants again.

At Lansdowne Road, I had good and bad experiences with Indian tenants. The first couple were a charming man and wife. He worked for British Airways. She always kept the place immaculate and delightful, very elegant and with pretty bowls of flowers. She was charming and alluring. They stayed for six months. About a year later they called asking if the flat was available for their son and his young wife. He was in London to study and the parents guaranteed the payment of the rent. I was hesitant at first but finally agreed. This young couple were very nice. I cannot describe the bedroom activity above my poor head (I had moved back into the ground floor flat by then). They were newlyweds so I suffered in silence! She was however a useless housewife, had no idea how to run a household. Sadly the rent cheques bounced. I was surprised as the parents had given me their assurance the rent would be paid. The young man had spent all the money on Christmas gifts for his young wife. The rent was low on his list of priorities. He apologized, but the next month he gave me another bad cheque. At the end of the year he asked if they could stay. I refused, their flat was absolutely filthy, bits of rice stuck everywhere. The wife was dirty and lazy. And they had broken the base of the bed while making love all night, I imagine some kind of record even for newlyweds!

On the whole, my experience has been that the worst kind of tenants are those who have had good educations in private schools and come from a privileged background generally. They have always had staff cleaners. They do not know what a dustpan and brush or a vacuum cleaner are. Girls who were all delightful, lovely to speak to and charming but knew nothing about housework moved into Elgin Crescent. They would ignore all shelves, cupboards and hangers. Everything was on the floor. The sheets on their beds were never changed. But these four ladies were nice and they loved the house. They phoned me one day to report they had seen a mouse. I was mortified. I made an appointment with the Council exterminator. He explained that because of the road works going on in Elgin Crescent, the mice ran anywhere, they smell food...no food, no mice! In the kitchen we found a frightful mess. Bits of food on the floor, greasy pans on the cooker, sink full of dirty crockery. The refrigerator stank with rotten food. It was unbelievable. The exterminator said: "This is the problem. Tell your tenants to clean and store food in dishes or you will never be rid of the mice or the cockroaches."

The best tenants have been single men. They tend to be clean and tidy, certainly more than girls. But mostly they avoid all housework, cooking and washing up, but eat out (or at their girl friends).

One other bad tenant was a cockney youth who rented my garage for £1. per week. He had a Japanese motorbike. One night at 2am the police awakened me, instructed me to open the garage. The headlights of the police car shone into the interior. A rough curtain was hanging across. They removed it and to my horror, hidden was a vast collection of stolen property. I was suspected of being in command of a gang of local thieves! Mrs. Fagin of Notting Hill. Fortunately the police soon acquitted me, the young man was arrested. Six months later he had the impertinence to arrive at my house and ask if he could again rent the garage. No shame, no guilt whatsoever. We live in immoral times in the big cities.

The infamous rent act of the sixties said all tenants were angels, all land-lords Rackman-type villains, exploiting the tenants. How wrong and unjust to condemn all landlords. These Acts destroyed the rental market. Perhaps these experiences explain why my last tenants were the worst. For two years they wrecked my house. At great expense I went to Court to obtain possession. The Judge sympathized, restored my house to me with damages. The cost of repairs was enormous. I have not had one tenant since then. So beware becoming a landlady.

Student at Homerton College – Cambridge

Hendon County College – 1941/1949

A portrait drawing of my husband by Feliks Topolski

Our wedding day, Caxton Hall, Westminster – April 23 1949

Mr & Mrs Roman Blachowsky

My parent's in-law

With our sporty red car

Henry Moore's "Madonna and Child"

In Spain

Up the mast of "Our Girls"

77 Lansdowne Road, London W11

With Sally

LIFE SEVEN

Life as an Hostess in Berkshire and in Corfu

It was 1960, commercial television had started and most actors were not happy with the financial remuneration offered and it was common knowledge that the original investors had become millionaires whilst the actors were paid very low wages. The actors' Union Equity was told they were paid £2. for 12 hours work. A scale of payment similar to the BBC's must be obtained. Equity approached the television company with unacceptable results; actors must accept our terms or be unemployed was their response. Equity ordered all their members to strike except those with an existing contract and a contract must never be broken.

So, I was out of work in summertime, with a mortgage to pay. During the Whitsun week-end I visited a friend who lived on the river in Pangbourne near Reading. An unexpected and fortuitous meeting that week-end took place with another guest, Grace Stafford-Jones, a delightful lady, a widow. She offered me a job as a hostess at her country club.

"You will earn a small salary but you will live in my house, and work in the bar, to greet members and their guests."

Her Club was apparently highly successful as it provided a much needed alternative to restaurants in the Reading area and hers' had an excellent reputation for fine cuisine. I accepted her offer. I hate unemployment. It would be a new experience, new people to study, a world apart from London.

Grace's house was a Manor house by a mill pond with willow trees, a gracious place, a comfortable residence. Her husband had been an artist and thus had taken great care not to spoil the environment. The Chef was from the Park Lane Hotel. He was a Scotsman and quite brilliant but unfortunately had a drink problem and had been dismissed from his position in London. Grace, recognising his talent nonetheless employed him and thereafter tried to keep him away from the whisky, especially between shifts in the afternoon, the evening clientele being very important. A cheerful chap when sober, his meals superb.

I agreed to work for a fortnight's trial. A new way of life, a new job, much better than being unemployed in London. As a resident, travelling from London every day could be avoided, in any case it would have been inconvenient and prohibitively expensive. The Manager was also a resident and had six dogs which I adored. He would pile them into an old battered car some afternoons. They knew their places. It was like a Walt Disney film. All the dogs in a row, big dogs, little dogs all sitting up and waiting to be driven away to the Berkshire Downs for a lovely run.

Eddy, the head waiter was a great help to me. He taught me about cocktails, which drink into which glass etc... The customers were exacting about this, so I learned quickly. There were also the basic drinks such as gin and tonic, whisky and soda etc..Vodka was not so popular at that time. I had a book behind the bar to help me when asked for cocktails I did not know. Eddy took me down to their fabulous cellar and showed me the different wines and champagne. I was learning fast about all manner of intoxicating drink. Personally, I have never been a heavy drinker, originally not through choice but through lack of funds.

My first time behind the bar, Eddy, nearby in the dining room, had told me to send for him if problems arose. Guests started arriving at about 11:30 for lunch and were interested to see a new face behind the bar. Eddy had told me to learn their names quickly and remember them. Members and their guests like to be greeted by their names and briefly engaged in light conversation. On that first day, a gentleman came to the bar and introduced himself. Mr. Jim Fisher who immediately informed me that he always drank "Mumm's Cordon Rouge" champagne and should orange juice be ordered, it must be freshly squeezed. "Yes, sir."

I poured the champagne for Mr. Fisher and his guest and was offered a glass which I accepted. He returned in the evening for dinner and I greeted him with Cordon Rouge! He offered me another glass but I soon had to return to work as other members were arriving. I concentrated on their cocktail orders, all with fascinating names and ingredients

Another evening, Mr. Fisher asked if I knew Berkshire. I told him I was a Londoner. He offered to show me the county of Berkshire during my free time which was between 3pm and 5:30pm. I thought he was rather cheeky, very friendly and a fast mover. I said: "I do not accept invitations from men who do not own a steam engine!

He replied: "I have one, I will bring it along and take you for a ride."

The next day, to my utter amazement and delight he did, smoke pouring out of the tunnel. He dressed me in white overalls, I climbed aboard, pulled the overhead bell and we set off. That afternoon we drove at least twenty miles around the countryside. I waved graciously like the Queen to the crowds who waved back... This engine was found for him in an Essex field, rusting. It was an old Foden steam lorry. His friends knew that his father had driven one of these for many years between Berkshire and Dover. Apparently England slopes all the way down to the south coast. I noticed the little pools of water by the roadside. That is where the drivers would stop to re-fill their water tanks and stoke up their fires. His grandfather told him that he would cook bacon and eggs on his shovel over the fire. In memory of his father's hard work, Jim's friends had bought this Foden for him which he had lovingly restored. It was magnificent. I have a photograph of myself on that first ride in this amazing steam engine

During the following few weeks Jim invited me to various events, all of which were new to me. We went to a local car racing meeting, an evening pigeon shoot and a barn dance. It was thrilling to see the cars racing up and down the country roads and lanes whilst not long after-wards we were in the adjacent fields at the request of the local farmers to shoot down as many pigeons as possible. I love animals and birds and the prospect of shooting any creature was abhorrent. But these birds destroy the crops by sweeping down and eating the first green shoot, like a flock of locusts. I learned that country people are not so senti-mental about animals and I could see their point. My lovely collie Sally from the Battersea Dogs' Home had cost me £1. and I brought her to the shoot. Jim's dog Ferdinand was a pedigree black Labrador worth £300. He was superb, a real hunting dog who obeyed his master's every command. Sally was wonderful to watch as we arrived at the edge of the wood at sunset. I told her to obey Ferdinand and she sat motionless and petrified by my feet. A lone pigeon flew on to a high branch, he was the lookout and would return with the others only if there was no present danger. The hunters (and the dogs) were well experienced and the unfortunate pigeons flew into a well-laid trap. The signal was given and the many blasts echoed through the misty early evening of tranquil Berkshire and one by one the birds fell from the sky whilst the lucky ones flew away in great haste. The order was given for the dogs to retrieve the dead pigeons and they returned quickly with the prey deli-cately held in their mouths. They returned to fetch more. These dogs could pick up an egg and not damage it. They laid the dead birds by their master's feet quite gently. Quite extraordinary behaviour by these brilliant hunting dogs. Indeed on another occasion, Jim laid an egg and a coin behind a tree and both were returned by Ferdinand in perfect condition. It was an education for me to realise that not all animals are good, some are considered vermin. The rabbits and hares are beautiful to look at but are a serious menace to the farmer.

The dance was held late at night so I could go after I finished work. The nearby barn had been nicely decorated, had the buffet and bar at one end and the band at the other. People from the surrounding countryside arrived for this splendid occasion. I had not realised that the English enjoyed life so happily. I danced merrily until 1 am. The drive home in the moonlight was romantic. Country life was most enjoyable, so unexpected.

I shall always remember my expedition with Jim into a remote area of Berkshire that was a reminder of 18th Century life. In the farmhouse lived a father and his four sons. He was about sixty, his boys were tall and coarse. Women were non-existent in this household! They stared at me as if I was a strange being from another planet. I suppose they had not seen a woman for many months in that wild remote valley. They were charming, in their way, practical men. We spent the day wandering about this beautiful country only sixty miles from London. Their lives were spent farming and hunting. At mid-day we had a rough picnic of slabs of cheese and hunks of bread and drank port wine. Actually rather nice. In the afternoon we went for another shoot and later on relaxing on the grass, the day's catch by our feet we shared out the dead animals. We had another drink, shook hands and departed. It was Cold Comfort Farm! Absolutely incredible and interesting that such a place existed in 1960, perhaps still, isolated from the 20th Century.

Of Jim's many business interests in Berkshire his first was a high precision engineering firm in Burfield. Jim would have gone to University when younger, but of a working class background he did not, as parental and social pressures were such that being a success was more important. He set out with great determination and created his own. So he built this plant from nothing and had become successful having taken evening classes in engineering. He showed me around the works. I was amazed by all these machines and skilled workmen.

There was an old Anvil and fire there which had belonged to his father. He had been a man who shoed horses in the village, with a hot iron and a hammer. In memory of his father, Jim kept it there. I wonder if all this is still in Burfield today. I asked him if Government contracts were extended from Aldermaston as specialized pieces of machinery were undoubtedly needed there. I specifically remember that he had installed a free emergency petrol pump outside the factory for passing motorists. He became a member of the Berkshire County Council and dedicated himself to the welfare of pensioners and children, and particularly the OAP's. some of the very first homes specifically intended for them were built in Berkshire, with his encouragement. They were built around pleasant garden squares. These flats were most comfortable. A warden was on site should anybody require medical attention. It is now called sheltered accommodation. I visited two of these places. They were quite excellent. Jim also spent much time helping the schools, not wanting talented children to be deprived of further education as he had been.

Apart from my various escapades with Jim I also very much enjoyed my work at the country club. One evening several young people came in. They had been water-skiing. Behind the bar was a new face to them and they ordered six very complicated cocktails to try my expertise. Eddy, the headwaiter, came to my aid, and we delivered the cocktails swiftly and accurately; never one be be defeated, I would recommend to any unemployed actor to work at different jobs during those difficult periods. I learned about wine, which glasses to use and above all about how a certain class of people lived in the country. It is a wonderful opportunity to study people in their natural habitat. An actor must be able to portray all manner of mortals, one day this experience may be essential to play such characters.

"The proper study of mankind is man."

One club member was a doctor who came to dinner every Thursday with his wife. After dinner his wife would play the newly installed fruit machines until she hit the jackpot. Sometimes this did not happen until 2am. The doctor slept in an armchair. Like an orgasm, his wife would not go home until she was satisfied. People are extraordinary. As hostess, I politely waited until madam reached the climax, a shower of small coins!

Another of Jim's occupations was the up-keep of the roads on the Duke of Wellington's Estate. He owned a gravel pit and so this was not difficult. One day we went to the House and called at the Estate Manager's office. The Duke himself arrived: "No money Jim, would you like half an acre of land instead?"

Jim enlightened me: "The wealthy are always short of cash."

I was surprised that the Duke had offered to part with any land. I always thought that landowners never, ever gave their land away but I suspect this was a joke between them.

Soon afterwards, the strike ended and I returned to work in London after a wonderful few months in glorious Berkshire and a proposal of marriage from Jim which I declined. I was fond of him but would only ever marry again for love.

* * *

The local police had invited me to a Christmas party in the Fulham Road where I had a fortuitous meeting with one John Patterson who rang me the next morning asking if I would work for him it I was not busy acting. I was unable to act then because I was receiving laser treatment for my eyes and could not face the studio lights. He offered me work in Corfu acting as an Hostess for Singles Holiday groups. I was to meet the single people as they arrived and introduce them to each other. A lively, friendly person was required and John thought that I would enjoy handling a great mixture of single people of ages ranging from 16 to 80.

I did not know Corfu, I had heard that the Corfiotes were a lovely and welcoming people, that they liked the English, having had such contact with Britain in their history. They had had an English Governor for fifty years who had married a local girl. They also had great Italian influence. Corfu was occupied by Italy for hundreds of years. They were not your typical Greeks. They were full of fun and their patron saint, Saint Spyridon is honoured at Easter time and many of the men are named Spiros after him.

I had read "My Family and Other Animals" by Gerald Durrell which had made me want to visit this lovely island, I agreed to go. I stayed for four months. I arrived in April 1976 at the tiny Corfu Airport.

John had received many suggestions over the years about the possibility of organising singles holidays. Many people who travel alone often complained that the holidays were full of couples. He decided to offer holidays where everybody would be single. He had recently returned from America and had started computerised friendships at an office off Kensington High Street. From these contacts, setting up singles holidays was quite simple.

So I became, the second "singles" hostess. The first lady had left to get married.

I arrived at my fabulous hotel in Corfu, where Durrell had written his books; situated in the mountain range in the north of the Island. Corfu is a long narrow island. This lovely hotel was built on a cliff, below was the swimming pool and the beach complete with a taverna. Across the bay facing eastwards was the main Corfu town. The hotel's owners realised that it was remote, 45 minutes to the town overland. So a motorised launch was introduced, in the morning to town and back in the evening. The hotel's attraction remained but it was now less difficult to go shopping for the day.

Facing east across the water was Albania only three miles away. We had been told that the Albanians were not friendly, their guns pointed in our direction. We were told never to venture further than half way because that is where the border is and we could be arrested and thrown into an Albanian jail; it all sounded so extreme.

The Greek owner at this exquisite hotel lived on the top floors and had accommodation for their personal guests. The manageress was English and had married a Greek. They lived nearby. The Hotel also had separate private villas let out to various guests. Some of these were for the use of the Hotel. It was wild, beautiful and very elegant. Thompsons were the only other Tourist company who had a representative on Kerkira, a very pleasant chap. The tourists were mostly British and a few Germans.

The Hotel had a pier at which little taxi boats could stop and take passengers. I became friendly with a family who had one of these boats; father, son, uncle and grand-pa. As an hostess, I was able to use their services. They lived near Ipsos. Some of my people wanted to explore the island by sea so I requested the boat to come along one morning at 9am. There was Kassiopi to the North and Benitses to the South, neither of these were populated at the time but were small fishing villages.

John Patterson had sent me notification of the people I was to receive at the airport on my first assignment. I made a cardboard sign "SINGLES HOLIDAYS" and positioned myself as to be seen when they came through customs. He had indicated to me which of the passengers might be difficult to deal with. It only happened twice. Most singles aged 25-40 were amiable, they just wanted to be in a lovely place and enjoy good company.

For an actress, it was a most interesting job indeed, meeting so many different people from diverse backgrounds, with varying occupations. All ages too; there were divorcees but usually just people who never found the right companion in their life and wanted a good holiday. I was pleased about that, thankful that the ladies had not come in search of a husband or the men for a bed companion! They were a friendly group of people, my job was to know them as soon as possible. From the moment they saw my sign at the airport I began to work. I could spot the troublemaker, the bad apple, very quickly. It was rare. They wanted to see this lovely island, many for the first time, and I was only too happy to show them around and act as their Hostess for the next two weeks.

I saw them through Customs followed by a 45-minute scenic drive North to the Hotel. I inserted the odd joke here and there when I was speaking and took note of the ones who laughed the most as they were the extroverts and would help me later in the programme to help break the ice. This usually always worked. As we drove along I told them of the two most popular drinks in Corfu, and indeed Greece. Firstly "OUZO" a very strong alcoholic drink tasting of aniseed, that clouds up when adding water or ice. The other was Domestica...not Domestos! Although it smells rather more like the latter. Mild Domestica is preferable when ordering your wine.

On arrival, they were checked into their rooms. I asked them to come down to the foyer bar at 7pm for drinks before dinner. People sat at different tables each evening. All problems or complaints, I would deal with. I had an agreed signal with Mary at the desk about the difficult customers, just a wink and she would understand that we had a difficult person to deal with. She would be extremely charming and do everything she could to make the customer happy again. It was the Hostess' job to create a good atmosphere and sort out any difficulties as soon as possible.

I was by the pool one day, observing my party and realised for the first time that it is not just the women who can be shy but the men as well. The defrosting period was usually about four days before a shy person would start talking to the others. I would help him along as best I could wanting him to have a good time. Others would jump in the pool and splash around and enjoy themselves, others would just sit silently. I would ask them why they did not go into the pool. All sorts of excuses, so I would get on the diving board and throw myself in making an enormous splash. Laughter relaxes everyone.

The beach had a taverna where you could have your lunch, food supplied by the hotel and later lie in the sun. This was a lovely alternative to going back to the main dining room, appropriate for lunchtime, less formal.

I arranged for them to have whole days out for the price of 10 r 180 Dr. We would go out in a boat, lunch included with plenty of wine, and I would inform them that we would not return until late afternoon. My Greek friends arrived with their little boat and we set out to see some unknown parts of the island. We would stop occasionally to have a swim in small uninhabited bays. We went as far as Benitses, passing "Mos Repos" the birthplace of Prince Philip. His mother who had become a nun was still living there.

We landed in Benitses, very happy campers indeed and wandered through a delightful orange grove. Hidden away we found a taverna where they were waiting for us with a glorious lunch After a splendid meal and much wine we practised our Greek dancing or went for a swim or slept under the vines. It was all quite lovely. We arrived back at the Hotel at around 5pm, quite exhausted feeling as if we had been living in Corfu for a week. Everybody was happy and relaxed, knowing each others names. I felt I had created a party atmosphere.

I suggested to the owner of the hotel that we might have a fancy-dress party one evening as there was no entertainment after dinner. The disco had thankfully not yet made its way to northern Corfu! People here for two weeks have nowhere to go in the evenings, no village, café or cinema. A fancy dress party would be fun. Nobody should spend more than a few shillings on their costumes, but must try to be as inventive as possible. We applauded them as they came out of the lift. Many were most original and imaginative. It was delightful and very funny, a good time was had by all. The Greeks were amazed as people arrived as sailors, trapeze artists, clowns, Aphrodite, a mermaid and a policeman.

On another evening we hired a small coach and secured hotel permission to miss dinner as I planned to take them to eat high into the beautiful mountains to a little village. It gave them something different and interesting to do. Arriving at the village, the driver said the streets were too narrow for the bus. We walked around these lovely cobbled streets. There was little electric light. This created the effect of walking around by soft candle light. We arrived at a delightful café with hanging vines, in the open air. To our huge surprise, there was a wedding reception in progress. The bride and bridegroom were there with their guests. We joined in the fun; an unexpected and memorable evening high in the Corfu mountains at a Greek wedding.

The food was delicious wherever we went. One evening we had one of their favourite dishes, a piglet roasting on a spit over an open fire, quite delicious eaten with fresh salads garnished with freshly picked herbs, such a beautiful flavour.

There was one guest I could never figure out. I found him somewhat amusing. He was Dutch and would always disappear up into the mountains immediately after breakfast never to be seen again until lunchtime, every day. I eventually asked him: "What do you do?...do you walk?...are you a climber?"

"No, no," he replied; I go out searching for tortoises, but have not had much luck at all, in fact none."

"Why" I asked.

"I was inspired by Gerald Durrell's book; his children always went out searching for these creatures."

"But that was long ago, maybe they are gone."

I imagine the poor tortoises never returned as I am told that Corfu is much modernised since I was last there. I am told that a major road has been constructed over the mountains to Kassiopi. Sad, I rather like the idea of tortoises roaming around in the wild.

One of our less bright customers hired a pedalo one day and went out too far beyond the Greek/Albania border in the sea and was picked up by the Albanian Authorities and thrown into jail. Back at the Hotel, we eventually realised that John had not returned from his pedalo adventure. We had to report to the Greek Authorities who were marvellous. Search parties were sent out looking for a drowned body. He was causing a great deal of trouble, as you can imagine. We couldn't know for sure if he had died. I was very worried about the outcome as I would have to report this to the British Embassy in Athens and in turn they would have to inform the man's family in Britain. The other guides told me that a death among one's customers is the worst thing that can happen, there would be inspections, everybody is distressed; it destroys the whole holiday.

The second day someone saw a boat in the distance. People came running and said: "He's back"

The Albanians decided he was not a spy and returned him to the sea border. They didn't want trouble with the Greek Government over this. A Greek boat held him and brought him to Corfu. He was not at all apologetic for the trouble and stress he had caused. What a great story he thought it was for the Tabloids back in England, that he had been captured by the Albanians. It would pay for his holiday. I was so angry. I took him aside and made him apologize to all the people who had tried to find him. I wonder if he ever did make any money with this story. I hope not.

Another unfortunate incident concerned a rather dim member of our group. He was about 23, very slim, very white and wore a tiny piece of cloth to cover his private parts. He came to me one morning. I noticed he was as red as a lobster. The poor boy was complaining of pain. He could barely speak. Thankfully I had a good supply of lacto-calomine. I told him to lie down on his bed and not use water on his burned skin. I fetched a doctor. This was serious sunburn. I applied the cream over his body and asked him what suncream he had used.

"None" he said!

This ignorance was so outrageous, to lie in the sun on the first day for three hours. I couldn't believe it, no suncream. He reminded me of Michael Crawford as Frank Spencer in "Some Mother's do have – em" a decent boy but not blessed with much grey matter. The doctor arrived and instructed him to stay out of the sun completely for two days while his skin recovered.

The next day we were to sail away for a day, he did not want to be left behind. I told him to wear a hat, a scarf and a jacket and stay out of the sun. Not long after we left, the wind caught his hat and blew it into the water. This boy was a walking disaster area. The boat turned around and my dear fishermen friends put out a net and retrieved the hat. Some customers! Some mothers...

Another evening I arranged to have a boat collect us at 8:30 to travel just 15 minutes down the coast to a lovely little taverna, I had met the owners, a British couple who had been classical dancers. They met in panto at Bristol and had married. They spent the summer running the taverna which belonged to his father and they loved it as it also gave them the opportunity to dance and entertain the guests in the evening. I told them I was bringing a party of about 24. Wearing lovely white shirts, black trousers and bright red sashes, they greeted all the guest. Drinks were served and they performed wonderfully and we then had a brilliant dinner. They cleared the patio and did a superbly professional display of Greek dancing. After dinner, all were invited to dance. They taught the novices. A superb and very enjoyable evening. These dances were usually for men only but these two always included the women. We stayed until 11:30 and then sailed back to the Hotel in the moon-light. I would not like to return, to find these innocent friendly parties have gone forever.

When all the customers had departed and the season was coming to an end, I stayed on for a bit of a holiday myself. It was September. I resided in one of the private villas. In one of the other houses came a Lord Somebody from England who was heading a cricket team for a match in Corfu. We know that there is English influence in Corfu but did I mention that in the centre of the town there is a full size cricket pitch?

It was in a bit of a mess then but I am told that in the 80's it was completely refurbished and is now quite lovely. I met some of the men in the local taverna who said I would make a good wicket-keeper. They would provide me with proper gear to wear.

It was a friendly invitation so I agreed to turn up to watch the match. I went into Corfu town early and watched them prepare the pitch. The match began. It was very funny indeed. The English batsmen were all skilled pros. At times the ball would be hit into the harbour and the Greeks would shout out "HOWZAT." A great deal of ouzo was consumed by the merry onlookers. The Ashes competition between Australia and England were nothing like this Corfu/Anglo annual battle.

I approached his Lordship and told him that his men had suggested to me the previous day that I would make a good wicket keeper. He looked frightfully pained and must have thought I was an eccentrically mad English woman. We find them everywhere. A gentleman by nature and disposition, he said: "Madam, would like a drink? Please take a seat."

So, in a pleasant ouzo daze, I sat in Corfu square with its delightful arched street facing the pitch, and watched a typical English cricket match.

※　※　※

Whilst thinking back to the events of my time in Corfu I have remembered an earlier trip to the Greek Islands. I was staying with a friend who was writing a book in Lindos on the island of Rhodes when I decided I wanted to see a working Greek island, one without tourists. I set off to Cos, in the south-eastern Aegean, north-west of Rhodes.

"Good bye" I said.

I went by bus to Rhodes town and came to the ferry which was heading for Athens We left the port of Rhodes and arrived at Cos. I descended from the ship. I was the only passenger leaving and I sat on a bench looking over the delightful harbour. Not a tourist in sight, the local inhabitants had probably never seen a tourist back then. It was lovely. A lady came and sat next to me and then another person and another. Who was this strange tall lady who left the ship? I should imagine that within half an hour most people on the island of Cos knew that I had arrived, they were very interested so I enlightened them by saying I was English, not German, an English lady from London, which amazed them. I asked if there was an hotel and they pointed to it, the only hotel, and I went along and booked a room for the night and thought I would explore this delightful working island. I wanted to see the Greeks as they had lived for centuries, no outsiders.

While I was in the bar having a drink a middle aged man came in and introduced himself and said he was the owner of the island's only industry, so I said: "Indeed, and what is that?"

"Sponges" he replied.

"We sell sponges to Europe, my men sail across to North Africa and dive for sponges. They bring them back full of unwanted creatures and various sea vegetation and here we clean them and separate them according to size and quality. Would you like to see?"

"Delighted" I said. So he invited me to have dinner that evening which was nice.

I looked around the lovely town of Cos. Up a hill was a very large church so I wandered up the winding path and sat on a wall overlooking this beautiful island. A little boy came up to me from a cottage. He bowed low, he was about ten years old. He spoke in beautiful English.

"Who are you?" he asked.

"A lady from London, England" I said.

He said: "I speak English, I learn at school."

"And very well, your teacher must be proud of you."

So he disappeared into the cottage and came out with a beautiful lady, his mother, a young Greek woman and she brought me a bunch of flowers and a packet of biscuits which she handed to me with a charming smile. It was the old world courtesy that you welcomed a stranger and offered them food. I thought it was really lovely. I asked the little boy: "What do you want to be when you grow up? He said:

"I will go to Athens, I want to be a doctor."

He was very decided about it. A very bright little boy.

"I am sure you will manage that one day, if you get to London come and see me." So we laughed and chatted, what a wonderful unexpected meeting. A little boy who wanted to be a doctor on this remote island and a Greek who had made a big industry out of sponges. The next day Dimitri took me to see the men handling the sponges. They were waist deep in seawater and cleaning them. Later they were taken to the factory and sorted out. I have a marvellous picture of him holding his prize catch which was about two feet wide and two feet long. He gave me a sponge as a present which I still have to this day. Next time whilst in Harrods purchasing a sponge, remember these men working for our pleasure. Cos was a paradise, today...well I imagine it is built up with tourist hotels and shops selling all manner of sponges.

LIFE EIGHT
Travels & Friends
(Ceylon – USA – Hellenic Cruises)

On my way to join my husband in Australia, I booked my passage an a new P&O ship, leaving from Tilbury Docks, the ARCADIA who's maiden voyage it was. A beautiful and luxurious ship. On a freezing cold January day, we sailed down the Thames, down the English Channel to a very rough and stormy Bay of Biscay, the Atlantic, Gibraltar and into the Mediterranean and onwards to Malta and Alexandria in Egypt. The voyage lasted two weeks and was rarely anything but blustery and cold. On the decks we wore very thick clothing. I travelled 2nd class, which was by far the merriest part of the ship. It was not possible to walk round the top decks. You were prevented by barriers which separated the classes. Before long the first class passengers wanted to join the younger people down below. Much to our delight, there were 30 British mariners going to join their ship in Sydney, Australia. They went by ship as there were no flights in those days. P.OS.H. (port out, starboard home) was how the British travelled to India and back (keeping the sun on the right side for both journeys). I was fascinated during the voyage to observe the pairing (or not) of the crew. The 30 handsome young men were delightful, loved dancing in the evening and were great company. They tried to avoid (usually successfully) the subject of marriage with the many Australian girls also en route to Sydney. When we sailed through the Suez Canal into the Red Sea there was a remarkable change in the weather and suddenly everybody on board appeared in bikinis as it was so hot. In this scant clothing we did not recognise anybody! A great time was had by all. We sailed merrily southward to Aden and across the Indian Ocean to Bombay. It was a lovely civilized voyage, far preferable in my view to flying. I fell in love with the Indian Ocean, 5 or 10 degrees north of the Equator. I am remembering the shimmering waters, so still, like shot satin and silk taffeta of exquisite colours. Out of this wonder we would see flying fish, like butterflies skimming aver the surface and dolphins leaping out of the water. I was reminded of Coleridge's Ancient Mariner, the vivid descriptions of a hot sea...

"The sails dropped down, down drop the sails,
Was still as still could be...

A wonderful poem, describing this beautiful tremulous tropical sea. The greatest of narrative poems.

I was shocked and much saddened at the sight of Bombay. We stayed one day. Within minutes of going ashore my handbag was snipped with scissors, hanging by a thread the perpetrator attempted to steal it, thankfully in vain as I resisted. I decided to go to the market, my earlier trauma notwithstanding. The overcrowding and extreme poverty was overwhelming. People sleeping on pavements, the crippled and blind begging. So many, so sad, so poor. Romantic, it was not. I returned to the ship as quickly as possible. It was sad that such a likeable people should live in this heat and terrible conditions.

And so we sailed onwards south to Colombo in Ceylon...

I had deliberately broken my journey and my passage allowed me to go no further for now. I had arranged to stay for a few days with a local family and would sail on to Australia later. My husband had met a fellow student from Ceylon whilst lecturing and rowing at Cambridge. He had kindly issued an open invitation to visit his family if ever we came to Colombo. His parents were in education and Government.

Roman stayed with them on his way to Australia. I was to stay two days with these delightful people and then catch another ship on to Perth. They were wealthy with splendid understatement, the house was quite stunning and their many servants charming. They showed me around Colombo.

Soon I discovered to my horror that there were no vacancies on ships to Australia for another month. I should have booked earlier from London. I told my hosts that I intended to spend a month discovering their lovely Island. Despite my hosts insisting on hiring a car, driver and guide for me, I wanted to travel by bus, train and on foot. They were most insistent, saying that English ladies always hired private cars. But I was determined. I went to the travel office, bought the necessary maps and booklets and read the history of the Island and then realised what a fascinating adventure this was going to be.

"It is a paradise, the garden of Eden. God created the world there... Adam and Eve lived happily there." I rhapsodised.

This was the last year of British rule before independence. Their new Prime Minister was a woman, Mrs. Bandenereika. Long before Margaret Thatcher. The people looked well fed, happy and smiling, most amiable, many speaking English. I said farewell to my friends: "I shall return in three weeks to join my ship."

They were appalled that I should travel alone by public transport. My bus and train journeys were lovely. I looked down towards beautiful woods and a river far below and could see people playing, bathing and washing. A great feeling of we well-being and happiness overcame me. My first visit was to Candy, three thousand feet up, where there was the famous temple of the Tooth. On a winding mountain road, a further three thousand feet up, we approached Nureylia, built by the British for their Diplomats' recreation in cooler mountain air. It was so high up but still the British managed to build a golf course. I saw many women in saris on steep hillsides looking like butterflies working extremely hard with baskets on their backs. As their hands fluttered over the tea bushes, I realised they were collecting tea leaves, throwing them over their shoulders into the baskets. They would be paid per basket-full each day. I commented to my fellow travellers that my friends had told me that the people of Ceylon were not a hard working people.

"Quite right" they said, "We do not like hard work."

They were not Sinhalese but Tamils from Southern India.

Many years later, alas, the always difficult harmony between the Sinhalese and Tamil peoples is finally put to the test when, after a succession of Socialist Governments, the Tamils of Northern Sri Lanka are constantly threatened with the enforced return to India. The Tamils have become prosperous and will not go. The young Tamils have formed the rebellious Tamil Tigers Army. There is great friction between them and the rest of the country, a tragedy. Civil Wars are actually taking place today. People once friendly are prepared to kill each other.

The new Prime Minister was a Communist. Immediately upon becoming PM of the new Independent State of Sri Lanka. she suspended the teaching of the English Language in the schools. Understandable but stupid as it is the international language of communication. More so with global trade and air travel. I wanted to return and see Ceylon but have been prevented by the fear that too much will have changed.

The most famous places in Ceylon are the three buried cities which are now major tourist attractions. Firstly I went to ANURADHAPURA. I was told to travel very early, catching the 4am bus before the heat of the day became unbearable. The driver would tell me when to descend and would point the way through the jungle. I stayed in rest houses around Ceylon, Government controlled hotels. I had a beautiful adventure. I descended from the bus and was walking through the jungle when I heard chanting in the distance. Through the trees came a delegation of men in saffron yellow robes with shaven heads. They were Buddhists. Their hands were in front of them, palms upwards filled with white and gold flowers. As they passed by me a great peace descended. One of them stopped so amazed at seeing me there alone. I said: "Are you going to pray?"

"Yes we are going to the Temple to pray."
"The flowers, you offer them?"
"No we take the flowers but we offer the perfume, it rises to our God Buddha."

Slowly they wandered on and disappeared through the forest. I shall never forget that magical moment. It happened like a dream.

I disembarked and the driver pointed to a jungle path. It was an hour's walk to Anuradhapura through jungle in the dark. I started off. There were strange morning sounds of various animals. Suddenly I heard voices that were very English, in fact they sounded like Peter Sellers' hilarious "posh" voices. I rounded the corner of the path and there before me were a group of men in RAF uniforms, British. We were mutually amazed. A single English woman coming out of the jungle. They asked: "What are you doing?"

"Trying to find Anuradhapura" I replied.
"Oh, we are staying there in the rest house."
"So will I when I find it."
"Not far" they said.
I asked: "What are you doing here?"
'We're filming" they answered.

"You don't look like a film crew" I said.
"No, no…"

They had been sent out by British Airways to canvass possible sights of
interest to tempt travellers on the forthcoming new routes to the Far-
East and Australia to stop and visit this beautiful island. They had been
filming the Buddhas and the Temples or anything that might be interesting in a brochure. But their main objectives were to find suitably
large surfaces of land to construct the necessary landing strips and
airports. I was there at the beginning when long-haul international
flights were still in the planning stage. It was important to respect
customs and religion, not to film anything sacred.

Now escorted by the RAF… I made my way to the rest house where we
had a very merry evening. These houses, delightful and cheap, have thin
roofs so during the night I heard some slithering noises and a chorus of
squeaking animals, basic jungle noises that can be frightening to a
novice. I particularly disliked the snaky oozing sounds. I was told the
next day that they were snakes. I loved the mosquito nets hanging over
the beds and grateful for their protection as mosquitoes eat me alive.
They are also aesthetically pleasing.

The second day I studied the Temples and Statues. In the evening we
noticed tables laid with special china and silver and a buffet with
marvellous food. The Indian men who were arriving to dine were very
handsome and well dressed. Mrs. Indira Ghandi, Prime Minister of
India, arrived and joined the party. It was thrilling. She too was visiting
the great shrines at Anuradhapura.

Two middle-aged Americans with an enormous chauffeur driven car
were touring Ceylon during the winter and they asked where I was
going next and I said to POLONNARUWA and SIGIRIA. They asked
me to join them. So, I was given the most luxurious ride in a private

limousine the size of the QE2. We reached Sigiria, a hidden city situated on a square shaped mountain, high up and surrounded for miles by thick jungle. Many centuries ago Sigiria was the bread basket of Ceylon and Southern India and was then surrounded by wheat plains; an area thriving with many people and excellent crops. It was farming country which grew enough food not only for the people but for export. Now it was gone and had reverted to jungle. On top of the mountain the rulers had built a City. We climbed up one side almost vertically on a very narrow staircase with one rope to hold all the way up. I did this accompanied by a guide. It was very exciting and most moving, but sad to think the surrounding plain was now jungle when it had been so prosperous. After visiting the famous reclining Buddhas of Polonnaruwa I returned to my friends in Colombo.

Before I departed I was swiftly taken to visit a rubber plantation. These trees are tapped into and it is the yield that becomes rubber. They gave me large Wellington boots to wear. My legs felt very itchy inside them. When I removed them horrible leeches were clinging to my legs. They are what the doctors in the West used to relieve blood pressure. They are quite horrible, you have to peel them off and luckily they do not hurt.

We drove back to Colombo for the final two days of my stay. Many occurrences of my stay with them could be highlighted but I was amazed that the grandmother of the house would wave a hand to one side after a repast and two strong male servants would bring an enormous high-back chair. She would be lifted into it and they would carry her up all the way to her bedroom. Also, whilst eating, one used one's hands to choose from a dozen tasty dishes, highly spiced and coloured – no knives or forks.

Before leaving Colombo I asked my friends if they were pleased the British were leaving.

"Not really, because we will have nobody to blame. At the moment if anything is wrong we can always blame the British. In future, alas, we will have to blame ourselves for the disasters of our own making."

A wise remark. As Shakespeare said: "The fault, dear Brutus, is not in our stars, but in ourselves, that we are underlings."

I had met some Australian, English and American professors who were working on the Colombo Plan at that time. This was an attempt to help Indian and Sinhalese peasant farmers to grow more lucrative crops and far more rice.

"We would show them how to clear a small area of jungle and prepare and fertilize the soil," They would be provided with tractors and required implements, and most importantly high quality seeds.

"We would go to a village and explain all this to the residents who seemed self-sufficient and happy to remain as they were, but we were trying to show them that with a bit more initiative they could grow so much more."

They would not only have enough for themselves but enough to send help to poorer areas of the country and eventually export to India where hunger and famine might occur. On the whole they were found to be fairly un-responsive, they did not wish to work any harder, not keen to learn of new technology and methods of advancement. This was understandable. The experts made two mistakes – the huge equipment imported did not suit the local fields, effectively useless – and they failed to comprehend the small village community mentality. They went away frustrated, and the villagers continued their own way of life. The team returned a year later and found that it had all been for nothing as everything had pretty much reverted to how it had been prior to their original involvement. The jungle was overgrowing again and the produce had not increased. It was, without question, an up-hill task. I have often wondered what became of the Colombo Plan.

So I bade farewell to Ceylon and my gracious hosts and left Colombo for the next step of the journey to Perth, across the Indian Ocean. You don't realise how far away Australia is until you sail slowly on vast oceans. Perth is delightful, situated on the western coast of Australia, thousands of miles from the far more inhabited eastern coast and in between just vast outback stretching into infinity.

* * *

It was April 1959 when I had the most exciting meetings with new people which transformed my life forever afterwards. I went on my first Hellenic Cruise. The Hellenic Society had been formed by a group of experts in the field of art, architecture, history, literature and archaeology. The great Sir Mortimer Wheeler the foremost archaeologist of his time, Sir Maurice Bowra, Vice-Chancellor of Oxford University and Warden of Wadham College; and Sir John Woolfenden, Master of Reading University, later Lord Woolfenden Director of the British Museum. These men were the lecturers on the annual April cruise to Greece. They created the Hellenic Society to spread the knowledge, culture and philosophy of ancient Greece. They urged all involved to retain Greek and Latin as essential requirements for entry to any great University. It was an inspired idea to start a Society to study ancient philosophy whilst on holiday. In the late fifties, nobody went to Greece much. In fact the popularity of Greece and its lovely islands did not accelerate post-war until the jet engine passenger aircraft was invented and the more affordable package tours were introduced. The British spent holidays at home. Only the adventurous or the wealthy went abroad. Going to France was a great experience. I had little money in my early life and could not consider going anywhere else, alas not even Italy or Spain. Greece was too remote, this new Society started one cruise a year. A Turkish ship the SS Ankara was used and Swan Tours administrated the cruise. The lecturers directed the inspiring educational programme.

I used to buy The New Statesman weekly magazine and had noticed an advertisement the previous autumn for the spring cruise to Greece. When I saw the list of the wonderful names. I thought one fine day I will go on that cruise and see Greece for the first time; a brilliant choice of destination, the country is resplendent with spring flowers under a clear blue sky. One felt that Persephone had returned from the underworld to paradise. My teachers at Walthamstow High School were fond of the teaching of Greek. We had the wonderful Greek Theatre, we learned Greek and Latin and there were replicas of ancient statues in the Art Room.

The following January (1959), I was offered a cancellation berth for £99 which I would share with four other women. I begged my Bank Manager to lend me the money and he agreed. I had not had a holiday for three years. With only three days to prepare for this new, rave travel experience I was told to take a cardigan, a raincoat and to read Maurice Bowra's "Greek Experience." I found a copy and spent twenty-four hours non-stop reading that classic enthralling book. I was ready for Greece!

On April 1st. we left from Victoria Station with the special guests and 300 passengers. We had lunch on the train heading for the South Coast. We sailed the English Channel and travelled to Paris on chartered ship and train. The French greeted us with rivers of champagne, escorted us across the city to board our train for the next stage of the journey to Venice. We were served a delicious dinner in splendid surroundings. Travelling by train is so civilized, a perfect opportunity to become acquainted with our fellow travellers. These people were lovely, lively and chattering, a quintessentially English group of retired professionals, former teachers of the classics and history, lovers of the Arts and Architecture. We all had these interests in common. After a good night's sleep we reached Venice the next day at lunchtime and I had many new friends. Hugh Reynolds, classics master at Skinners School in Tunbridge Wells, the Rev. Waddy, Head Master of Tunbridge School, a scholar of Roman History who had two of this three daughters with him. Sir Mortimer Wheeler, Sir John and Lady Woolfenden. To this day I am still in regular contact with Andrew and Bridget Ganly from Dublin – the Pottingers, Piers was thirteen at the time and is now a father of four. Camille Durnley from San Francisco and Peggy McIntire of Miami.

The train arrived alongside the ship. We walked up the gangway and were shown to our cabins. Luncheon was served on the top deck and we sailed slowly away, the vision of San Marco sublime. The salmon was exceptional, the wines delicate. My table companion was a writer, Nina Epton, famous for her books on love, the Spanish, the French and the English. The first port of call was Delphi a day later. The most wonderful introduction to Greece. Hugh Reynolds was so overwhelmed he knelt like the Pope and kissed the ground saying: "I've taught Greek all my life after Oxford and now at last I have saved enough to come here."

It was a great adventure for us all. The company was excellent. Delphi, a superb drive skywards through the olive groves to a magnificent site, my favourite temple and theatre in all of Greece – a memorable start to a holiday. I walked through the temple, stood on the stage of the amphitheatre and looked up. The Lecturers were sitting there and called for me to recite. I could say that I "played" Delphi when I got home so I recited Shakespeare: "Our revels now are ended…we are such stuff as dreams are made of. And our little life is rounded with a sleep…" Amazingly I later found that I had been heard further ways high up in the stadium. The accoustics are astounding.

At the time there was only one tourist coach, ours! On a more recent trip there were dozens, it was too crowded. Some of us stayed and watched the sunset beyond the olive groves and saw the moon rise over the temple. I shall never forget that. Greece was covered with spring flowers and one was reminded of Tennyson's poem "The Lotus Eaters."

From there we sailed to Athens to visit the Parthenon. There was no path at the time. Sir Mortimer stood on the steps before this great temple. We were the only tourists. We looked down over Athens and felt the magic of that ancient civilisation.

We next went to Mycenae and Sir Mortimer in his Stetson hat stood at the Lion Gate and told the story of Helen of Troy and of Agamemnon; describing it all with a thrilling actor's voice making the history come alive so vividly. The following year I returned and had the pleasure of walking round the Museum at Delphi with Sir Maurice having the exhibits described in perfect detail. That was a great moment of my life. His wit, rendition and enthusiasm were spellbinding.

Many of the staff on board were students of classics and archaeology. Sir Mortimer had allowed approximately thirty to come free. They helped around the ship, elderly people might require some help. These young people were a lively addition to the holiday atmosphere. It was a generous idea, extremely successful and much appreciated by all.

Camille and I were always the last for breakfast, loathing the early starts...not helped by tea which was too weak! You were not obliged to sit at the same table every day. That way I met as many new people as possible. Most people do not travel alone like myself. A very elderly lady sat down for afternoon tea in the lounge. I asked what she had done for a living. She said she had been one of the first ever female surgeons. In The late 19th Century women were not allowed to be surgeons, medical doctors perhaps but generally women were not welcome in the profession. Women were not permitted to see the nude body of a man so could not be a surgeon. She was determined to be a surgeon and cut her hair short and dressed as a man, she had a contralto voice naturally, and pursued her studies as a man. How I admired this extraordinary old lady. Now there are many women doctors, they must salute these brave ladies who preceded them.

Being the only actress on board, I was asked, at the end of the cruise to express a vote of thanks to the lecturers and staff on behalf of all the passengers. At the last celebratory dinner, the lecturers make witty speeches about the passengers, who are affectionately referred to as the "culture vultures." They wanted someone to respond. My friend Andy Ganly, a witty Irishman, helped me dress in a heavy tweedy suit, men's boots and a tweed hat, my hair tossed, a rope around my body carrying various tools and saucepans. He would introduce me as "Madame Avoir du Poid" an archaeologist just arrived by helicopter who would make a speech about her most recent dig the audience would not wish to miss. I went away during the last course to be transformed into this ferociously butch explorer and was announced after the speeches from the lecturers. Everyone was stunned including the lecturers but as soon as I spoke everyone realised that it was Eunice behind the disguise. They rolled with laughter. I began my few words imitating Sir Mortimer and announced the following day's bogus programme beginning at 5:30am and other dotty items. At the end, I thanked them seriously and sincerely each in turn. They had such enthusiasm for their work, were friendly and informal.

Laurence Waddy, the Head Master, had been writing a musical in his spare time. When I returned to London he telephoned me and asked if I would come down to Tunbridge Wells to see a performance of the completed oeuvre and give him my honest opinion. I liked it enormously but couldn't praise it. It was a good amateur show. The next morning I told him firstly there are no memorable tunes, no conflict between the characters which made it boring. It is too sweet and not exciting. I do not like being cruel but a professional critic must be honest. I enjoyed my visit to the school thinking how lucky the boys were to be there. I certainly understand why some parents would go without holidays and luxuries in order to pay for their children to receive the best possible education.

During the following year's cruise Sir Maurice lectured quite brilliantly on the Delphic Oracle. He came in after dinner and began the lecture in Greek. There was a solemn hush as most of us did not have a fluent knowledge of the language. Of course he knew what he was doing, he had a tremendous sense of humour. He continued for ten minutes and a great feeling of gloom descended upon the audience. He then stopped and said: "Which, translated is..."

Followed by hilarious and outrageous translations of the Delphic Oracles. I was honoured to be asked to dine with him. It is sad that Greece was ruled by fascist Generals because Sir Maurice stopped going, refusing to return while they were in power. Sadly, he died before he could see Greece again.

The last year of his life was spent at Wadham College. He died suddenly. When I was touring with Hermione Gingold, the final week of the tour was at the New Theatre in Oxford. I wrote to him and asked if he would like to see two old actresses in a dreadful farce. He wrote back and in turn invited me to visit him. I went in the afternoon. I arrived at 2:30 in a taxi carrying a bottle of Napoleon brandy which I knew he liked. The porter opened the door of the College and Sir Maurice came across the pavement and helped me out of the taxi. What a marvellous moment. We talked of Shakespeare and the theatre and laughed all afternoon. He told me that he had bought a house on the outskirts of Oxford in which to retire and then found that with a cook and housekeeper he was not able to afford it. How disgracefully these great men are treated. He was offered a small flat within the College where he could be cared for. I thought the new Warden would dislike such a neighbour but Sir Maurice said he hoped to spend the first year of his retirement travelling to the places he liked in France as a young man. Then write the second book of his autobiography and translate several more Greek poems. I asked if I could come and see him again sometime.

"Certainly."

But alas it was not to be. He died. I was greatly saddened I would never hear his wonderful rolling tones again or enjoy his great fun and wit. It was a great loss to England, but his books survive…"The Greek Experience" is a classic. I retain many memories of him.

I remember a journey from Dubrovnik to Venice at the end of another cruise and during the last morning at 9am we held a general meeting to praise or complain about the trip. It was a merry meeting. We talked about various subjects including the noise made by the guides in the museums. The present increase in the number of tourists must be intolerable. Headphones and personal descriptive machines are now common place and are much preferred. He invited me for a drink afterwards and for three hours we sat in a bar and talked about the arts, particularly Shakespeare and poetry. Our conversations were not always high brow but always wonderful. We were drinking brandy, it was far too early for such merry making so we became quite tipsy as we approached Venice. It was a wonderful end to a holiday spending three hours listening to Sir Maurice Bowra. As we parted he asked: "Eunice, if you were stranded on a deserted island and were told that you could have one play of Shakespeare only, which would it be?"

"Too difficult, but I suppose it would have to be *Anthony and Cleopatra*."

"My choice too" he replied.

And quoted from the piece at length. And further added: "We could play the roles ourselves, what a production it would be. You Cleopatra, me Anthony."

Indeed, I can still laugh at the image of rotund Sir Maurice and six foot Eunice playing this greatest of love dramas!

That was the end of my wonderful holiday on the S.S. Orpheus with its splendid crew. Before going to the airport in Venice we visited the Islands of Murano famous for its coloured glass factories (many of which I found to be a bit flashy), and Torcello with its lovely church. Thank you Sir Maurice.

Other souvenirs include Laurence Waddy suggesting that we write and perform a revue in which the Lecturers would take part. Lord Woolfenden wants to do a Noel Coward type satirical song called "Passengers." He would wear a dressing gown and have a long cigarette holder. He was excellent. Another gave a nonsensical history lecture, a parody of himself. I repeated my acclaimed performance as the intrepid archaeologist. The revue lasted forty minutes. I insisted we rehearse at 7am with the small Italian orchestra. One of the students from Cambridge played the piano brilliantly so he accompanied the performers. Laurence had written a song for me called "Statues." I still have a copy of this witty song that would have suited Noel Coward or Beatrice Lillie. It was performed wearing not much more than a bikini. In the first instance I was "archaic" in which I stood very rigid with a fixed grin, then "Greek classical" and finally "Decadent Roman." Fortunately I had a slim figure and was nicely tanned, I caused a sensation on board this Hellenic Cruise. There was an informal family party atmosphere in those days. Time and so-called progress has no doubt made the cruise more formal. The new ship, the Minerva, is very elegant and beautiful but the old hilarious days were less pompously academic and much more relaxed.

For twenty-five years I travelled on many other cruises. To Turkey and beyond. Our arrival on the Bosphorous was timed to sail into Istanbul at dawn. We sailed along the coast of the Black Sea, the Russian south coast and the north coast of Turkey. The ship sailed very slowly as we approached ancient Constantinople. The sun rose over the magnificent mosques through a slight mist. A flock of birds flew round and round the ship on cue, like ballet dancers, as if to welcome us. We could see the extraordinary city on the hillside and could hear the call to prayer which resounds throughout Istanbul six times a day. It was magical, East meets West. The friendliness and smiles of the people within the great hustle and bustle of the markets were intoxicating. One day I left the ship with a fellow passenger having decided not to go on the guided tour. We went down to the seaside and found a charming small mosque. Inside were the most beautiful carpets, people knelt and prayed to their God. On the beach, children were playing, some splashing in the water and some flying kites, running up and down whirling the long strings. The kites appeared mad, gorgeous and like giant butterflies. We played with the children who saw us as friends not tourists, with laughter and fun.

Later we sailed to Odessa where the atmosphere was much changed as we moved into Communist territory. Long ago the French and the Italians had built the villas along this coast. We were taken to the famous steps where the Russian sailors rebelled in 1917 when the Tsar was overthrown and a Communist society installed. The beauty of the coastline was spectacular, like the South of France. It was sad that the people on holiday stared at us without smiling. We smiled and waved to no response. You tell that they had been told never to fraternize with the wicked visitors from the West. As we were admiring one beautiful view on the City tour, teenagers marched by with their teachers in regimental file. They wore white blouses and blue ties, the same uniform and looked very smart. We were not allowed to film, they looked straight ahead as if ordered to do so. They were a young army disciplined and polite. They were on a strict politically supervised holiday. The beautiful villas were now sanatoria for workers who had worked hard all year. Their reward was a holiday on the Black Sea. The beaches segregated parents from their children to their mutual enjoyment. The change between the two cultures was very apparent. Perhaps, in the year 2000, parents everywhere would prefer this holiday arrangement as teenagers are now so independent. This was very much a Police State and it was clear that they did not want us there. On one of our coach tours we were lectured to by a University graduate on dialectical materialism. We found this quite unnecessary and asked her to stop. She was perplexed by this. It was quite insulting, we did not like to be indoctrinated on Communist theory.

The coastal scenery is a delight but we constantly felt under observation, it was depressing. When we sailed into Turkish waters the mood changed. This is where the classic novel by Rose McCaulay "The Towers of Trebizond" is set. It tells of her journeys on a camel, carrying a Bible, to this unknown part of Turkey. The people greeted us with laughter and dance, waved and were so merry and bright. So human and friendly after the Russian cold shoulder. The Black Sea trip was nevertheless much appreciated. It is historically important. The main trading area between East and West, from Europe through Turkey to India and the Far-East. To follow this historical route was a pleasure I shall never forget.

On the west coast we called at the important port of lzmir. From there we embarked on a two hour coach journey to Aphrodesia. Alexander the Great marched his armies south over the barren mountain ranges here when suddenly they arrived at a deep river valley with trees and water. Aphrodesia. He built a city there. A small museum now exists as a tribute to the great man and contains many superb busts. Bodrum in South Western Turkey was a small seaside village. It is now a fashionable yachting centre. I went ashore and there were no other women in the streets, they were all at home minding the children and being house-wives; Turkey, a country of men, sitting drinking coffee and smoking. As our coach journeyed across the open country, one of the wheels fell off and rolled away down the hill. We slid along one-sided and stopped. They sent for another coach. They were unaccustomed to tourists. We visited SIDE where there was an ancient city close to the beach. There are Greek and Roman remains everywhere. Now, years later, the tourist industry has transformed Turkey much like Spain and Greece have been transformed. I am so happy I travelled B.T. (before tourism!).

We went swimming after lunch and I lie on my back, looking up at the sky and imagining I was in heaven when suddenly I felt something pinching my bottom and a jolly Turk popped up next to me. I swam back to the shore…the Rape of Helen of Troy avoided and not arrested for indecency! Women in bathing costumes was an intoxicating sight. Today, no doubt: nudity is commonplace even in Turkey. When the ship left the Black Sea to return to the Aegean, the moon rose. The soft light shimmered over the water. SWAN always timed such moments as perfectly as possible, some of the dining tables were put on the top deck so that we could enjoy every moment sailing in moonlight through the Bosphorous.

I visited Beirut before the war when it was the banking centre of the Middle-East and every bit as elegant and chic as Paris. I decided to fly to Palmyra the great buried city in the desert, once the great trading centre on land between the East and the West. I went in a small plane accompanied by Sir Maurice Bowra. We flew over the high mountain range to reach the vast desert of golden sand which I had never seen before. I looked down at this endless expanse of bright yellow. The dunes creating a mirage of ocean waves. After landing our party of twenty or so proceeded to explore the colonnades of gigantic golden pillars rising out of the sandy wilderness. We were met by the top archaeological experts in the country, there to welcome Sir Maurice.

They told us that an oil prospecting company had discovered, while digging for oil, deep down under the sand, a great door and beyond it a graveyard thousands of years old. Sir Maurice was invited to take us to see this site. We were the first visitors there before these works were removed to a museum. Flashlights shone into the darkness and before us were rows and rows of coffins. Each one had a beautiful sculpture of the person inside as they wished to be remembered, young and beautiful, with a dog or needlework or some personal treasure. Sir Maurice could barely contain his excitement. It was as if we were discovering these treasures for the first time after centuries. It was truly a wonderful moment. We returned outside to photograph this incredible place. Queen Zenobia had been the ruler there, very tall, like myself apparently. When conquered by soldiers of the Roman Empire and taken back to Rome as a prisoner she was not defeated, but married a Senator and enraptured the Romans. Palmyra was such a great city once long ago, a sad reminder that we all come to dust in the end. I stood by one of the pillars to have my photograph taken and for once felt quite petite. Sir Maurice said, to my delight: "You are the reincarnation of Queen Zenobia."

The visit to Knossos in Crete was amazing. I fell at home with the Cretans. Sir Mortimer's remark remains in my mind. He said: "Where did the Cretans come from? We don't always feel so sure that they are Greek in origin. They were the original Philistines that you read about in the Old Testament. They would have sailed westward and discovered this rich island and conquered it."

Another useless but delightful piece of information was given on the beautiful island of Cyprus. Our coach stopped over-looking a bay.

"That is where the love Goddess Aphrodite had her amorous adventures" said the guide. "If a lady swims in that bay at midnight her virginity will be restored."

Why bother? I thought.

Petra in Jordan is in a deep gorge with high mountains on each side. You leave your coach and walk over a rocky dry river bed for a mile. The lovely pink city carved out of rocks and built on this rare site for protection for the people who lived in the city. If under threat of attack from the gorge, defending themselves was relatively easy. We were permitted to gain access on the back of a mule helped by a local guide.

I met the Right Reverend Dean of St. Paul's, Eric Evans, on my last cruise. A great and kind man who loved everybody he met. He lectured on the cruises accompanied by one of his beautiful daughters – both actresses – Alex and Georgie. His wife Linda did not come as she suffered from sea sickness. He gave a superb lecture about Christianity as we approached the Eastern Mediterranean on our way to Jerusalem. I also met Doctor Patrick Moore on my journey to Petra and Egypt. He lectured on the stars. He would go on the top deck at night and point out the glittering stars and the constellations to us. He was much loved by the entire company throughout the cruise.

"Do you ever use notes" I asked him .
"Never."

But he does have a brilliant collection of his own photographs of the universe which he showed the audience as part of the lecture. He was extremely kind and attentive to me because of my blindness. I hadn't intended to go ashore on some excursions it they were hazardous. I feared falling over. He immediately offered to escort me anytime. As he is over six feet tall with a strong right arm I felt confident. He insisted on taking me around the streets of Jerusalem for four hours. What a dear kind man. He held my arm firmly the entire tour. I can see a little through a thick fog, not at the main subject but with some peripheral vision. Patrick Moore showed us an amazing photograph, in Arizona six enormous dishes were pointed to the stars and would be the greatest power ever directed towards the Universe. The result of this experiment was an image of a dark black hole with a misty area in the top left hand corner which they could not identify. Was it another galaxy? I offered an opinion: "Was it God?"

I told Patrick that astrologers might bring forward a more romantic theory of the creation of the Universe. They state there was a "Big Bang," how simple, how boringly scientific and ordinary. This vast Universe with billions of stars and galaxies started with just a bang! Why we are here is a great mystery. It was a great privilege to meet this wonderful man who's BBC television programmes "Stars at Night" have been entertaining us for nearly forty years.

Now, the ORPHEUS with a Greek crew is in Athens taking tourists on shorter trips around the Aegean Greek islands. My heart and my memories and my love stay aboard forever. In wonderful company I saw the ancient world of the Mediterranean civilisation.

＊　＊　＊

A television advertisement offered a trip to the United Stales by air and the return aboard the QE2. Travelling in this manner would allow me to truly appreciate the distance between the two continents. The flight to New-York is seven hours. The crossing to Southampton is five days and would be a new experience. My friends lived in Chicago and at that time the main hub for all of the United States was JFK airport in New-York, from there I changed aircraft and flew on, (in recent years several airlines have instigated direct flights to many American Cities, there are several to Chicago every day) arriving after midnight. I was met by Bob, his wife Polly and their children Laura and David, respectively eleven and nine at the time and greeted with a bunch of flowers and a red carpet which Bob had arranged... Welcome to America! I felt like the

Queen. We drove to their lovely home in the exclusive suburb of River Forest where a champagne supper awaited. I stayed one month and a more perfect introduction to the United States of America one could not imagine.

I had met Bob in 1943 when he was working in British/American Counter intelligence. We always kept in touch after the war. He married Polly and brought her to meet me. Having always stayed at the Hyde Park Hotel, they had started renting an apartment in Sloane Street as their home base during their annual visits to London and would motor to Paris and tour Europe. Polly and I grew fond of each other and I considered them both my dearest friends. They had been to London on many occasions and had always urged me to come and visit them. It was difficult, for many years after the end of the war, many restrictions hampered our desire to travel further a field than France. A £25.00 maximum expenditure existed on holidays abroad and there was no dollar exchange. The Heitners had lived in Los Angeles where he was Head of German at U.C.L.A., from there they moved to Texas and eventually settled in Chicago.

It is very hot in Chicago in the summer – I found air-conditioning a joy, the ideal indoor temperature at the touch of a button, but in America the windows remain shut unlike in England when at the first hint of mild weather, the windows are swung open! A fascinating discovery was the supermarket where everything was wrapped air-tight in cellophane, a huge variety of produce beautifully packaged and presented. A somewhat different approach to fresh food in comparison to Portobello Road! I thought however, the customer does all the work, unlike the little grocers in London where one is provided with a personal service.

All the houses were openly accessible which I loved, no gates or high hedges as in London where privacy is desirable. Each property had an immaculately kept lawn with a walkway from street to house. There were flower beds everywhere to admire, many trees and no rubbish anywhere. Bob showed me the ingenious system which kept the grass so green, an underground network of sprinklers which were activated automatically at set times. I had never seen anything like that before. There were no people in the residential streets, it was too hot. You went everywhere in your air-conditioned car. People stayed indoors during the summer. I noticed there were no birds in the trees. In London they are my little friends and I missed their chirping. I imagine it was just too hot for them too. There were no parked cars in the street, every house has its own garage. These houses were built in varying styles from English Tudor to South of France, Spanish and Italian. The Heitner's was in the style of a French Chateau. Frank Lloyd Wright had designed twelve houses in River Forest, West Chicago. Some were inhabited and privately owned, others were museums. I saw one, an extraordinary design; open plan, clinical, clean with elegant cool plain wooden surfaces. Japanese and Scandinavian in inspiration; an architect ahead of this time.

Chicago is the United States' second city situated on the shore of lake Michigan. universally known as "The Windy City" because of the strong North wind blowing off the lake. The downtown area is peppered with amazing skyscrapers built of bold designs, not uniformly rectangular as was in Britain but of all shapes many with black glass surfaces reflecting the sky and the clouds creating the illusion of the building floating past. My favourite edifice of white marble glowing in the sunshine is by the lakeside. Many skyscrapers in central downtown were flood-lit by night in a kaleidoscope of colours whilst others proudly displayed their newly erected huge metal sculpture by Picasso. In view of the surrounding architecture this ultra-modern work was the perfect choice.

A canal runs through the heart of Chicago on which ferry boats take visitors out to lake Michigan. A complicated system of locks and barriers work expertly. Some years ago, to prevent the flow of rubbish into the lake, the current was reversed. An extraordinary feat. The panorama of the city as seen from a boat on the lake equals the New-York skyline. Chicago is a noted centre for the Arts with the world famous Art Institute containing paintings by many famous impressionists. Opposite is the home of the Symphony Orchestra. There is a complex of Technological museums to rival any in London; long wide avenues with beautifully decorated and lighted stores that would shame Harrods.

Polly was a member of the most elite "Fortnightly Club" whose members were wealthy and well educated women. Polly took me for luncheon followed by a lecture. An old period house was the setting for the twice monthly meetings. The ladies were chic which made the sight of this particular lecturer all the more surprising. He was wearing a brown Stetson and a fringed leather jacket with a gun in his hand (one hopes a fake). The subject was the discovery and exploration of the Mississippi River. He burst into song when recounting stories of Tom Sawyer and Huckleberry Finn's adventures from St. Louis to the Golf of Mexico.

On another afternoon a lecture was given on the Theatre. At question time I asked the speaker if he agreed with the three great English classical actors who stated the following:

"The duty of an actor is to be heard" RICHARD BURTON
"Know your lines and act by instinct" LAURENCE OLIVIER
"Know your lines and don't bump into the furniture" NOEL COWARD

Acting ability, the desire to be another person in another time and place with a different voice is a strange and wonderful occupation. It has

survived miraculously for thousands of years. In the forthcoming
century of undoubted endless technological invention in virtual entertainment I do hope that live theatre will survive. I am quietly confident.

Because the United-States is such a large country, it is only in the
theatres in the big cities and specially New-York where actors can train
for their profession. In England the repertory companies supply that
need. To become a name in the theatre in America is a major accomplishment as the experience cannot be as intense and varied as in
England. I have, however, seen great American productions of
Shakespeare and Ayckbourn with convincing English accents.

On that occasion I was introduced to the Grande Dame of Chicago Art
Societies. She was charming, quite elderly and lived on Lakeside Drive.
The Chicago Symphony Orchestra travels abroad and the city regularly
receives visits from great foreign Opera Companies. Donations are
received from members of the public and the major patrons are thanked
and rewarded with their names in the gala programmes. She asked me to
sit next to her at the luncheon, a great honour, and subsequently invited
me to join her the following week in her box at Symphony Hall for a
Beethoven recital led by resident conductor George Solti. A memorable
evening in many ways, at one point he turned and requested that
members of the audience should try and refrain from coughing quite so
much!

Many years earlier, I had been on a trip to Dublin to visit some friends
whose theatrical parties were attended by Michael McLearmore and
Hilton Edwards. I wanted to go west to Galway and visit the place
where the first airmen landed in a bog, their mission to cross the
Atlantic. In Galway, after initially checking into an hotel, I discovered a
small building with four pillars in the front which it seems was a cinema.
One of the feature presentations was a film on the life of the great
pianist Arthur Rubinstein. The gentleman in the box office did not

encourage me to enter as he was hoping for an empty house and a much anticipated few hours in the local public house: "You don't want to see this film. It's an old man playing a piano."

"Yes, that is just what I want" was my reply to his impertinence.

A tall man also ventured into the cinema whom I discovered was from Chicago. Mr. James L. Riedy. Extremely fond of London theatre and concerts, he had recently arrived in Ireland on his way back to Chicago where he was a lecturer on the Arts. We were staying at the same hotel. The next day he went to the Isle of Aran by boat and I visited Keats country. In the evening we met for dinner, compared notes and exchanged personal details so as to keep in touch. He was returning to America via Shannon and I to London via Dublin if I could escape from my friends' endless parties. James and I have remained friends to this day, he is now retired and living in Costa Rica but his marvellous book on the great city of Chicago "CHICAGO SCULPTURE" with his own photographs is a testament of his work. It is still on my shelf and I cherish it.

Bob Heitner also had several books published as a "GOETHE" specialist. He gave me his latest publication and proclaimed: "Another boring book from a boring academic, Eunice."

Of course I disagreed and said these books were most precious.

Whilst I was in Chicago, Jim had invited Polly, Bob and myself to dinner. He lived in a studio in a less salubrious neighbourhood. There were other guests, married couples, teachers…We were served a delicious Margarita (my first) in a glass with salt on the brim. Jim is a gourmet cook, he spent a great deal of time in his kitchen and eventually we were presented with a sumptuous trench dinner of several courses. As a bachelor, Jim had become increasingly tired of eating out. Inspired by his local open-air market he enrolled at a cookery class. Let this be a lesson to all bachelors around the world, it can be done!

Two charming teachers of my acquaintance told me that their son was taking Drama at the University of Dallas in Texas. He had played Hamlet during his last year at High School. He now had a part in a Noel Coward musical. They asked me to go to Dallas to see his performance. For two days we drove South with overnight stops at two roadside motels, an amazing journey across the central United States. The land is so flat you could see the curve of the Earth. The maximum speed was 55mph which seemed slow on the enormous highways across vast plains where the wheat is grown and the cattle roam. We arrived in Dallas for lunch and were in our seats at the magnificent University auditorium as the performance was about to begin. Their son was handsome and suitably urbane for the part, tall and well spoken but it was difficult to judge his acting ability as he was the compère of what was essentially a revue. After the performance we visited his lodgings. He played the classical guitar for us quite expertly. He was a talented shy young man who, when fourteen years old had won a prestigious American competition for classical guitar. He was impatient with Drama School elementary classes. He wanted to act greater parts straight away at University.

"The procedure is slow..." I told him, "...be it here or at a Drama school in London."

I told him that firstly he must be physically fit and take vocal exercises. "Acting parts do not happen until the 3rd year of training."

But, "Mime and improvisation are boring," he interjected.

He had every attribute, good looks, voice and intelligence. I hoped to see him on Broadway some day.

Over the years I have returned to visit Bob & Polly in Chicago. I attended Laura's wedding. She had studied at Harvard and received an Honours Degree. There she met her future husband, David. He was a graduate and was working for an oil company. The ceremony was magnificent and they honeymooned in the Caribbean and settled in Denver. He had a new job in the same field and Laura decided to begin training for a law degree. On one occasion, I was flying to Los Angeles from Chicago to visit Jane Seymour. At Laura's suggestion I stopped over in delightful Denver snuggled in the majestic Rockies. They were living in a cottage an hour's drive from the centre of Denver. I was horrified to hear that breakfast was at 5:30am as they had to be in the office at 7am and wanted to avoid the morning traffic. They hoped that I would be all-right on my own until 5pm when David would return from the Gym. or ice-skating and Laura from class. The Art Gallery was apparently not to be missed and I would enjoy exploring Denver. The centre of the City was being pedestrianised and the work would take three months. I thought in England it would take three years! The Gallery was indeed a joy. I noticed an equestrian statue of a cowboy looking eastwards to the prairies.

A few years later Laura and Dave moved to Houston and two years ago were sadly divorced. They have two young children. Laura has since re-married.

One year I decided to accept Bob and Polly's invitation to spend Christmas and New-Year in Chicago. It was the coldest winter for a hundred years. The lake was completely frozen. They had moved to a condominium on the 22nd floor of a downtown building. All visitors were announced by the duty doorman. A semi-private high speed lift took me aloft, there were only two apartments per floor, Bob and Polly met me as the elevator doors opened. The building was remarkably self-contained with all services and even a post office located on the lower-ground floor. Their apartment afforded stunning views, surrounded as it was by glass walls. From the large kitchen table I was dazzled by the white frozen vista on the horizon. We were so high we could see to the west great clouds of snow rolling in from the Prairies direct from the North Pole. The temperature was -20C and the snow flakes huge. The few cars that were parked in the street below were completely covered. The night views were wonderful. The tall buildings a mass of twinkling lights covered with snow resembled huge concrete Christmas trees. O'Hare International Airport was shut down for the first time, the snow was so heavy the runways could not be cleared.

At term time, everybody was told to stay at home. Most of the traffic had come to a halt. The city was still. We thankfully were warm as toast, all electrics in good order, unlike England where the first snow flake brings the country to a full stop. One morning I was stunned at the surreal sight of a young man suspended from a cradle outside the window of the condo scraping the ice off the windows and laughing heartily. Bob announced that he intended to walk to the University, Polly insisted that he wear ear-flaps as he would probably get frost bite. He returned one hour later, the University was closed. His nose was bright red, his ears frost bitten! The Chicago Herald Tribune described this time as a period when "cabin fever" was beginning to settle in. This is because of people being stuck indoors for too long with each other and going mad, threatening divorce. Polly asked me to stay for a month, so I cancelled my proposed onward trip to California and remained as the referee until the snow began to recede and normality returned to the household. I shall never forget the incident of the rice pudding. Bob, a lover of all things English expressed a desire for rice pudding with skin on the top, one of Prince Charles' favourites I am told. Bob asked Polly to make one. She was not keen, so I offered to make a special English rice pudding. When the pudding was ready Polly removed it from the oven forgetting that the top of the stove was still very hot and placed the glass dish on that surface and left the kitchen waiting for it to cool. Minutes later a fantastic noise emanated from the kitchen, the glass dish had exploded, the pudding mixed with broken glass was now all over the walls, the floor and ceiling. Polly became hysterical, so I took immediate charge of the situation: "Polly, go and lie down."

"Bob go to your study and translate something"…

"David go to your room, lock the door and don't come out until I tell you."

They obeyed very quickly and without discussion, this was Eunice as they had never seen her before. I cleaned up the mess and calm was restored to the household. Perhaps I saved their marriage. I had never heard of rice pudding on the ceiling, an Edward Lear nonsense escapade.

From Chicago in midwinter, Bob suggested that we should travel to St Louis and visit his relatives and the family home. The Heitner family had come from Germany at the beginning of the 19th century and founded a soap industry. Polly pointed out that the roads were ice-bound and snow-covered but nevertheless we set off. We were the only automobile on the road south, ice everywhere and the snow-covered plain stretching to eternity. The sky was crystal blue with brilliant sunshine. There were abandoned cars on the highway in dismal scenes of wreckage. St. Louis was covered with snow. There was nobody about, but the next day Bob took me for a drive. There are many beautiful parks and hills and a renowned Art Museum which we visited. We were the only people there, a treat to see the pictures in such glorious conditions. The trees outside were covered with icicles glittering in the sunshine like chandeliers. We drove to the Mississippi so I could see the one hundred year old houses which were restored and preserved for posterity. They looked enchanting on the banks of this mighty river.

On my way to Houston I stopped in glorious New-Orleans for a few days. I stayed at an hotel recommended by the airline. It was small but comfortable and the black owner very jolly, congenial and friendly. I am quite used to travelling alone. I chose a full day's tour which included lunch. The architecture and the slow pace were most charming. It was pointed out to us that the whole city is built over water apart from the delta of the Mississippi. The guide showed us a cemetery which was literally sinking into the water. I wanted to go out in the evening but was advised not to, so I consoled myself with a river trip the next day on an old Showboat vessel. There were a group of sailors on board on their leave. I was escorted around the old plantation houses by girls dressed in 19th Century costumes.

I had acquired some bottles of gin as a gift for my friends in Houston and realised as my flight was about to depart that I had left these behind at the hotel. It was too late, the crew informed me that we were about to take off. Farewell gin. They must have thought I was crazy: "Gin, gin where is my gin?" I cried.

I felt quite at ease in Texas. Everything is so large. My hosts in Houston were Dr. & Mrs. Graft. Dora is Puerto Rican, a lovely lady. Her husband, Homer, is German of origin and was an E.N.T. specialist at the Houston Medical Centre. Dora met me at the airport and I told her that I left the gin behind. She was very gracious about that. They had five children who wanted to meet this lady from England. I spent most of my holiday sitting on the floor playing with their lovely children and grand-children. The four year old girl was quite intrigued by me. She would return from nursery school with her mother and the daily tea ceremony would take place in my honour. She would quietly come into my room when I was resting and would stare at me in wonderment. She loved stories and I would draw pictures of cats and rabbits for her. She was entranced. She once came in and did three somersaults telling me that she had just been doing that at school.

"Can you do it" she asked

"No, my dear, I'm too old."

She and I became great friends. She would sit next to me and watch me draw, a charming child. I often think of her, she must be a teenager by now. It was a lovely family atmosphere. There was one big general family room where all worked and lived throughout the day. Dora loved all kinds of machines, cameras and recording equipment. She was also an excellent needle-woman. She showed me some of the exquisite patterns she had made on her children's clothing. Homer left for the hospital every morning at 7am and would return at 4pm and would usually listen to music from his vast Opera and Classical collection. It would fill the house. At 5:30 it was the daily cocktail hour and a gin and tonic would be offered with sparkling conversation of the day's events. He would then retire to the kitchen and prepare the evening dinner which would be served at 7:30 and always be delicious.

"I wish I could train someone to be like you" were my words to him!

I invited Dora to go to the theatre but Homer did not like her to be out in the evenings so I asked the Jones's instead. I had planned to stay with them during the latter part of my stay in Houston. He was retired and loved to make things in his workroom and she was tall and elegant. Their house was minimalistic, almost Japanese in look and atmosphere. They introduced me to a diet of natural foods, no fish, meat or eggs. Although somewhat sparse the food was good as was the liberal quantities of Californian red wine. Mrs. Jones showed me yoga. I was quite slim at the time but still could not quite manage the lotus position. We sat on mats, very relaxing. Part of my training as an actress was to learn how to relax for short periods, so I felt at ease practising yoga. They would rise at dawn before the extremes of heat and traffic and go bicycle riding to keep fit. It was all very different from the Graff household.

We went to their splendid Arts Centre where there is one fairly small auditorium to see a play by Ayckbourn. I had been apprehensive of Ayckbourn by Americans but was pleasantly surprised. The accents were good as was the production. It is very possible that some of the actors were English. We also went to the University Music Department where they also have a lovely theatre. We attended some of the concerts given by the students. It is no wonder that the standard of music in America is so high. My friends also had a ranch for the week-end. In Texas everything is big, vast expanses of land reaching the horizon where the cattle industry thrives. We ate some of their corn beef from a tin. Considering how swiftly most Americans like to eat in restaurants, the size of the steaks on their plates leaves one baffled. During my stay in Houston I was taken out to a grand house one afternoon for tea. It was quite a long drive on the outskirts of the city. We arrived at a high and impressive gate where our identity was requested by an armed guard before we could gain access. This is how wealthy people live in America. It was a very select neighbourhood, much the same as Jane Seymour's residence in Los Angeles. The American spirit is as expansive as its landscape. Virtually every race on the planet is represented in one region or another. It is amazing that they have constructed a nation of people in fifty States under one President living harmoniously, a great achievement. The country is known for its hospitality and generosity of spirit. The English are very popular in America. They are always fascinated by my accent. If I mention that I have worked with Benny Hill they are ecstatic. They love my deep actressy voice and I too am fascinated by their various ways of speaking our same language. It was George Bernard Shaw who said: "Two nations separated by a common language."

I have been back to Houston in recent years to visit with Bob Heitner, now a widower. He wanted to live closer to his daughter Laura. He bought an English style house and decorated and furnished it elegantly. Alas, dear Bob now lives in a nursing home as he is suffering from Alzheimer's disease. But with new medication he is now able to write to me. I hope soon to visit him and see Laura, her two children and meet her new husband; and of course the Graffs whose son visited me recently in London with his Asian wife.

* * *

Ever since my first visit I have always adored the Golden State. I have friends in San Francisco, Carmel, Los Angeles and La Jolla. My first port of call was to see Camille Durnley whom I met in 1959 on my first Hellenic cruise. We were always the last for breakfast, we became friends in adversity! I had an open invitation to visit her in California. I had been visiting Polly and Bob in Chicago and decided to prolong my trip and fly west to San Francisco. It was a wonderful surprise for us both. She lived on the far side of the bay across the Golden Gate near the University of Berkeley which she had attended. Camille and her husband met me at the airport in the evening and we drove to their home. The cold Pacific waters meet with warmer bay waters and swirling clouds of golden mist are formed sweeping over the bridge. The setting sun was shining through this amazing cloud; my first sight of San Francisco was enchanting. No coincidence that Camille's house was Italian in inspiration as she spent many holidays in Tuscany. Three sides surrounded a lawn in the centre. At one end up steps was the swimming pool under lovely tall pine trees. An ideal situation and I swam under the trees every morning. Their extremely kind and generous hospitality was overwhelming. On my first Saturday a party was given in my honour. Camille had invited several of her friends, mostly lawyers and academics. At the end of the dinner, her husband stood and invited the guests to raise their glasses to: "Our wonderful friend from England."

These extremely sophisticated people raised their glass to me. Overcome, somehow I replied thanking them, such wonderful people.

I was taken to see Berkeley campus – it is such a famous University –

there are more people with honours and glory from there than anywhere else in the world. More Nobel Prize winners have studied there than at Harvard or Yale. Bob and Polly told me that their nephew John Rosin was at Stanford University (also in the Bay area) taking a second degree. He invited me to see his campus the next morning. I spoke to Camille and asked if I could take the day to visit with this 28 year old student. John arrived the next morning at 8am in his old banger calling me Auntie Eunice. I laughed because most cars in America are as big as the QE2. I had trouble squeezing into this one! His lodgings at Stanford were humble to say the least. I sat on the arm of an ancient armchair and it promptly fell off. I offered to buy him a new one. All American students are not wealthy. San Francisco is blessed to have two such famous Universities.

John drove me to Carmel-by-the-Sea rather than let me fly or take the bus. I was going to visit my friend Jack Wood. We drove south along the beautiful coast and arrived at 4pm. Jack was a teacher and I wondered if he would be home. We drove along the main street to the beach and telephoned. He had just come in from work and said he would join us. Carmel is chic and sophisticated. Jack said we would drive to Big Sur and have dinner there overlooking the Pacific. The drive to Big Sur is stunning, with mountains dropping down into the sea. Many famous film stars live there and in surrounding areas which are unspoiled. The coastline is unique and memorable. I stayed one day with Jack in his lovely town before flying to LA. to see Jane Seymour.

On a subsequent visit to San Francisco I stayed with another friend Bill Peralta and Jack came up from Carmel to meet us. It was a glorious day and he drove us around the sixty seven hills of San Francisco in his convertible VW. He played soft music on the car radio, cockney London tunes for me. We motored up and down the hills and whirled over the Golden Gate Bridge to Sausalito for lunch followed by a drive through the great pinewoods, some over 200 feet tall. Possibly my fondest memory of San Francisco was a visit to the outstanding and hilarious revue: BEACH BLANKET BABYLON. It is so original with hugely funny headdresses, one – the entire city of New-York in perspex; outrageously comic costumes and Pythonesque dialogue. The show is running forever and is a great showplace for aspiring comedians. An evening I shall never forget. Thanks to Jack and Bill for taking me.

I had been Auntie Eunice to Jane since her childhood. At first she had wanted to be a ballet dancer and I had encouraged her, her parents seeking my advice. An unfortunate knee injury ended her ballet studies and her aspirations in that area. She later decided to be an actress and trained at the Arts Educational Centre in London. She often said: "I want to be an actress, like you Auntie Eunice."

I told her she needed lots more training and experience. She decided to try her luck in Hollywood, if not successful she would return to England.

So I left from the charming Monterey Peninsula Airport and was met by Jane at LAX. I shall never forget the wonderful picture of the beautiful young Jane with long flowing hair running across the tarmac to greet me with a huge hug. She led me to her enormous truck-like car. We drove to her rented house. She had arrived in Hollywood at a time when beautiful unspoiled English girls were in demand and she received constant offers of work. Jenny Agutter lived down the road, also there to seek her fame and fortune. The next day Jane had an interview to obtain the elusive Green Card which would give her permanence in the United States. That evening we had been invited to a birthday party. I would be staying for a few days with Doctor and Mrs. Sobel (friends of the Heitners). He was Head of German at UCLA. Jane returned at 5pm with her Green Card so it was to be a double celebration that evening. Jane told me that it was extremely difficult to obtain and that they had asked many probing questions about her film work, the money she earned and the American Income Tax she had paid. She proved to them that we was not a burden on the State. She paid her own rent and was never unemployed. She was also given a full medical examination. Finally she received the card and could now work in America as well as in her native England with the two Equity trade Unions satisfied. One unexpected pleasure was when Jenny Agutter and Jane were being photographed for an English magazine at Disneyland, two English actresses enjoying a day out. It was a great and memorable day.

In the early 80's she played the part of Mozart's wife Constanza in the play AMADEUS on Broadway opposite Ian McKellen, which I saw. At supper afterwards she confessed a preference to television and film work, not really enjoying working on stage. She was right and was making the best decision, agreed that she did not possess the necessary technique or projection for the live theatre; much like Elizabeth Taylor who's talent on film cannot be denied.

Jane has changed, she is an American intent on improving her image, career and fame. But as a wife and mother of four she remains English. She has family reunions at her English "home," St. Catherine's Court near Bath. I do see her from time to time in England.

Los Angeles is a big and sprawling city which made me feel lost because I never went anywhere alone. The Sobels escorted me round the UCLA campus which is beautiful with hills and trees and parks. The building which houses the German Department is stunning, an Italian architectural construction with a golden exterior. I went to a David Hockney retrospective where his most famous painting "The splash" was on display. He has lived in California most of his life although born in Yorkshire and is one of the world's most famous painters. I was most interested to see a retrospective exhibition because it explores the evolution of the artist from Art School to the present day. His was a vast exhibition of great wonder, a remarkable painter of originality and imagination. A section of the show came as a complete surprise; in a dark room there were a great number of beautifully lit miniature theatre sets with scenery designed by Hockney from diverse productions. As an actress I was fascinated. I wished he designed more for the theatre in England. Another area consisted of collages of hundreds of photographs taken at a party. The work was called "The party.".hands, feet, heads, wine glasses put together to form one picture. Hilarious and entertaining and original. These days, I am sad to say that my sight has gone which makes viewing magnificent works of art almost impossible. I avoid the crowds, go early and put my face close to the picture.

Leaving L.A. and the lovely Jane behind, I moved on to La Jolla to visit a lecturer I had met on one of the Hellenic cruises. The Reverend Laurence Waddy. He had been Head-Master of a school in Tunbridge Wells and had decided to come and live in California and was now a lecturer of Roman History at the University of La Jolla south of Los Angeles near San Diego. He very kindly came to collect me and we drove in his large open top sports car to his bungalow and afterwards showed me around his campus in La Jolla. As an Englishman he could not preach in a regular Church and thus had been permitted to use a school hall. The altar was on the hall stage. The service was informal with families and children in their prams. The music was provided by a small band and a guitarist, no organ music. Amateur actors played a scene from the New Testament. There were a few hymns, a most unusual and original Church service which became very popular. Coffee and soft drinks were offered to the congregation afterwards.

So farewell to California, farewell to the migrating whales along the Pacific Coast, farewell to San Francisco and Los Angeles and farewell to my lovely Jane Seymour to whom I have spoken recently, she was preparing to film with James Bolam and is writing a children's book inspired by her twin sons born four years ago.

*   *   *

I go to America every two or three years and those holidays are always special. One year whilst in Los Angeles I decided to visit Las Vegas and the Grand Canyon. I flew from L.A. over the mountains to Las Vegas. Below there appears only to be endless desert when suddenly a bright sprawling city appears. One must try to arrive in the evening to appreciate the glitter from above. What a place! Only the Americans could invent Las Vegas. In the past dedicated to gambling, it has in recent years become more family friendly. As you arrive there are fruit machines in the airport lounges with hundreds of people playing at every corner. Quite bizarre. Everybody, everywhere gambling. I spoke to some French people who had not slept for three days. They told me of flying trapeze acts without safety nets above their heads at one of the hotels. Some of the artistes virtually nude but nobody took any notice all concentrating on their one arm bandits. I asked a taxi driver to show me around town. We drove up and down the Strip and I saw the fabled hotels where the stars were appearing. It was brief, it was unforgettable.

I flew on to the Grand Canyon in a small aircraft landing on the rim of the great crevasse. I am a lover of paintings all the more inspired by the talent of my late husband The colours dominating the azure over the Grand Canyon were quite unique, the sky becoming the canvass of a great painter surrounded with endless diversity of paints. One morning I arose at dawn and the heavens were scarcely to be believed; subtle colours of pale blue blending into shades of mauves hovering above the Canyon. It is up to three thousand feet deep The bottom is barely visible and the amazing rock formations change patterns and colours as the sun rises and the golden light shimmers In the heat of midday, the rays transform the Canyon walls from russet to a blood red tapestry and in the evening fades to purples and pinks. It is a different place all the time. On the zigzag paths inside the Canyon you can see the intrepid travellers on mules making their way to the river below. Time has had no effect here for ten million years. There is an extraordinary sense of timelessness and ancient tales of what Mother Nature has carved out of this land. I was completely enraptured for two days. The brochures had not exaggerated the colours and the beauty of this place.

* * *

One year, after a holiday in Chicago. I decided to fly to New-York and subsequently tour New England during the glorious fall colours. All actors have wanted to stay at the famous Algonquin Hotel, home of the celebrated "Round Table" at which sat the cream of the literary set for their weekly convivial dinners, it was earlier this century and Dorothy Parker was perhaps the most renowned. She had great wit and is still quoted avidly. The Hotel is situated near 5th Avenue in Midtown Manhattan, a short walk to most Broadway theatres; the persistent summer heat, the oppressive sky-scrapers limiting the air circulation and the extreme humidity usually enticed me into air-conditioned taxis however. The Algonquin although historically thrilling remains unfashionable and somewhat archaic. It was so hot in my room that I called room service and asked if there was some kind of air cooling system. The bellboy pointed to a box in the window. He kicked it a few times. It made sounds like an aircraft engine. I thought it would come away and crash down to the street below.

I had expected New-York to be much like the West End of London, but it is actually quite different. There exists a vitality and energy unparalleled and everything moves at a great pace. There is electricity in the air, that was my first impression. There are so many different people from various ethnic minorities, adding to this amazing melting pot of races, Spanish, African, Jewish and European.

There is endless choice of activity and my main interests were Opera which I attended at Lincoln Centre and the Museums. I visited the

Metropolitan and the Guggenheim situated opposite each other on the upper East Side on Central Park.

Memorably, I attended a matinée of a revival of a famous musical. I sat next to a short elderly gentleman who asked me at the interval if I was English. I told him that this was my first visit to his great city and I was there to see a few shows, get a taste of the city and later tour New-England. At the end of the performance he insisted on escorting me back to the hotel. He thought I might be in some danger. I towered over him, I wondered who was being protected!

The next morning I was leaving for my tour, my new found friend asked me to get in touch on my return and he would show me around the Wall Street area. Lovely.

We left from the beautiful Waldorf Hotel on Park Avenue in a luxuriously huge air-conditioned red coach. There were 39 passengers, mostly American from many States. We went north to Boston across three mountain ranges, then back south along the Hudson River. As we left New-York each passenger was invited to stand and introduce himself or herself to the other members of the tour. We took the front seats in rotation as to allow everyone to share the opportunity of the best view. The English should do this. We had the most erudite guide blessed with great fluency, a graduate who expertly described the interesting sights, including the residence at the man who invented the Biro pen!

Each night we stayed at different kinds of hotels. The Hilton in Boston. Further inland in the mountains were lovely Inns, each with its particular style and cuisine; French, German or Italian...always delicious. The colours of the trees, scarlet, gold, orange and yellow are unique in the autumn sunshine. The time I was married to Roman made me appreciate vivid colours and extraordinary beauty all the more and this was a rare treat.

I was soon back in the Big Apple and meeting my matinée friend down in Battery Park which I attained by city bus, on my own....a proud moment. He had mentioned a visit to the Stock Exchange to which I was much looking forward, I had never even been to the London Exchange. In fact we went to the Chocolate Exchange where the deals being made were not concerning stocks and shares but tons of cocoa. To me his hive of activity was like watching a well-choreographed Broadway musical, the brokers all shouting at once constantly referring to the board above for the up-to-date prices. The gesticulation and arm waving reminded me of the tic-tac men signalling the prices at a race meeting. It was so exciting. This was a world I knew nothing about, commercial market trading by experts for us to be able to eat delicious chocolates and those naughty Mars Bars! An ear-piercing siren signalled break time and I was introduced to several members, many English who asked me questions about London and for some extraordinary reason asked me to sing an English song. Naturally I duly obliged and belted out "My old man said follow the van" to great applause and for an encore I performed "Any old Iron." The Cocoa Exchange has not heard such melodies before or since. I thought I might be thrown out for this behaviour but the boys enjoyed my songs and were most courteous. So, I had made my début at the New-York Chocolate Exchange. It had been one of the most wonderful mornings of my life, thrilling, unexpected and hilarious. My escort then took me to lunch to meet his sister

We walked for ages through a fairly unsavoury area near the docks. I wondered where he was taking me, eventually arriving at a shabby door. We entered. At the top of the stairs was his sister, a comfortable looking woman of about sixty who said: "Welcome to the most famous fish restaurant in New-York City."

We ate splendid fish and drank delicious Chablis. How kind these people were. I wanted them to be my guests for lunch but they insisted that I was to be their guest. I had assumed that after luncheon we would return to the Algonquin before going to a show in the evening. But no, they had plans. As a surprise, they took me to the world famous Radio City Music Hall to see the equally famous Rockettes.

It was my intention to reciprocate their kindness by asking them to dinner but they wanted to return home. We had a drink at the hotel and said goodbye. I invited them to stay with me anytime in London and the following year they did come to London and I was able to return their hospitality. I showed them around, especially to unusual places not often visited by tourists. We went to Simpsons in the Strand which they liked very much because it was so English and the food is first class, their speciality being roast beef, roast potatoes and Yorkshire pudding. It was a great joy to entertain this retired couple from New-York.

Before I left New-York I decided to take a day trip to the Nation's Capital in Washington DC which included a tour of the White House. The city is elegant, the design French in inspiration. The architecture quite splendid, specifically the Capital Building and the White House. During my tour of the President's official residence I noticed that the portraits were of former Presidents with their wives. At No. 10 Downing Street you see paintings of former Prime Ministers but not one with a wife, Margaret Thatcher there in her own right. For a comparatively new Country it is interesting that the Americans have clearly appreciated the role of women as supporter of their husbands. Europeans are more male orientated with the little woman at home, a hostess and mother; supportive not obtrusive.

My friends. Dr. and Mrs. Heitner from Chicago told me that their son David was attending University in the New-York area. David had arranged to meet me at The Battery where we took the ferry passing right by the Statue of Liberty. His University were producing Strindberg's "The Father"; another evening of merriment! It would be performed in the round in a tiny theatre. We arrived and sat in the front row. We were so close that at one moment a prop. lamp being thrown across the stage missed me by inches. Thankfully I ducked. Lecturers played the major roles and were professional. It was an unexpectedly enjoyable evening as all too often amateur productions can be gruesome.

I went to visit my English friends, Mr. and Mrs. Piers Pottinger who had been sent by his Bank to work in New-York for a few years. They invited me to their period rented apartment in Brooklyn. It was almost like Kensington, they lived on one floor of a Victorian type house, known as a "brown stone." They, however had a cockroach problem and the exterminator would come round once a month to deal with it. In New-York this is a major problem, caused by central heating.

On this occasion I was returning to England on the QE2. I said farewell to my two new friends, with echoes of the Rockettes resounding in my ears, left the Algonquin the next day and headed for the docks for a 3pm sailing. Crossing the Atlantic by ship gave me a real idea of the distance to Europe. I arrived to discover that I was to share my cabin with another lady and that a farewell party was in progress. To my utter surprise, when I reached the cabin, I discovered that the party was for me. My friends decided that I must have a celebration to see me off. The lady with whom I was sharing joined in and a good time was had by all. We embraced and said Goodbye. We departed and I shall always remember the Manhattan skyline and the Statue of Liberty, a symbol of hope for millions of immigrants to this wonderful country.

The QE2 has a reputation for great cuisine, efficient service, civility and comfort. I was placed at a table with six other people. All were younger than myself. There was a handsome young American on his way to the Guild hall School of Music and Drama to study to be an actor who was delighted I too was in the theatre. There was a British Diplomat returning from several years on a remote Pacific Island. He would find London very changed. He was refreshingly working class, not Oxbridge, and great company. He made me laugh hilariously about his exploits on his Pacific Island. There was a delightful Japanese girl who spoke very little English. We translated the huge menu for her. I loved listening to her repeat items to me in her fractured English. There was also a young couple at our table, I offered to change but all agreed that we were compatible. A most debonair and personable Frenchman was also with us. We entrusted him with the choice of wine, at the end of the sailing we would share the bill. For five days we could enjoy discos, floor shows, cinemas, casinos, gyms and a swimming pool. We intended to make full use of everything available to us. At the end of the voyage, the Frenchman insisted on settling the wine bill as his father was a wine merchant and he could not possibly take our money.

We arrived in Southampton, I was home and back to the real world, to my life of hard work which I have always enjoyed.

On another occasion, during one of my numerous subsequent arrivals in New-York, I was flying in from the West Coast when the pilot alerted us to a hurricane warning. Elsie or Dorothy I think. Our flight was diverted to Pittsburg where we waited to see what would develop. Sitting on the tarmac, my imagination ran wild. I wondered would New-York still be there when we eventually arrived? Would the Algonquin still be standing?... Sometime later we were invited to change aircraft and arrived in New-York. The hurricane had whirled away out to sea and missed Manhattan. That night I had dreams of an English lady being blown to heaven in her nightdress as the Algonquin Hotel floated away into space.

* * *

I arrived in Miami on the 26th of January 1998 to stay in wonderful

Coconut Grove at 3753 Matheson Avenue, happy at the prospect of being spoiled during my recovery from the truly terrible consequences of my fall on July 13 1997. It was heavenly, with massive palm trees and many beautiful flowers everywhere. There was a lovely bird bath; I managed to entice the birds to visit, even wild parrots – pure delight as they splashed in the bath and ate the food. In London my wild birds entertain me in the same way – sparrows, blue hits, starlings and blackbirds. The house had two floors. My apartment was situated on ground level with French windows opening from my bedroom with a view of a glorious garden. The sky was always blue and pink in the morning, deepest azure by sunset. It was breathtaking and comfortable. I spent three weeks resting, contemplating the wondrous scenery. I was in Heaven. The leaves fascinate me, how nice of God to design such beautiful plants, these palms with extraordinary varied smooth leaves, some thin, some spiky. The king palm, so lovely, like a duchess dancing at a ball with a feathered head-dress. I was told to beware of the coconut palm as the falling coconuts can cause severe head injury. Here I lay on my bed on a Saturday morning wanting to be nowhere else in the world. I wished that I could afford a private let for all my friends in England to come and visit, fly out and have a drink with me under the king palm trees. Eventually I began dictating this autobiography on cassettes. I had started writing long hand but found this far too slow because of my blindness, but writing is best because editing is immediate and automatic.

Two days after my arrival, a tornado struck. The authorities requested that everyone go home early from work as the storm would hit in the late afternoon. Great gales blew with torrential rain pouring like waterfalls, trees were blown almost horizontal, but the beautiful giant palm did not snap. Later in the evening, the night sky was alive with endless flash lightning with surprisingly little thunder. Suddenly there was a loud noise like an exploding bomb. It was very frightening. I thought the house had been struck but I later discovered that a very old tree nearby had been hit by lightning and had collapsed, luckily away from my house. Immediately, the power was cut and I was plunged in complete darkness. At about 11 pm, I attempted to contact my friends by telephone and to my great surprise the line was functioning. Roberto and Renaldo came immediately to rescue me, although I told them not to bother bringing candles and torches. When they begged me to return to their place, I refused. I had survived the blitz in London for six years, this tornado was a spring breeze in comparison. The centre of the tornado was in North Miami, about twenty miles from Coconut Grove. The calm after the storm was marvellous with the blue sky returning, the plants and vegetation luxuriously verdant. This had been my first twister, fortunately I was not whirled into eternity. In North Miami, 1500 homes lost their roofs and at the airport aircraft were over-turned. Thankfully this was the only storm of its kind during my stay in Miami.

Our favourite restaurant in Coconut Beach is "NUNZIO," very Italian, the food, Mama and Papa Naples atmosphere is absolutely wonderful. Reasonably priced with the best pizzas I have ever tasted, thin and crispy with delicious toppings. We would habitually dine out there two or three times a week. So delightful, we became friends of the family.

I did not cook a single thing the entire three months I was in Miami. Roberto's lovely friend Renaldo very kindly did my shopping and so I never entered a supermarket. There are so many restaurants, I was particularly fascinated by the ones that advertised "All Day Breakfast." One evening I went for a late supper and had a full breakfast. Marvellous. I have been very independent all my life and have been extremely fortunate to have such endearing friends around me who care for me. My friends in Miami took exceptional care of me for three months. I am overwhelmed by the kindness and generosity of all my American friends. I will always remember the large limousine in which they would take me for our evening dinner. I was so spoiled during my stay in Miami. It contributed enormously to my recovery.

Their visit to me that Christmas in London, had been a joy for all. I had the house decorated, lighted and ordered a huge tree. I was unable to walk but they did everything, shopping, cooking etc. They are my dearest friends.

I would happily live in Miami permanently during the winter but from May to October it is unbearable for me, far too hot and tropical. Thankfully everywhere is air-conditioned. I prefer being able to wander in the fresh air in our parks in London. I would be too sleepy and lazy in the tropics. Anyhow I am sure that my friends will come over and see me in England when their busy schedule will permit it. Dr. Roberto Vitale whom I met on an Arts Treasures Tour to Moscow and St. Petersburg many years ago is Doctor of modern languages and speaks French, Italian and Spanish and travels regularly to Europe, particularly to those Mediterranean countries. He will pop over to England and see me when it is possible. His close friend is Renaldo whose father is Chinese, mother Spanish and was originally from Cuba.

My other great friend is Dr. Hector Vasquez, also originally from Cuba. In 1960 his parents had been deported by Castro with thousands of talented Cubans. Spanish is now widely spoken in Florida, the young enjoy life in Florida but many older Spaniards would like to return to Cuba after the death of Castro. That may be impossible. I had spent the previous Christmas with Hector and his family, it was ten days surrounded by his delightful Spanish relatives with parties every night. A huge Christmas tree, sparkling and splendid stood in an elegant white walled reception room with dramatic pictures on the walls painted by his brother, a dental surgeon.

Naturally I have also met many of their friends and acquaintances and particularly appreciated meeting Mrs. Jane Pyle, a musicologist. I was invited to stay on her farm. One evening she gave a celebration dinner for me and a dozen friends. The very old, delightful, detached house was quite isolated and one could see a horse in the paddock, chickens and dogs everywhere. A huge bonfire lighted the sky at night, we ate glorious food and drank splendid wine. Then to our great delight, Jane's husband lighted a terrific fireworks display, magical it was, like a tropical Guy Fawkes night! Knowing these people makes for a lovely social scene and I enjoy their visits to me. They love London and the English countryside, our theatre, music, art galleries and our parks. An international friendship of great warmth.

One week-end we travelled Southward to Key West. I loved the Keys and especially Key Largo and was amazed by the succession of extraordinary bridges linking the small islands and appearing to be resting on the sea. The architecture of Key West is colonial in inspiration I suppose and many of the men you see look like Ernest Hemingway. He had lived there and his former house is now a museum. Alas, quite recently, a major hurricane hit Key West and much was destroyed; I imagine that the authorities will protect the heritage and re-build in the same style, charming white wooden houses with balconies.

On another occasion we flew to Orlando for a weekend enjoying Disney World. It was clean and tidy and expertly organized and administrated. The English should take note. Despite the millions of people who visit the site every year, endless queues are rarely seen. If there is any wait there is a vast choice of restaurants at which to enjoy food from all over the world. Apart from the various enjoyable rides and games there is also Epcot which has models of many of the world's famous buildings. I enjoyed the jungle ride and loved Fairyland. One evening we went to a show that was like an old-fashioned Music-Hall. The audience sat at tables. There were beautiful chorus girls and great tunes. I went backstage to offer my congratulations to the many English artistes. A member of the audience is crowned Miss Statue of Liberty at the end of each performance. That night, when they saw me, I was destined to be the star. I was hurriedly dressed in the long costume,

Disney has imagined everything for them, and pushed to the front of the stage. I felt quite at home. Luckily I have a photograph of myself as the Statue of Liberty. Another part played by Eunice! If one negative comment might be expressed it would be, in my opinion, that the children have little opportunity to use their own imagination. But still, thank you Walt Disney for a quite brilliant experience.

One memorable day out was at The Everglades National Park, a vast expanse of marshland infested with crocodiles and many rare bird species. We took a tour which is specially designed for the tourist and is safe. Also, there is a place called Parrots Park, where these beautiful birds are trained to perform for an audience. We sat in a semi-circle to see the show and the birds appeared to be happy. I felt a huge admiration for these colourful parrots. The whole day was quite unforgettable as they counted numbers and obeyed all instruction with grace and expertise. But as I love birds, I prefer them to be free to fly away. Such is the variety and vitality of life in Florida, from the Everglades to the beautifully renovated art-deco buildings in South Beach.

With Jim Fisher and steam engine in Berkshire

In Corfu

15 Prince's Street,
Reading,
Berks.

3 September 1974.

To all at 'Dateline'.

I should like to write a letter in praise of
Eunice Black, who acted as your courier at the
Nissaki Beach Hotel this summer. While I was
staying there in August, I was full of admiration
for the way she carried out her duties, sometimes
in difficult circumstances. Not only did she
organize many boat trips, excursions and visits
to tavernas with extreme efficiency, but she also
made everyone feel relaxed and happy by her irresistable
cheerfulness and fascinating sense of humour. She was
discreet in dealing with people – which is not always
easy! – and encouraged everyone to come to her with
any problems, without 'forcing' herself on them. I
personally was very grateful for her presence. I came
on my own and, although I got on quite well with most
people, I still felt the need for a friendly chat or
a laugh (which never failed!) with someone with whom
I had something in common, and Eunice was always there
when needed.

I know that the job was only taken on in an emergency
and Eunice may not be willing or able to take it on again,
but I should be delighted if you could persuade her to
do so when I go on my next Dateline holiday.

With best wishes,

Yours sincerely,

Hward

Hennie Ward.

Praise indeed

Dr. PATRICK MOORE CBE FRAS   FARTHINGS,
                                               WEST STREET,
                                                 SELSEY,
                                                  SUSSEX.

Myd dear Eunice —

Things have been a little tricky, but
I phoned twice with nil result. MARCH 11
Friday. Can I take you out to lunch on that
day? If not, let me know another — my fax is
            .... phone is   . All
news then!!!!

            Much love

With Patrick Moore on an Hellenic Cruise

With Patrick Moore on an Hellenic Cruise

BOWRA, Sir

(Cecil) Maurice, Kt. cr. 1951; F.B.A. 1938; M.A.;
Warden of Wadham College, Oxford, since 1938;
b.8 April 1898, y.s. of late Cecil A.V. Bowra, Chinese
Customs Service. Educ.: Cheltenham Coll. (Scholar)
New Coll. Oxford (Sch.).   First class Hon.Mods. 1920;
1st Class Lit. Hum., 1922; Hon.Fellow1946; Conington
Prize, 1930; D.Litt. 1937; Hon.Litt.D. Dublin; Docteur
h.c. Paris, Aix. Joined R.F.A. 1917; served in France
1917-18. Fellow and Tutor Wadham College, Oxford 1922-38;
Prof. of Poetry 1946-51, Vice-Chancellor 1951-4.
President of the British Academy 1958-9. Commandeur de la
Legion d'Honneur.
Publications: Pindar's Pythian Odes, translated (with
H.T. Wade-Gery) 1928; co-Editor of the Oxford Book of
Greek verse, 1930; Tradition and Design in the Iliad, 1930;
Ancient Greek Literature (Home University Series);
Pindari Carmina (Oxford Classical Texts), 1935; Greek
Lyric Poetry, 1936; co-Editor of the Bxford Book of Greek
Verse in Translation, 1937; Early Greek Elegists, 1938;
The Heritage of Symbolism, 1943; A Book of Russian Verse,
1943; Sophoclean Tragedy 1944; From Virgil to Milton, 1945;
The Creative Experiment, 1949; The Romantic Imagination, 1950;
Herioc Poetry, 1952, Problems in Greek Poetry, 1954;
Inspiration and Poetry, 1955; The Greek Experience, 1957;
articles in the Classical Review and the Classical Quarterly.
Recreation: None
Address: Wadham College, Oxford.   T.4045.

On an Hellenic Cruise

FROM THE WARDEN
TELEPHONE NO. 44048

Wadham College
Oxford

Monday.

Dear Eunice.

Delighted to hear you are in Oxford. Could you come & have a drink at 6 on Friday? No answer unless you can't.

Yours ever
Maurice Bowra.

With the Very Reverend Eric Evans, Dean of St. Paul's

With Jane Seymour and Jenny Agutter, Disneyland, Los Angeles. 1977

The Keach family in 1995

With Joanna's son Julian at the annual C.I.D. ball, London 1977

**Doris Hare on her 90th birthday
at Denville Hall**

Robert and Polly Heitner

Beryl and Bill Roskelly with Hector Vasquez at Glyndebourne, 1977

At my christening in the crypt of St Paul Cathedral

As the Statue of Liberty – Florida   **In Miami during my convalescence**

Where most of the dictation took place in Miami

Roberto with Joanna and Renaldo, Christmas 1997

Joanna

Leonard Amborski

LIFE NINE
MY EARLY YEARS, SCHOOL DAYS, MY FAMILY

"no mewling and puking, no creeping like a snail
unwillingly to school; a joyous leap into wonderland"

One of my great pleasures as a child was to sit on the iron balustrade in the front garden and fall backwards into the privet hedge covered in white flowers. I would lie there thinking this was heaven until I was dragged out and taken indoors. Brothers and sisters do not always show their affection when young, but it is lovely to have a large family. They are fond of you, loyal without sentimentality. You learn quickly when surrounded by older people. My mother was 42 when I was born and my father 47. Her previous baby, Lucy, was born when she was 36. I was a surprise; I hope a pleasant one. Unfortunately for her, I had been born after the Great War had started in 1914. So it was a shock to have a new baby as her husband and her son William joined the Forces in France. I am constantly amazed at how much I remember from my early year. My sister Lucy and brother Fred were the closest to me in age and they were told by my mother early on that they would have to help take care of me. As you might imagine, they too were young and found baby Eunice a burden. They would wheel me up the hill in my perambulator and then, hoping I would die or that it would overturn at least, push it back downhill as I hurtled at vast speed. I would be out of their care for a while... But I would survive these onslaughts and run back up the hill, find where they were and at the top of my voice shout through the letter box: "Let me in! let me in!"

Children do not always love each other. They are self-absorbed, selfish.

When I was young I was never one to be left out of things. My sister Lucy would take me to the swimming pool at 7am before school. She could swim and I could not. I was left in the shallow end, shivering, with the water nearly up to my eyes while she continued to play with her friends at the other end of the pool. With the inexpressible frustration of a four year old, I demanded to know: "What do I have to do to swim?"

Lucy and her pals came over and said: "Put your arms forward and your legs up behind and kick out and then towards the middle."

I was very proud of myself when I managed it, spluttering my face downwards in the water. My sister stared and cried: "Oh look! little Eunice can swim."

So, older family and lots of determination can make one more advanced for one's age. I am often asked: "As the youngest, were you spoiled?"

No, I certainly was not; not when you are the 9th child and there is nothing unusual or outstanding about you.

I was born at 13 Lloyd Road, a terraced house, Walthamstow, London E17. Upstairs, there were three small bedrooms. Downstairs, one long corridor led from front door to back with a small earthy garden at the rear of the house. All the houses were laid out in this way up and down the street. The front parlour, the special room, was seldom used. It was select for Sunday visitors. As children I never remember us playing in there at all. The fireplace had an open fire with fascinating velvet decorations along the top and sides with bobbles of velvet which I thought were entrancing. In the centre of the room there was a glass dome under which was either a stuffed bird or an arrangement of dried flowers. These were the height of fashion. There was a precious clock that was made of black marble and was probably quite valuable. It chimed regularly. The curtains seemed huge and also had velvet bobbles, there must have been a mania in Victorian times to put them on everything. In the window, on a stand, there was a large bowl containing a gigantic aspidistra; each week the leaves were cleaned with a damp cloth. The parlour was the Valhalla of the working class home.

An early memory was that of a very tall man in full military uniform picking me up in his arms. It must have been my brother William on leave during World War One. My sister later told me that those few steps taken towards William were in fact my first. I also remember being called the "coon" by my other older brother George. I was so called because I was born with a mass of very black hair and not as a result of a corruption of the name Eunice. It is strange that I should remember these two moments in particular. I was called "Coonie," it became my nick-name and just the other day my sister called me that without thinking. I said nothing, but it made me think that after all this time such a term of affection, as nick-names are, was still being used. A sign, that although poor, we were a happy and affectionate family.

The kitchen is where the family did most of their day to day living. The scullery, beyond the kitchen, was dominated by a giant copper under which a fire was lit every Monday morning to wash all the family clothes and linen (if you had or could afford any!). There was a large oak dresser in the kitchen which held the plates etc, the pots and pans, and the cooking utensils. The cupboard doors at the bottom of the dresser had been removed and replaced with a curtain. All the family shoes were kept there. Charged with minding baby Eunice when she was a young child, but wanting to play with their friends, Lucy and Fred (who were great pals) decided to hide me among the shoes in this curtained area. Perhaps that is when I first enjoyed the mystery of the actor's hidden presence behind curtains. I drew them apart and peered at an audience.

I remember that our family of nine made the house feel very crowded indeed. And so, like many others, we were street children. We played hopscotch, skipping and hide & seek. It was neighbourly, innocent and friendly. There were places of interest nearby that we could explore. Such as the park and the barrows in the market in Walthamstow High Street which I loved. When I see the children running and playing around the stalls in the Portobello Road Market, it reminds me of my early years. Most children find markets of all kind mysterious and interesting. They are full of colour, shapes & smells. A wonderland.

I admired the Lloyd Park Museum near Forest Road. It had been the home of William Morris. We thought this marvellous pavilion was the residence of a King. There was a theatre and a lake. It was a place of grandeur and mystery to explore, our idea of Buckingham Palace. Epping Forest is beautiful. We would be taken there on the tram, as exciting a journey as a trip to the Moon might be today! Ours was a far more simple childhood. We made up our own fun and used our imagination to create adventures. When I was born, we did not have radio, television or cinema. We did have an upright piano and toys and table games such as Ludo, Snakes & Ladders and playing cards; and these provided our entertainment.

One day whilst in Walthamstow Market with my mother, we became separated. I was four years old and no longer held her hand. I was terrified; it was a crowded busy day. I can see the street corner and people bending down over me. Thank God my mother came along, rescued me and we returned home. You can understand why little children become so afraid if separated from a parent or a loved one. At that age the world is full of giants, dragons and strangers. You hold tight to your mother's hand whatever.

I remember being taken into the school playground to see an eclipse of the sun. We were told to bring a piece of smoked glass. George put a candle flame to a piece of glass. This was the protection for my eyes. The world went dark, the sun was black with a golden outline, like a black football on fire. I thought it was about to fall out of the sky. Another time, a crowded street gazed in wonder at a huge cigar-shaped balloon passing overhead. It had a gondola suspended under it. A Zeppelin. It did not prove effective in combat as it was easily pierced and exploded. The Great War did not enter my world as it was waged abroad, elsewhere. Many years later I saw the musical "Oh What a lovely War" and at last I understood the horrible waste, horror and misery that my brother William and my father had suffered when I was a child.

My acting career actually began when I was five. I went to Blackhorse Road Infant School in a class of 45 boys and girls. On the first day, the class teacher, a stern tall lady who filled me with awe, instructed us to stand and speak our names clearly one at a time. I said: "Eunice Holden" in my deep contralto.

"Come here" she cried.

Nervously I walked to the front of the class and stood by her side, trembling.

"Don't be funny" she said.

I wondered if maybe she thought I was playing a game with her. So, I learned at an early age the dangers of being a comedienne.

They also realised that I had excellent talent to memorise and would be good in the school play. My first performance came during parents' visiting day when I recited "Sir Patrick Spens" at great speed. A lengthy ballad. My eyes fixed on a ceiling electric light. I was terrified. Even my mother sitting in the front row could not give me confidence. Later I played Joseph in the Christmas nativity play with rather less stage fright. I was Joseph and believed every word. My first experience as an actress feeling I was another person. I remember every moment of that baptism of fire.

Later in Junior School I was very lucky indeed to have Miss Ridgeway and Miss Curtis as my teachers. They were dedicated lovers of theatre and poetry. We learned a great many poems from the "Golden Treasury," including "Ode to Autumn" by John Keats which I was later to recite as the school teacher at the beginning of Tony Richardson's film "A taste of Honey."

"We want you for your voice" were his words!

We spoke clearly and loudly and learned to project. It was wonderful training. Those teachers were a wonderful inspiration. I was able to read when I was four and had a capacity to learn quickly. My mother and my teachers agreed that I should be sent up to a higher grade immediately. Unfortunately they were somewhat ahead of me and I had difficulty at first catching up, with mathematics in particular, but it soon improved.

In the classroom there were written Shakespearean quotations pinned to the board such as:

> *"Speak the speech,*
>   *As I pronounced it to you.*
>   *Trippingly on the tongue..."*

A whole speech from "HAMLET" Act 3, scene 1, was on the wall facing me. "HAMLET" I thought, what does a small village have to do with anything!

They took us to see Miss Marjorie Gullan's lovely Ladies Voice Choir in Woburn Square. I don't think they exist anymore but they were quite unique. To use the human voice in such a manner, to speak the verse as if sung with music of it's own; contralto, soprano, just like opera singers, but without instrumental music. Later when I became a teacher I introduced this type of choir and it became very popular indeed with my teenage girls. They loved poetry, spoke clearly and listened to the beautiful sound of the English language when spoken not sung.

When I started at Junior school we moved to a newly built house on a Council Estate facing the edge of Epping Forest. It had a large garden, back and front and was situated at 217 Hale End Road, Woodford Green, Essex. Epping Forest was given to the people of London by Queen Elizabeth I and still remains open to all. It is long and narrow in shape, about 10 miles long going North. It still has wild deer and rabbits. We spent much time outdoors after moving to our new house. We had a pussy cat. It was like heaven for us and we loved it. Along the street, other families were arriving and we soon made new friends. We also loved playing in the Forest which was safe, unlike today. We played Robin Hood and Maid Marion, cowboys and Indians, climbed trees, made little caves and hid in them. Playing tag, we'd count to one hundred and hide leaving little marks on the trees to be found by the pursuer. It was exciting.

Children love clowns, they perform acrobatics, have pointed gargoyle laces, are grotesque and wear outrageously baggy clothes of vivid hues. They have enormous shoes, they fall over, throw custard pies and are the epitome of disasters of every kind. And we laugh. In Epping Forrest, my young friends and I, discovered an old man who lived alone and slept outdoors under a bush. He had a wooden leg, was shabby, unshaven. He pushed a wooden box on two wheels which contained all his worldly goods – a few cardboard packets. We thought he was a sad clown, or a wicked ogre. We called him "Peggy wooden-leg." We laughed at him sometimes and threw stones. He turned on us, growled and swore wicked words. We ran away at high speed. I realised later the sadness of an old man who was homeless, friendless, without family and was probably a casualty of the Great War. But children so young cannot understand, nor should they. But it is sad, that in the year 2000 homelessness still persists. This new century must bring solutions.

After an afternoon playing in the forest we'd cross the fields and return to our own gardens. It is awful that some are obliged to live in concrete jungles; the outdoors is so important to children. Nowadays many cannot play free from fear in our city streets, our parks and forests; young people sit indoors watching television, pressing knobs and are entertained by others. In retrospect, I am happy that I was young when we amused ourselves with our friends and were not afraid.

Our teachers always encouraged us to the front of the class to act out any subject we happened to be studying at the time, such as Literature or History; the "Wind in the Willows" or Christopher Columbus' travels. They also founded a Drama Club which met one evening a week and said that any profits derived from the performances would go for World peace keeping at the League of Nations in Geneva. This Drama Club was a marvellous stepping stone to my eventual career as an actress. Gradually I lost my fear of standing on a stage. Later as a visiting teacher, I was able to recognize in others this fear of facing an audience. Student teachers facing a large class of teenagers for the first time can also become speechless with fear.

They sent us to competitions (known as eisteddfods) in Stratford East in London where we would recite various poems or act playlets. The prizes were fabulous books and I often won and proudly took my prizes back home to show to my brother George. He filled our house with books and classical music and I wanted to start my very own collection.

Our move to Woodford made us feel, like our neighbours, that we had gone from being inner London cockneys to outer London refugees and as we were on a Council Estate, we were all brothers in spirit. My mother realised early on that we were considered the low-brows of the area, the working class, because we were situated near Highams Park where people could afford to buy their own detached or semi-detached Edwardian houses. The English class system divided us, we Council house tenants were far too near for comfort. The working class had moved in to their area and we were made to feel a different species. As a child I was not aware of class distinctions. The Council house "divide" was new. Soon I had middle-class friends who were equally unaware of class distinctions. When I was invited to tea at their houses, the parents were amazed that Eunice from the Council Estate had passed the 11 plus scholarship and was top of the class.

"Do your brothers write your essays? You have classical books and records."

I made friends and my mother invited them into the house and out into the garden where laughter and singing, books and music, always prevailed. In later years some of my middle class childhood friends said that the best part of their education was when: "We invaded your house."

There was always so much of interest there. They were people who were not snobbish although much wealthier than us.

The houses were extremely well built and are still standing today looking immaculate. I am happy that my mother had the courage to up-lift us from the grime and the crowded 1920 slum of central London to the relative paradise of a new house in Woodford Green.

I was sent to Church as soon as I was old enough. It must have been High Church of England and I loved it. The procession of the Clergy and Choristers was rather theatrical I suppose. I loved the music and sang loudly when I knew the Hymns. I was in awe of the building itself and the language used therein and being there was my passage to heaven. At Sunday school I was given little pictures of biblical characters which I stuck in an album. They told you the stories from the Bible. I was wide-eyed with wonder and found the Bible readings absorbing, imaginative and completely truthful. When young I was not critical and going to Church and Sunday school were activities that I loved. I do not understand why today people are against young children receiving religious instruction.

"You are converting them to Christianity, how dare you?" they cry.

There is surely nothing wrong with that, you can reject it later it you wish. But as a child it takes you out of yourself and introduces you to the spiritual, to the meaning of man's relationship to others in love and brotherhood. Surely it cannot be wrong to be made aware early that there is more to life than acquiring material things, that spiritual matters are even more important.

In my teens, I became a disbeliever. I became cynical and critical and clever, thought miracles impossible. I had heard of Karl Marx who had said: "Religion is the opium of the masses."

Didn't quite know what he meant, as I did not know the meaning of opium, nor did I know what or who were "masses of people." You become critical at that period in your life. Adults, in wars have ruined the world. You the younger generation will restore order, peace and justice to a new Jerusalem. It is a pity that each generation does not necessarily succeed.

I am most grateful to my parents for giving me, despite their poverty, a healthy beginning to life. I have an excellent heart, good lungs, blood and bones. I had four brothers, all over six feet tall, handsome and intelligent. That inheritance of good genes is most important in life and will keep you in good stead throughout your life.

From an early age my mother talked to me about politics. In Walthamstow west, the many times re-elected Labour MP was Val la Touche McKenzie. A kind, gentle old man with a flowing moustache. West Walthamstow was full of prosperous factories. There was always plenty of work. I now lived in East Walthamstow and the MP was Sir Brograve Beacham. My mother said to me one day: "I've joined the Labour Party; there will shortly be a General Election and you must help me as I have volunteered to deliver pamphlets through all the doors in the area."

She said that she had also joined the Co-operative Society, a working class enterprise that offered dividends with each purchase, providing a sense of self respect for the poorer people.

She gave me a huge pile of envelopes to be addressed to all the houses in the locality. I delivered them by hand. I was eleven years old.

She then said: "I am going canvassing, I shall knock at doors and try to convince people to vote Labour."

I accompanied her from door to door. I became politically aware at an early age and the first sparks of socialist idealism began to enter my head. I discovered that some people were very poor and should not be, some were hungry and all was not well in the world. Some were much richer, some were unemployed. I had read about the poor miners who had marched all the way to London from Yorkshire protesting that they were starving, were paid only shillings a week. I began to question the inevitability of poverty, began to question the class system. I realise now in old age that every single country has devised its own class system. It is an almost natural route in the development among all races, the haves and the have-nots! The energetic and the lazy, the ambitious and the unambitious, the able and the stupid; summed up by George Bernard Shaw in his classic play "PYGMALION" spoken by Alfred P. Doolittle (perfectly well named!) the dustman: "..there are the deserving poor and undeserving poor. I belong to the undeserving." Quite right.

At high school, aged 12, I was also on the net ball team. I had started to get very tall by then and my being a junior was often questioned by teachers and players from opposing teams. We also played hockey which was considered rather middle class back then, maybe still. We played on Saturday afternoons either at home or away. But always during the interval we had an opportunity to meet the girls from other schools whilst enjoying some lemonade or orange juice.

The school uniform had to be bought by one's parents. My mother was a widow and had very little money. It consisted of a black velour hat with a band and a badge at the front, a green tunic to match and a white blouse, black bloomers, a liberty bodice instead of a brassiere. We had no bosoms at that age, but later we did wear the brassieres. The school's colours were bottle green and yellow. Very glamorous without realising it, we wore long black stockings with a seam up the back which went right up to our crutch! We attached suspenders from the liberty bodice onto the top of the stockings, no garters. We were required to have a pair of gym slippers, and a school blazer with a large badge on the left breast pocket.

My dear mother went to Walthamstow High Street to the Saturday stalls and found some rather horrible green wool material. On a hand-operated sewing machine she made my tunic for me and other required items. I cannot imagine what I looked like compared to the other girls who had the official uniform. God knows what the teachers thought of me. Well, I didn't know or care, it was a wonderful school and I was very happy. Each form elected a prefect and I was to be the first with a badge on my tunic. Joanna, who was to become my life long friend, was in the same class and was the games' captain.

We had a marvellous Physical Education teacher, Miss Squire. When in the gymnasium performing various activities, I unfortunately discovered that the sleeves of my blouse were becoming undone and the seams on my bloomers were splitting. Very sadly, my mother's eye sight was failing and although these were her best efforts, the garments were quite simply not stitched up properly. Bless her. Eventually my mother must have been contacted by the school authorities and was requested to acquire the correct clothing for me, which somehow she did. I had that one outfit until I was 16 years old. By then I had started making my own clothes. My sister Deborah bought me the necessary Butterick patterns, she taught me how to sew, which I did and made my own clothing. I enjoyed this practical work and found that I had a flair for it. Maybe I inherited some manual skills from my mother's father and his father before him who were cabinet makers in Islington in the 19th Century. Extraordinarily, my brother had bought a Meccano set for me and I adored it despite the fact that this was traditionally a game for boys. I made scale models and followed the instructions to make a bridge or a lift. I was absorbed with my screw driver and little nuts and bolts. The other entertainment provided by my mother was an upright piano. I do not know where it originated. There was no radio yet and certainly no television. We had one weekly visit to the cinema…so the piano was marvellous and she paid a local teacher 6p a lesson to teach Lucy who became a very good pianist. When I was old enough to start taking lessons, wishing to emulate my sister, the piano, very sadly, disappeared one day. I came home from school to find there was just a shadow on the wallpaper.

"What has happened to the piano."

My mother said: "I have had to sell the piano in order to pay for your school uniform."

My mother went to Woolworth, then known as the "six penny" store, a heavenly gift for the working class, nothing was more than sixpence. Ideal for those unemployed or poor. Incredibly, my mother would buy second hand spectacles there. The National Health Service did not exist yet and no medical services were free. If you needed to go to the Doctor, Dentist or Optician; you had to pay. My mother would not spend money on such things unless absolutely necessary and thankfully I remember always being well and healthy. Having toothpaste in the house was a special treat, normally it would be a pinch of salt on the brush. My mother would always have boracic powder or ointment on hand. It was cheap and good.

For breakfast we would have porridge with milk and sugar and a lovely dollop of treacle or golden syrup. I was sent off to school feeling warm and healthy. I was growing last and these foods were good fillers; she prepared suet puddings both with meat & potatoes and also as a dessert with raisins and currants and the odd bit of peel, and they were delicious. She went down to the butcher in the High Street and bought fresh suet and cheap off-cuts from which she made very good soups which were inexpensive, added a few vegetables and the result was a healthy diet. Today, these traditional dishes have become fashionable again in smart restaurants, very ironical.

Many of the women were widowed during the 1914-1918 War and were bringing up families on very little money. School dinners were not introduced until 1922. Those women used their common sense and were very resourceful. We were healthier then because we ate less out of necessity. Frozen or convenience foods did not exist. We ate fresh fruits and vegetables and more often than not walked to our destinations.

Unusually tall and thin for 17, I do remember regularly feeling hungry despite hearty breakfasts. At morning assembly we sang a hymn and a lesson was read by the Head Mistress. We would then kneel, and one morning I fell over. The teachers immediately picked me up and took me into the rest room. What was wrong they inquired?

"Her period?..."
"The mumps, what?"
I sighed: "Just a square meal is what I would like please."

I had not eaten much in the previous 2 days. They sent me home. That day I realised, perhaps for the first time, what a terrific struggle life was for my mother to keep us alive with such humour and love. My brother George, who never married, supported us with his entire salary from his job in the Civil Service. She and George kept herself, himself, Lucy, Fred and me. How they managed I cannot imagine, but we were well taken care of. That diet was similar to war rations to which we were all subjected later from 1939 to 1952.

We would walk to school most of the time or might sometimes take a bus. It was a quarter of a mile to the bus stop and a penny ride would take me to Wood Street Station and then I would walk a further half a mile uphill, round the Church and into the School. It was an extra penny to remain on the bus and travel up the hill and those with more pocket money would do this. We went home for lunch and thus did this journey four times a day. I would set out in the morning, meet my friend Mary French on the bus. At Wood Street she would carry on and I would walk the rest. It happened occasionally in the winter that my mother did not have the 4 pennies for the bus and would tell us the previous evening that we had to get up early the next morning and walk the two miles. I knew the short cuts and I didn't mind at all. It didn't happen often. She didn't like me walking in the rain and quite apart from that it caused the shoe leather to wear out faster. These days there are terrible traffic problems at school delivery times because everybody uses their cars and nobody walks anymore. There is also the sad and terrible prospect of a young child being abducted or molested on their way to or from school. A sad comment on the violence of the present age.

I expressed the desire to go to Walthamstow High School, which I had visited a few years earlier when Lucy was a student there. The Head Mistress, Miss Norris, had theatrical connections and had invited Sybil Thorndike, a leading classical actress, to open the Greek Theatre she had had built in the grounds with a performance of MEDEA... When choosing High Schools I declared that I wanted to go to the place where the woman had killed her children!

What a change from junior school! We now had several teachers presiding over several forty-minute periods. The classrooms had a long blackboard, a platform and a desk for the teacher. I loved our French teacher. Mademoiselle Grimaud who was from Lyon. She was quite marvellous and taught us her native language with undoubted accuracy. Miss Jacob's teaching of Geometry & Algebra etc., was competent no doubt, but a little complex for me at first. I had History with Miss Newmarch who had the seemingly magical ability of making the subject come to real life. Her hair was parted in the middle and platted into circles over each ear giving the impression of earphones! Miss Hall was like an old Victorian governess with big flat shoes, a high waisted skirt and blouse. She taught us poetry.

I had my moments of naughtiness. I once encouraged the class to make stick-on white teeth out of paper, stand up and show them off when Miss Hall entered the room. We all got into trouble for that one, and God forgive me, I was the instigator. But mostly I was well behaved as a prefect and Miss Park told me much later that they had decided upon first seeing me to give me some responsibility as an incentive to remain well behaved...

We all loved books at home and all had Library cards that we used frequently. George, in any case, was a great lover of books and our house was always full of them. Miss Park, my English teacher had a great gift for her chosen career and also encouraged me to read. She was a marvellous teacher of Literature and loved all things theatrical. Walthamstow Public library in the nearby High Street was first class and I can never forget the helpful gentleman there who would find all the books I needed to do my homework; I hope it is still there and maintains its wonderful reputation. The afore mentioned Val la Touche McKenzie had arranged (all those years ago – late 20's, early 30's) for there to be quiet places for children from difficult and noisy homes to do their homework. Fortunately, my home was quiet and loving. The public baths were near the Library and I loved swimming. We could go at 2pm and be back at school by 3pm for the last hour I loved going with my school chums, that was great fun.

Miss Park once asked George if she could take me to Stratford upon Avon for a day's visit to see a play. My brother agreed and thanked her. She had told him that she thought I should be an actress, but should get to University first. On arrival in Stratford she asked what I thought of the new pickle factory down by the river. A pickle factory? She was joking, attempting to convey her dislike for the modem architecture of the building. The new Shakespeare Memorial Theatre, as it then was, and which is now one of the RSC's homes. This, I think was 1931. On another occasion she took me to Cambridge to visit the avant-garde Festival Theatre, which was more or less in the round, rather like a circular Mermaid Theatre. I was knocked sideways by the under-gradu-ates and their performances. God knows what the play was, they all wore half & half, head to toe costumes; one side white, the other black. This was 1932, I fell in love with Cambridge and dreamed of returning one day as a student.

Many moons later, I met Miss Park on a bus. I was going to visit the School. What a surprise that was. Great hello's ensued, she was wearing a flat cap on her head and had clearly forgotten it was there as she was wearing another hat on top of it. That was Miss Park! She lived to 78 and we always kept in touch; she came to my wedding. When I was working in the West End she would come and see me and take me out to tea between shows, at The Ivy or somewhere. She would say what a terrible play it was and what was I doing in it. I had to earn my living.

I was extremely fortunate to be in the class of Miss Annette Park, who was an Oxford graduate and loved to direct plays. She made great use of the Greek theatre and of the school stage. Usually we would act Shakespeare and other classics but at Christmas time we were permitted to do send-ups and revues. To think that we had such literary delights in East London; it was a wonderful school. When cast in some of Miss Park's plays I felt I was becoming quite experienced and behaved like a real pro. I always knew my lines and projected well which was very important especially in the outdoors. It was at this time that I became, I suppose, unconsciously, fond of the theatre and performing. When I played Agamemnon with a black beard in Euripides' play "Iphigenia in Aulis," my mother came to a performance. Afterwards, still in costume. I asked if she had enjoyed it. Upset, she said: "You wicked man..."

"Mother...'tis I, Eunice," I cried.

It would seem I had given a convincing performance...

Miss Park also instigated a form of contest whereby we would select some scenes from various plays by Shakespeare to perform and after an initial elimination round conducted by Miss Park, a famous West End actor would come and judge the finalists. I chose Coriolanus which they thought was a brave choice. Later I also played Prospero and Brutus. My fear lessened each time I performed one of those difficult roles. She did indeed give us same unforgettable experiences. Miss Park and her colleagues followed us throughout our years at High School. They didn't marry and were totally dedicated to their chosen vocation. And thank God; it is we who benefited from their wisdom. I am very fortunate to have had teachers of such calibre who inspired us, without being patronising, with a love for the best in art, painting, music and literature.

Because I had played the leading character of Marlowe in "She Stoops to Conquer," Miss Park asked me if I would direct a production of this play. It came as a lovely distraction after the very hard months I had been through taking my A Levels which I accomplished in History, Geography and Latin. We rehearsed for 3 weeks and performed at the end of the term. Afterwards I was completely exhausted and slept for 2 days. I now realised the level of concentration and energy required to do such a full-length play. To much acclaim, Dora Bryan and Tom Baker appeared in this play many years later at the Old Vic Theatre. I was privileged to see their great comic performances.

The 1933 summer term came to an end and Miss Norris asked what my plans were. I had thought of being a doctor but was dissuaded when told of the monetary requisite and that grants were virtually unheard of in those days for women. They were allocated to the men as women would get married and become housewives. Further, with 3 million unemployed, women had to give up work on marriage by law! I then suggested I would like to be an actress perhaps. She was horrified. I didn't understand her reaction considering I had been in all the school plays. Maybe I could get a scholarship to R.A.D.A...

"No, no, no," she went on...
"You should consider becoming a missionary in darkest Africa..."

Well no thanks. I was not interested in that. According to Miss Norris, there was only one avenue left. I should be a teacher. For that there was a small grant, and a place at Homerton College, Cambridge.

"Cambridge" I wondered...remembering my visit there with Miss Park. "Is it not the case that Oxbridge colleges are exclusively for the very rich?" I asked Miss Norris.

"...No, my dear, those who are bright and intelligent can qualify." George recommended that I take this option as I had nothing to lose. If I didn't like teaching, I would still have a degree which would be most useful in the future to obtain a good job anywhere, even though teachers were taking pay cuts to help the desperate financial predicament caused by the crash of Wall Street which began in 1929. I thought, I must be able to take care of myself, be independent. "Fine, I will go to Homerton, it will be lovely."

So, I was directed into teaching. As time went on I came to enjoy it more and more and I had a regular income. For the time being my acting and directing ambitions would be satisfied with work with amateur groups.

I was 19 years old and had no money to spend during the long vacation before going off to College. I learned very young that money cannot give you much pleasure if you are void of imagination. I don't ever remember being miserable. It you have a loving home you could get through anything. I was not due at Homerton College's first term until September and was delighted when Miss Park approached me with an offer to direct a group of graduates, who had formed a Shakespearean Society, in a production of Midsummer Night's Dream in the Greek Theatre at their old school. Miss Park told me that she had already started rehearsals but that she did not have the time to continue. Would I take over? I was so young, not sure, but confident. I thought of this as an opportunity not to be missed. After all she had trained me well and I had no fears. I started work with these older people who accepted me immediately as their Director. A huge relief. We worked out all the movements and the distribution of the characters. So you see, this was to be my holiday. No money required, just a little for the tram journeys. Two of my friends from the 6th form, Joanna Barrett (later Mrs. Christians) and Edna Willesden got involved with this project. Edna had received training as an artist and would design the sets and costumes and Joanna who was learning classical ballet at the Rambert Ballet School, then at the Mercury Theatre in Notting Hill Gate, managed to get some time off and would imagine the choreography. She would also be the lead dancer which would be a vast improvement on the clod hopping dancers usually associated with amateur productions.

I went down to the boys' Grammar School and asked if any of the boys would like to be in the play. I approached the Music Master and asked him if he would arrange the music, form an orchestra and conduct Mendelssohn's – Midsummer Nights' Dream. He agreed. I asked the Science Master if his boys could see to the lighting. They were all extremely cooperative and enthusiastic. I do not know how I had the impertinence and the cheek to ask all these people to help. I became so immersed in the project and just wanted to bring this marvellous play to life with this very fine cast of actors. Harry Hyde, the senior French Master of the Grammar School was to play Puck, and very good he was too. Miss Park & Miss Norris asked how it was going and had we fixed a date yet for opening night? Yes...and could they prepare the programmes for me? I did not want any daytime performances. The Dream is for an evening audience, with all the magic that the Greek theatre could bestow. One day during rehearsals, I was surprised to see a London Electricity Board truck arrive with what appeared to be miles of cables.

"What is this?" I enquired.
 "We are here to arrange the lighting for your play, Miss."

The Science Master and his boys had done us proud I thought. He, myself and the electricians went through the details so as to provide the best possible effects. The finale with Oberon and Titania's reconciliation, with the Fairies and all; it would look just marvellous with these brilliant lights. I have never seen The Dream at the Open Air in Regent's Park but this, mine own production, moved me enormously. I can still see it. By the way, I had not been able to resist playing Oberon myself and have the opportunity to recite Shakespeare's breathtaking poetry... The lights dimmed and we flew across the stage passed the central altar up to the great porch and on into the night...and we left Puck alone with a diminished spot light on him...

"Give me your hands if we be friends...
and Robin will restore amends.."

The production was an immense success, with queues forming down Church Hill. Banners were placed in the High Street and elsewhere announcing Shakespeare at the Walthamstow High School. People came from miles around to see for the first time in 1934, an open air production of Shakespeare's masterpiece.

The following year I was asked to do "As you like it" and the next "The Tempest" and "Twelfth Night." Looking back, these summers directing Shakespeare, were the best holidays of my life. This will seem incredible to modern generations of students who now travel extensively during the summer holiday, and at such an early age. But I was more than content and in those days you didn't think of travel. I have not been back to that lovely Greek Theatre at Walthamstow High School for a very, very long time. I do sincerely hope that it is still there and being used to the same effect as it was in my day, but I doubt it.

My mother had waved me off at Highams Park Station as I was leaving home for Cambridge to be a student.

"Be a good girl" were her last words to me as I waved her goodbye to start my new life away from home. At Liverpool Street Station I changed trains for Cambridge. I was a day late, having been given permission to arrive on Sunday because I had directed and performed in the Greek theatre the night before. My dear mother had attended the last performance. I am glad our good-byes were said there with Shakespeare and the memory of a lovely evening in London town.

* * *

My father died in 1942 aged 72. I thought he had died after the Great War in1920. George must have known he was still alive yet never told us or took us to him. I would like an explanation out of curiosity. George, a kind & good man decided what was best for the family, of that I am sure. My mother was born on 12 December 1872, married on 16 September 1894 and died on 4 November 1934. My father was 27 and my mother 22 when they married at Holy Trinity Church in lslington.

Wishing to forget the horrors of the 1914-1918 War, my eldest brother Bill emigrated to Regina, Saskatchewan in Canada and became a farmer. He wanted to leave Europe and all memories of those years. It was 1930 when he came back for one month. I looked out of the window at No. 217 and said: "There's a Holden walking up the path."

There was much rejoicing. He wanted to make one visit to see his family. Fortunately we still lived in the same house. It was a happy reunion. I have a photograph of him. He went back after a month and we never saw him again. Dear Bill, died a bachelor in Regina. In his will, he left his final possessions to any surviving Holden brothers or sisters. Lucy replied to the Canadian Authorities that there were 5 siblings alive. We each received £200. How kind of brother Bill, whom we did not know, to think of us at the end of his life.

My brother Albert Edward was born on 4 January 1903, married

Phyllis Sandel in 1932 arid died on 20 August 1994 at the age of 91. He trained to be an engineer during a seven-year apprenticeship but became a City of London police officer working at Snow Hill Station near the Bank of England and the Mansion House. He had two daughters who have recently come into my life having found my details in their father's personal papers after his death. Another brother Frederick Charles was born on 17 April 1907 and died on 6 February 1978.

I remember George more as a father than my brother. He was the one always there caring for everybody and certainly caring for me from my birth. He was born on 8 September 1899 and christened George Thomas. He died on 14 July 1972. I was glad that I was at his bedside in hospital in East London during those last days of his life and sat with him, not knowing the end was so near. The nurses allowed me to sit with him from 10am, I held his hand, his eyes were closed and he was very ill. I thought that he would get better. At 7pm, I said that I would go and return the next morning. I lived in Swiss Cottage and arrived home at 8pm. As I walked through the door the telephone was ringing: the nurse said that as soon as I had left, he had died. It was a terrible shock but I was with him almost to the last moment. He was a good, kind, funny and generous man. I was very lucky to be cared for by him from childhood. There was lots of fun; friends calling in all the time, chatting and laughing.

When I think of how limited funds were it is amazing that he took me, in my teens, to the "Ballets Russes de Monte Carlo," to classical theatre and to some of the classic Aldwych farces. I am sure the sexual innuendo of the latter went right over my innocent young head. But I do remember laughing a great deal. Little did I know that years later, I would play in "Rookery Nook" myself, firstly playing Aunt Gertrude and later the housekeeper, directed by Ralph Lynn himself, the original silly fool innocent hero.

When I was 10, George said: "You are going to school today to take a scholarship exam; I want you to do your best. We think you are quite good…if you don't pass you will not get the scholarship but in any case you will go to the High School as we will pay the fees if necessary; but of course the scholarship is preferable."

I did not let him down…I was first out of 1200. I left very grateful to my teachers at junior school and especially to George for his support and encouragement.

I have so many marvellous memories of my dear brother George. I remember following him around as a toddler, in the garden, helping him to plant runner beans. I would hand him beans. He would plant them in and I would watch them grow. Eventually I would help to pick them. They were delicious. He also built a garden shed. He was no mechanic, and I would hold the nails and hammer for him. He was not very good at this. He repeatedly banged his thumb. It would bleed. I would tie it up with a bit of rag. We planted bulbs and wait for the tulips to come out. He loved flowers and so did I, still do to this day. He planted a vegetable garden at one end. He would explain to me how all the vegetables would grow. I thought it was fascinating.

Nobody, in those days could afford a car, cars were for the rich or middle class. George joined the CTC and his long holidays were spent cycling all over England and France with his friends in the Club. He also joined a yachting/sailing club where he could go as a member of the crew. I still have a copy of the "Yachting Monthly". He and his very good friends went down to Burnham on Crouch in Essex to join their yacht. They entered the sailing competition of the year, quite an adventure and considered by some to be dangerous. Expert sailing was required. They sailed to Norway and back and that year George and his friends won. The account of that voyage was given in the magazine with photographs. In one, George and his friends look starved, worn out and appear like convicts. They were very happy to have survived and were back in harbour. The crossing to Bergen was stormy but with a southwesterly gale behind them, the sailing was very fast. The return journey was extremely stormy and the main mast had snapped during a storm.

I remember George staggering in, looking very thin and haggard, hair matted…Thank goodness he was home safe. He had survived on cold tinned food for all that time. There was no time for cooking as they were constantly in fear of the yacht overturning in the enormously high waves. I remember George with great love. He was an adventurous man who made many friends everywhere. For his holidays he used his long legs and his brave spirit. He always encouraged me to go abroad. When I was 17, our Headmistress announced that they were sending a delegation from the school to Geneva to witness at first hand the important work being done at the League of Nations. George acquired my first passport for me. I had not expected to go to Paris and France until I was earning my own money. My friend David Thomson who was Master of Sidney Sussex College, Cambridge, came round one day and said: "Eunice should not go with a school group, she should come with our Cambridge University group with the undergraduates."

So it was to be. What luck; my first journey abroad was with undergraduates from Cambridge. To visit the League of Nations and beautiful lake Geneva and Paris was an unexpected joyous occasion. I was attentive to every detail from the moment we left as I would be reporting back to my school.

We went by train through Paris. I remember being served lunch in an elegant Hotel. At 17 years old I was served delicious and, to me, exotic French food which we had not seen before. Each plate contained a huge artichoke. There was a great silence. Nobody knew what they were or what to do with them. I felt like putting one on my head as a hat. Finally, one of the more understanding waiters leant forward and showed us what to do. When I returned to school I stood on the stage and told of my travels. Teachers and students listened in awe. Travel abroad was a great, rare experience. Travel to the whole world is commonplace now. Like Puck in Midsummer Night's Dream... "I'll put a girdle round about the earth in 40 minutes."

I had started to realise how good George was to us and to appreciate everything he did for us. I hated asking him for money. He was so generous. He never expected any thanks. He was a lovely man. During the long holidays from Cambridge I took care of the household, Fred was back from New Zealand and George kept us all. During that time I also directed four Shakespeare comedies in the Greek Theatre.

During the 1939-1945 War, George was sent to North Wales with confidential Inland Revenue documents. He hated leaving London and returned after a year. He was in a reserved occupation He was now 41. He would have been conscripted later if necessary. I went to visit him in Llandudno on one of my leaves from my war work with children in London (1939-1946) and spent a fortnight with him. We were very amused on how different the people in North Wales were to those in London. They would speak Welsh when we passed by. They were not friendly. The landlady of my hotel asked for my ration book immediately. She removed all the coupons. She served us minuscule meals, but it was war. We expected smaller meals. On my last day, I stumbled into the kitchen by mistake, the whole Welsh family were there around a table groaning with delicious food. I realised that most of our rations went into the family kitchen.

After the war, George and Fred became like a couple of bachelors sharing the house at 217. I married and left that home forever. When George was ill for months, I visited him every day and on Saturdays cooked him a lunch. We had long talks. There was a great rapport between us; especially when talking of the arts and of travel.

"You're not going to put me in a home?"
"Never," said I.

So I bought 119 Elgin Crescent close by and modernised it, made it a home especially for George and myself and any others. Alas, he died before that could happen. So farewell George, always in my heart.

My elder sister Florence Deborah was born on 15 July 1900 and died in 1981 in London. Her husband, Philip Bernstein died a year later in Santo Domingo in the Dominican Republic My other sister, Lucy Isabelle Charlotte was born on 6 March 1909 and is still alive. The three sisters were interesting, three different characters like Chekhov's "Three Sisters." Deborah was fourteen years older than me and Lucy five years older. We were totally unalike. Deborah was beautiful and always extremely elegant, remarkable considering her background and up-bringing. She left when she was nineteen when I was starting school and I don't remember her living at home at all. She went to live in Bloomsbury, working as a secretary and shared a flat with others who sympathized with her left-wing beliefs. She quickly learned about the Arts in general. She loved galleries, music and the classics.

By 1924 the Russians had recovered from the 1917 Revolution and the USSR began trading with the West and opened their first office in the City known as A.R.C.O.S. Its purpose was to promote the new Revolutionary Workers' Paradise and to establish amicable relations, basically wishing to impress the West. Most of the staff were Russian and were paid much better salaries than their British counterparts. Deborah met Philip at A.R.C.O.S., both aspired to be a part of an organisation supporting the Revolutionary Russian Party and were attracted by the higher wages.

Philip had planned to become a doctor. Unfortunately, a year into his training his father died. As there were no grants in those days he was forced to abandon his dream and went out to work instead. He was a brilliant intellectual. They eventually married. From then on Deborah could afford to shop in the smarter stores.

When she came to visit us on Sunday I assumed she was an aunt not my sister. She always looked like a princess in the most exquisite clothes. She too had seen the visiting Ballet Russes de Monte Carlo and was inspired by their fashionable appearance. She was one of the first to wear twenties style transparent chiffon summer clothing with black and yellow floral patterns. To my great horror I could see a black silk undergarment underneath. I thought this was wicked and naughty. She brought exotic little jackets for me that none of my friends could afford. I did not want to wear them, they were too pretty and too expensive.

Deborah and Philip talked to George about the latest books, writers, art exhibitions and theatre. I sat entranced, it was part of my education although I did not realise it at the time. For me, they were wonderful visitors who might have been from another planet. Deborah took me to her flat in Ebury Street near Victoria Station and told me that several famous people lived nearby. Noël Coward upstairs and the writer George Moore next door. It was an artistic neighbourhood, convenient for the West-End. Deborah was an exotic creature. When the war broke out in 1939 I reported for duty in London and remained for six years. Philip was Jewish and left England in 1940 when it seemed me might lose the war and Jews would be persecuted. He went to Trinidad and in 1942 Deborah who by then had a flat in Swiss Cottage, left to join him. She did not want to lose her flat during her absence and insisted that I live there until the end of the war. I enjoyed living with my two brothers and was not thrilled at this prospect. However I did acquiesce to her demands. The flat, located in an old-fashioned Victorian house with a huge garden, consisted of two large rooms, kitchen, bathroom (with an antiquated water heating system known as a geyser, like an Ascot) and lavatory. For the first time in my life I was living alone and did not like it at all. The rent was £2.50 per week which was half my salary. I started teaching evening classes at the Holborn Institute to earn extra money to survive. Travelling during the blackout was difficult and tiring.

After the war ended, Deborah returned in 1946 complaining how shabby the flat was. I said: "There has been a war Deborah dear, we were not permitted paint or glass for repairs."

"No matter my dear" she said.
"The flat is yours now, I am going to live abroad."

Before her departure, she invited ladies from the Diplomatic Corps for tea and asked if I would act as waitress. I was intrigued to see what these women were like who were lucky enough to spend the war in the West Indies. I dutifully made the tea, used what was left of the best china, prepared the sandwiches and cakes and handed them round listening to their every word. They were dressed beautifully in contrast to shabby Londoners but I thought they were the most stupid women I ever met. They gossiped like actors in "The School for Scandal." I had imagined they would be sophisticated and academic.

In July I started six weeks school holiday and decided to go to Switzerland to see a country which had not been at war, to see the bright lights and smell the clean air, but mostly I wanted to eat non-stop for a fortnight. France was not yet allowing visitors and so after Calais the train went non-stop to Geneva.

Deborah was changed, she had become a typical middle-class British ex-pat wife living with servants in the Colonies and had developed a superior attitude. Her original political inclinations were to the left but her time in the West-Indies mixing with a more upper class social set had altered that. At first she was friendly to all. She now disliked black servants.

"They cheat and lie."

She remained in the Caribbean for 30 years, but moved, leaving Trinidad for Santo Domingo in the Dominican Republic. She much preferred residing in a Spanish country. Her husband became extremely prosperous, they had made artistic and intellectual friends. One a wealthy Swiss man, had a house twenty miles along the coast where they spent week-ends, a luxurious high-life. Many years later, I spent two weeks there at Boca Chica. Lovely for a short stay but the tropical paradise made me lazy and indolent.

When Deborah reached fifty-five years old she returned to England bored with the lifestyle, the people, the parties and of surviving on the BBC World Service and listening to classical music. As a loyal wife she had stayed longer than she might have. She moved to North-West London where her husband bought her a flat. She lived there until she died. She was happy to be back.

She was hugely critical of many things and especially disliked television, at first (always enjoying mine however) but eventually acquired a set of her own. She enjoyed visiting Art Galleries but the theatre less and less as her hearing failed. Beautiful Deborah, always much admired by men, would not admit that she was growing older. Her new flat was near Eton Avenue in Hampstead, NW3. On the first floor lived a female doctor whose Jewish family had been exterminated by the Nazis. She had managed to escape. A lovely lady who lived alone. The top floor was taken by the local Council for social housing. There was a constant stream of parents, children and prams. Thankfully a quiet couple finally moved in. As a tax exile Philip was permitted to came home for three months in any one year. Although geographically separated, they remained devoted and this arrangement suited them both and continued until her death.

Late one night, in the darkness she tripped on a rug. She managed to raise the alarm and her sister-in-law who lived nearby arrived shortly thereafter with her husband and she was rushed to hospital. She was ill for a year, in and out of hospital. The leg never recovered and finally developed gangrene; sadly amputation was the only course of action and she refused.

"I shall go to my grave with two legs."

Philip arrived in haste from the Caribbean and she died two days after. She was 82. She was a remarkable woman with great intellect who could have been another Mrs. Thatcher. She had a lively mind and loved politics. She was well read and spoke fluently. She had made the most of her life considering her humble beginnings. I thank her for introducing me to the Arts, the theatre, paintings, all things Spanish, travel and an elegant dress sense. She and Philip's conversations with George made me more sophisticated in my tastes. I talked in class of Aldous Huxley. My teachers were amazed at my knowledge of Segovia, Henry Moore and Argentinean Tango dancers.

My sister Lucy looked after me when I was a child and was very good indeed. I have a picture of her, hair dragged back in a plait down her back with squashed faced little me aged three. She is wearing a huge apron covering her frock holding my hand outside the house in Lloyd Road. She left high School at seventeen after one year in the sixth form. She played the piano beautifully and spoke French and Spanish. Many talented individuals left school as soon as possible to work and help the family finances. Deborah dominated her. It was she who arranged her first job interview but George told her to take a Civil Service Examination where she became a clerk. She married Bob Waugh in 1939, an accountant who had been to public school. A year later she gave birth to Joy. They evacuated to the country for a short time. During the war I did not see my brothers and sisters. Lucy had a second daughter Elizabeth, Betty. By then her marriage was unhappy. Her husband drank too much, money was short. She was a devoted, wonderful mother to her two beautiful and intelligent girls who were her whole life. They became teachers, Betty had a degree in French from Southampton University. Joy went to Homerton College, Cambridge, married banker Jim Escombe and travelled the world. Lucy was the only member of our family who had children apart from brother Albert. Betty sadly died at the age of 42 from multiple sclerosis. From then on Lucy devoted herself to Natasha her grand-daughter until she went to University at the age of twenty. Lucy, now in her nineties lives in Hackney. I hope she lives to one hundred and receives a telegram from the Queen!

❊   ❊   ❊

During my life I have had have had six close women friends, many were fellow students at Homerton College. In two short years from '97 to '99 I lost four, Hylda, Muriel, Beulah and Ruby.

Hylda Mandy became a head-Mistress and worked until her retirement at sixty. She had been the daughter who stayed at home to look after her widowed mother. She was a wonderful teacher with a great sense of humour. She taught infants. She was the youngest Head Teacher in Clapton East London. She transformed a Victorian building into a magical place. She transferred later, with her mother, to Southend to a modern infants school in a superb new building situated between a middle class estate and a working class one: a difficult but interesting job to get them to mix at the age of five. The children had no prejudices but the parents did. Hylda was a genius, a lovely lady. She soon calmed all fears and created a happy lively school.

My other dear friend was Muriel Young (later Griffith). She too was a Head Mistress at an infants' school in West London.

Beulah Hastop was a gloriously titian-haired singer and musician. She married a Naval Officer with whom she travelled the world. She had a son who became a doctor.

My dearest and oldest surviving friend is Joanna Christians. We were at High School together at the age of eleven. She was extremely good at dancing and athletics. We had one hours' dancing each week which she loved as did I. It was most unusual, we did Polish, Greek and Ballroom dancing. We danced to Chopin. Our wonderful Gym. teacher Miss Squire who had been a ballet dancer herself loved incorporating dance with gymnastics. God Bless Her. I became friendly with Joanna because we both loved the theatre. She hoped to be a classical ballet dancer and I hoped to be an actress or a doctor. We had ambitions. We have remained friends for 71 years, a source of great joy for us both. Through war, marriages and geographical separation we have always somehow kept in touch. It is a God given friendship. She is most kind to me now that I am disabled and blind. We are the same age, both love the Arts and the Classics. She too has a great sense of fun and humour. I am happy she achieved her ambition to became a ballet dancer. She was in the Ballet Rambert and Ninette de Valois' Company at Sadler's Wells in the thirties. She served in ENSA during the War entertaining the troops. She met her husband and went to live in Swansea. She has one son Julian who lives in Malta and a grandson Marcus, aged eight.

My other long-term friendship is with Mieke Frankenberg, the actress Jane Seymour's mother. She had married Dr. John Frankenberg in the forties. Having attended my wedding decided that marriage was a good thing. I attended theirs and a year later their first daughter, Joyce (Jane), was born followed by Sally and Anne. The three sisters. I was so lucky to be friendly with this lovely family and was accepted as Auntie. I loved playing with the children as they grew up. Mieke is Dutch and had been married earlier when she was very young to a Dutchman and went to live in the Dutch East Indies. She was captured by the Japanese and interned in a camp. She worked as a nurse and was freed by the

British at the end of the war. She came to live in London and worked at the Dutch Embassy. She is a practical jolly lady, a marvellous mother, a great cook and an accomplished hostess. She and John and family were extremely happy. It was a joy always to go to their house and play with their children. So much so that the children wanted to be actresses, "like Auntie Eunice" I had played with them a lot, dressing up and having fun in their Wendy house. I was unlucky in not having children of my own. I was devoted to the whole family and still am. Jane has become very famous in Hollywood and is married now to her fourth husband. Bravely, in her forties, she gave birth to twin boys in 1995. She has had great success. The result of hard work, talent and beautiful looks. So I hope that this 4th marriage is the lasting one and she continues to be successful and happy. Mieke is devoted to their children and is unfortunately now a widow. John died a few years ago. I am so glad she has such happy children and grand-children now she is old. I have known the family for 53 years.

I have few surviving friends in my neighbourhood but since 1954 when I met Bill and Beryl Roskelly in the communal garden we have remained firm friends. They have lived at 149 Elgin Crescent for nearly fifty years. Bill played the cello in the orchestra at Covent Garden and Beryl was a painter/teacher at The Slade School of Art. They had three boys under the age of ten, and two dogs. It was an immediate friendship that has lasted to this day. They are also so kind to me in my present situation. Bill has said: "Eunice I am your panic button, we will come to your aid anytime."

The boys have been very successful. When I was in "Crackerjack" with Leslie Crowther I took them to the BBC Television Centre to see a live performance. They were so excited it is talked about to this day. One has made a career in the Army and is now an Officer, another is a Parson and the other a businessman often travelling to Poland. It has been marvellous to see these boys grow up to be such handsome and prosperous human beings. But most of all to know another very happy united family.

Since 1956 I have known the actor John Dunbar. He too is my age and has retired to Torquay. We met when I left Cambridge and started as a professional actress. One Christmas, both unemployed, we were working for the Post Office sorting and delivering the mail. We met in the cafeteria at a 2am breakfast break. We noticed each other reading the New Statesman weekly newspaper which sparked an immediate conversation on the Arts. He lived at Chalk Farm and I in Swiss Cottage. At 7am we walked home together every morning. We are friends to this day and still correspond on a regular basis. During 1998 I had a period of convalescence. Joanna and I went to Torquay and stayed at the Gleneagles Hotel. John lives nearby and it was a lovely reunion. We are now ancient but have remained close. John has always been in work, he is Scottish, had lived in Hampstead for most of his working life playing character parts. Character actors are in a way more fortunate than stars because they are always in work. John has played lawyers, doctors and respectable civil servants. For years he was in Doctor Finlay's Case Book with Andrew Cruikshank, both on radio and television. I saw his last performance at the Exeter University Theatre when he played in "No Man's Land" by Harold Pinter in the Ralph Richardson part. A brilliant production. John travels regularly to Plymouth to see classical touring productions.

A more recent acquaintance and friend is Dame Anne Warburton who was on the sleaze committee when the Conservative Government was in power. She was Head of Lucy Cavendish College, Cambridge. I met her on an Hellenic cruise. She invited me to visit the College. It is one of those rare Colleges for mature students who wish to obtain a degree in later life. The house was donated by Lucy Cavendish, a wealthy Cambridge resident, to establish a seat of learning for older students. Eventually other properties were added and it is now quite large. His

Royal Highness the Prince Philip Duke of Edinburgh, Chancellor of Cambridge University, was guest of honour at a luncheon I attended, to present the College with a certificate of full membership of Cambridge University. A great achievement. They depend on private contributions so I have become a benefactor. I admire anybody who makes the effort to go back and continue their education. Dame Anne was the first Principal, an amazing lady. I hope we remain friends for a long time. It was kind of her to invite me to the College and meet some of the students. It should be a project encouraged by any Government.

One extraordinary meeting I will always cherish was with the poet Walter de la Mare whom I met in 1931 and who remained a friend for many years. I was in the sixth form at High School. I was chosen to go to Paddington Stations by taxi, to meet him. He would arrive at 1pm from his home in Buckinghamshire. We would recognise each other as follows; he in a large soft trilby carrying books and I very tall in a green school uniform. We met instantly. We travelled eastward to Manor House.

'What 's the name of this road?" he asked.
"Seven Sisters, next is Tottenham Hale, then Forest Road to Epping Forest."
"Ah," he sighed....
"Once upon a time there were seven sisters named Lucy, Sarah, Jane, Penelope, Muriel, Doris and Deborah. They played together in Epping Forest and in turn were the wives of Robin Hood', and so he continued. I sat enchanted the entire taxi ride to school, where he spent an hour reading his poetry – especially "The Listeners." As he left for his return journey to Paddington he gave me a signed book of his poems. I treasure it to this day.

One of my dearest friends was the late Dean of St. Paul's Cathedral, the very Reverend Eric Evans and his wife Linda and their two daughters

Georgie and Alex. It was a great loss to London and to the Church of England when he died two years ago because he loved humanity and was not pompous or overpowering because of his high office. He loved music. I had the great pleasure of going to an evensong which he was conducting at the Cathedral. He led me down the main aisle and placed me among the choristers as he knew how much I love music. When I first met him on a cruise he asked why I did not go to his Sunday Eucharist. I told him that as a child we moved house, my mother was ill. I too was ill so I was not baptised. The dear Dean said he would baptise and confirm me in one service in St Pauls. In London he telephoned and said he was writing a proper service for me and a date was fixed. It was an overwhelming honour. The service took place in the Crypt and he chose the Bishop of Fulham to confirm me because he was so tall. It was one of the great days of my life. As we came out onto the great steps of St Paul's facing west to a glorious sunset, the bells were ringing. I looked up to Heaven and thought of my cockney mother who, I am sure, as an Islington mum was looking down on her youngest daughter and smiling at this special baptism.

The congregations at St. Pauls always had a wonderful atmosphere with love and affection in the air. His sermons were always entertaining and interesting. Everybody felt that they were loved by him spiritually. His family were warm and friendly. When I visited the Deanery I found his wife Linda taking care of their sheep dog and a mass of new puppies. It was homely and informal. Their daughters were in the theatre, Alex working in television at the BBC. Since their father's death, they have moved to a cottage near Gloucester where they had lived for seventeen years prior to St. Pauls. The Dean was given the Honour of lying in State within Gloucester Cathedral. I went to his Memorial Service at St. Pauls Cathedral, a remarkable tribute to a great man. In attendance were the Mayor of London and entourage in full regalia, the entire Cathedral Choir and teachers; representatives of all the senior Royals and every facet of London life came to pay homage to dear Eric.

One sad morning shortly before his death, I was told that the Dean was ill in hospital with emphysema, a chest complaint, and was breathing with an oxygen mask. He was able to return to the Deanery for a short time. I spoke to him hoping he had recovered and invited them to a celebratory lunch as my yellow roses were in full scented bloom. One morning he telephoned and said they would come, he was to be allowed to leave his bed from 11:30am to 2pm without oxygen. We sat on my balcony in Elgin Crescent, surrounded by hundreds of roses. Alas, he passed away only two weeks later. I, like thousands of Londoners mourned and we cherish his memory.

One of his telephone calls will always remain a fond and funny memory: "How is my favourite Dame?" he said.

"Panto?" I replied!

He had a glorious sense of humour, had been a joy on the Hellenic cruise both as a lecturer and friend. I miss him so much.

(Clockwise from top left)
My father
George, Eunice & Mum 1930
Eunice & Lucy at Branscombe 1931
Lucy with Joy 1940
My mother 1932

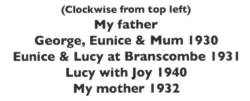

(Clockwise from top left)
Eunice age 10
Deborah and Lucy
1970
Deborah and
George 1970
My niece Joy at
Cambridge 1960
Philip Bernstein
1931
Deborah 1924

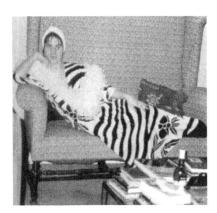

(Clockwise from top left)
My niece Betty's 21st birthday; Betty with Philip Bowen;
with Jim Escombe; my great-niece Natasha; My brother Albert with
his daughter Jill

A recent gathering of surviving Holdens

My nieces Jill and Jeannette (Albert's daughters)

Drawing by George Holden

Top: The Greek Theatre, Walthamstow High School

At School, in full costume   **Ron Dubock**

In the Greek Theatre, 1930

Midsummer Night's Dream in the Greek Theatre, as Oberon (centre)

In the Greek Theatre (with Joanna extreme right of photograph)

FINALE

My chief characteristics are that I am an optimist, always a survivor and that I will never be defeated. I passionately love the ARTS – poetry, Shakespeare, architecture, painting and classical music. They are our spiritual blessings.

To survive our most horrendous personal disasters I suggest that one should consider three possibilities:

Yes,
No,
Compromise.

Ponder for three days, think of the cost – both financial and spiritual; and the personal and long-term effects. Come to a decision, A or B, no compromise Then act. Say: "Merde alors!" three times, then drink two strong gins and tonics. Do not indulge in self-pity. Remember indecision is a killer of future hopes and plans. Remember dear Shakespeare's advice: "The fault dear Brutus, is not in our stars but in ourselves, that we are underlings.

So, this is my life. So unlike the Queen Mum's life throughout the twentieth century. She, born into a life of privilege and wealth into the upper orders of the British class system, becoming Queen of a great Empire witnessing its decline; bravely surviving a long widowhood – a remarkable, well-loved lady. I stood in line in the crypt of St. Paul's Cathedral to be presented to the Queen Mother. She is the patron of the Cathedral. She attended a tea party and chorale serenade in her honour.

When she shook my hand I bowed and said: "Your Majesty. I am a Londoner – a great admirer."

She giggled. I was wearing a sombrero. I did not wish her to think I was Spanish!

The Queen Mother and I have shared the adventures and inventions of this amazing century past. She from a position of power and responsibility and me from the other end of the spectrum. But I have had the freedom to fail or succeed by my own efforts and do what I like. I doubt she would exchange her life for mine. I certainly would not exchange my freedom for her demanding and restrictive life. Freedom to experiment, travel anywhere, discover and develop one's own talents and character and hopefully to help others. These are more important than the pleasures, responsibilities and headaches imposed by vast wealth and the disciplines of Royal protocol.

I, her subject, born in the East End of London into the bottom end of the working class have witnessed the same times with little money, no welfare state and since schooldays, no parents.

But we have both survived.

Long live London and the English traditions of humour, tolerance and a love for gardening and dogs; for eccentricity and originality.

This book may be read from front to back or from back to front…I was born on the 23rd October 1914…

ENVOI
HONOURS LIST
MY FAVOURITE THINGS

Music: Bach, Mozart, Schubert, Chopin

Painting: Magritte, Toulouse Lautrec, Turner, Bonnard

Actors: Olivier, Schofield, Tim West, Michael Caine

Actresses: Ashcroft, Edith Evans, Judi Dench, Maggie Smith

Comedy: Spike Milligan, Ken Dodd, John Cleese, Marks Brothers,
                Dora Bryan, Joyce Grenfell, Bea Lillie, Victoria Wood

Dramatists: Shakespeare, Wilde, Shaw, Pinter, Ayckbourn,
                Stoppard, Bennett

Authors: Austen, Dickens, Waugh, Trollope

Musicals: Oklahoma, Oliver, Guys & Dolls, Three Penny Opera

Books: Hitch Hikers Guide to the Galaxy, Diary of a Nobody,
                The horse's mouth

Comic genius
Of nonsense: Edward Lear, Lewis Carroll, Spike Milligan

Sculptors: Henry Moore, Rodin, the Greeks, the Egyptians

Scriptwriters: Denis Norden and Frank Muir

Originals: Tony Hancock, Tommy Cooper, George Robey,
                Noël Coward

Theatre
Directors: Peter Hall, Richard Eyre, Trevor Nunn, Komisajevsky

INDEX OF NAMES

Lightning Source UK Ltd.
Milton Keynes UK
UKOW06f1542180915

258888UK00001B/23/P